Namaste

MY EVEREST JOURNEY

Emma Després

@iamselfpub
www.iamselfpublishing.com

Contents

Note:
This book is based on a true story that took place in 2007. All names of those involved in the trek have been changed to protect identity.

About the Author

Emma is passionate about many things, but especially family, yoga, Reiki, Guernsey, Nepal, the moon, sea swimming, writing, soaking in the bath while reading a good book, women's health and wellbeing (especially fertility), realising our potential, and living a life of purpose.

Based on the beautiful island of Guernsey, Emma teaches a regular schedule of yoga classes, as well as running yoga & wellbeing retreats and offering Level One and Level Two Reiki attunement sessions.

Emma is the published author of Dancing with the Moon, an honest account of her spiritual journey through IVF, pregnancy and early motherhood. On Emma's website at www. Beinspiredby.co.uk, you will find a number of free yoga videos, and meditation and relaxation audios.

We all have a story to tell and this is
mine – it is not the whole story, but it is a story
nonetheless. It is a journey, really, my encounter with
the Himalayas and the Divine, as she danced and cast her
magic and changed my world forever.

Namaste

"I honour the place in you
In which the entire universe dwells.
I honour the place in you
Which is of Love, of Light and of Peace.
When you are in that place in you,
And I am in that place in me,
We are One.
Or quite simply...
The light in me meets the same light in you."

For my Mum and Dad, for giving me wings to fly and a place to call home.

And for my brother, Ross, for setting me free.

Prologue

*Good luck? Did he really say good luck? Do we need good luck? Hello, checking in with yourself. Emma, have you any idea what you've actually let yourself in for here? I mean isn't it about time that you started to consider your current reality, standing here as you are in Nepal, about to get on a flight up into the Himalayas and trek, did you hear that, **trek**, all the way to Mount Everest Base Camp, as in base camp of the tallest mountain in the whole world? I mean you've never trekked anywhere of any significance in your life, and I'm not quite sure that practising yoga every day on your mat constitutes adequate training for a trek of this magnitude. How on earth did you find yourself here?*

Introduction

Bird of prey,
bird of prey,
flying high,
flying high,
take me on your flight.
"Bird of Prey", The Doors

Beep, beep, beep.

It is the middle of the day when we arrive into Kathmandu. I'm jet-lagged and tired, and all I can hear is the incessant beeping of horns. The air is hot and sticky, thick with dust and car exhaust fumes; I've never known air like it before, and I'm struggling to breathe.

We travel by a decrepit minibus through the chaos of the outer city, along potholed and dusty roads, up, down, *bash, bash*, weaving in and out of cars, *beep, beep*, motorbikes, people and the odd cow munching through a pile of rubbish at the side of the road. Then more horns, more potholes and the air still so heavy; it's a completely different world to the one I've left behind in Guernsey.

My eyes dart all around as we pass through brightly coloured and bustling streets on the outskirts of central Kathmandu. They are lined with endless small shopfronts teeming with people. Women wear saris in every colour and bright material hangs from the shopfronts, making for a vibrant scene. Even the signs above the shopfronts, written in both English and the Nepali script, Devanagari, are eye-catching, many of them hand-painted in reds, blues and yellows.

The buildings are built higgledy-piggledy, all crammed together in different colours, (light blue, burnt red, purple, pink, light orange and grey, for example), and different heights. They look like they'd collapse so easily in an earthquake (little did I know then). The heads of the concrete pylons, which line the roads, are covered in a spaghetti tangle of hundreds of electric wires; some of them loose and hanging down, and others tightly wound. How does anyone know what they each do? The wires cross the streets too; a world of wires that I've never seen before, hidden as they are under the roads back home.

It's sensory overload for me as I try to take it all in. Chaos prevails and I struggle to understand how anyone can function in it, let alone have any control over it. Dust fills the air and there are yet more wires hanging precariously over the uneven and rubbish-strewn pavements.

I smile to myself – it might be chaos, I might feel like a fish out of water, completely out of my comfort zone, as if on another planet that I don't yet know; but I'm here. I've made it, finally, into the maelstrom which is Kathmandu!

* * *

I am in Nepal with a UK-based charitable and adventure organisation, which supports projects in developing countries around the world. However, it has not really dawned on me even now – as I notice with some relief that the minibus is stopping outside the gates of a comparatively elaborate house in a decidedly less elaborate area of town – exactly what I am doing here; I mean, I have a vague idea of course, the chance arose and I took it, but I have not really given it too much thought.

It was never a conscious decision to trek to Everest Base Camp; I simply signed up for some voluntary work in Nepal and later discovered that the trek formed part of the package. I had dreamt of visiting Nepal and the Himalayas for many years and my patience had finally paid off. The opportunity presented itself without any effort on my part; I didn't even bother to read the fine print, I just went with my heart, it was as simple as that.

Not only did the opportunity land in my lap, the timing was perfect. I had qualified as a yoga teacher in Byron Bay, Australia eighteen months earlier and I had been living back at home with my parents in Guernsey for almost a year, trying to make a go of things, working part-time as a company secretary (which had been my previous full-time professional career) in the offshore finance industry, which afforded me the opportunity to live my dream of teaching yoga, practising Reiki and writing.

However, dream or no dream, home or no home, these were challenging times. Back living with my parents in Guernsey, I missed the freedom of my yogi/traveller/writing life in Byron Bay, which had been my utopia. My feet were itching for further travel, for the opportunity to tread a different path, get off the beaten track, view life from a different perspective and glimpse the bigger picture. I was struggling with trying not to get caught up in the energy of life on a small island, an offshore finance centre no less, 40 sq km and filled with approximately 65,000 people!

There were other reasons too – I was thirty-one years old and had been in a four-year, on-off relationship of comfort with a most wonderful friend, which I knew deep down was not going anywhere. I was struggling to let go because he had been my knight in shining armour and rescued me when I was at my lowest ebb in life, the same year I found yoga. Essentially, I was still searching for my soulmate and life partner and was aching for this connection and to bring new life into the world one day together.

Plus, while I had made a number of attempts to conform to the accepted (and expected) so-called 'normal' life – the education, career, mortgage, pension, accumulating assets, status and so on – it just wasn't working for me. It made my soul feel confined and my wings clipped, so much so, that I ended up getting awfully depressed, which is also part of my story, depression that is.

Instead, I was drawn to the more spiritual, esoteric, nomadic, unconventional and thus unacceptable way of life that has found me flitting around the globe, furthering my yoga practice, exploring my spirituality and sense of self, embracing different cultures and attempting to live from my heart – so much easier in principle than in practice!

So, this trip to Nepal came as nothing short of a blessing for me. Not only are volunteering trips considered socially and conventionally acceptable these days, thus escaping the "When are you going to settle down, Emma? You can't just keep travelling your whole life, what about your pension?"-type comments I was getting sick of, but also I was rather keen to experience the perceived 'spiritual' energy of the Himalayas. I wanted to just 'be' yoga, rather than simply 'do' yoga, (we are spiritual beings having a human experience after all), allowing my essence, my inner teacher and my light to shine and guide me from within. Oh heck, my soul just wanted to grow.

You see, this trip also coincided with my questioning the current labels and ideologies of yoga in the West with its emphasis on what type of yoga you do. I mean, yoga is yoga; surely, to define is to limit and aren't we seeking freedom from limitation? But clearly not, for at that time it seemed to me that everyone had something to say about a 'right' or 'wrong' way to teach and practise yoga, not simply teachers, but students too (although aren't we all students really?).

For me, this seemed to go against the very nature of yoga itself and I had the sense that yoga had to be much more than simply what happens on the mat. I had grown tired of the pressure (admittedly my own, life is one big mirror after all) to read yoga book after yoga book thereby fuelling the "Have you read this book? Have you read that book? So and so says we should do this or do that for our spiritual transformation"-energy pervading yoga and, indeed, spiritual communities.

I had become increasingly aware that this energy and my reaction to this energy, (yes, yoga teacher or not, I still react to stuff), was doing me no favours whatsoever. All I really wanted to do was to live yoga in its entirety, on and off the mat, to experience and feel it for myself, allowing myself, my soul, to be touched by my own sense of spirituality, rather than limiting myself to the experiences, feelings and thoughts of other practitioners and seekers, many of whom have placed themselves on spiritual pedestals regardless of whether their actions are in accordance with their self-held ideals.

Furthermore, I had recently realised that in my effort to 'do it right', yoga had been controlling my life rather than enhancing it – like so many others around me, I found myself striving rather than evolving. I was well aware that it was time to take a break from the yoga books, be open to my inner teacher, wisdom, whatever you want to call it, and the teachings of others in their many guises, and simply enjoy and experience all life has to offer. Also, it was time to be free, take a risk, face a few fears and just have a good old time in the process.

I thought to myself, I have climbed many mountains in my mind these last few years, I have overcome many obstacles, I have taken a new career path, I have lived on the other side of the world, I have turned my life around; surely trekking in the Himalayas will be easy in comparison. Little did I realise how the transformative energy of the Himalayas, and beauty of Nepal, would impact my life.

1

We're just two lost souls
swimming in a fish bowl,
year after year,
running over the same old ground.
What have we found?
The same old fears.
"Wish You Were Here", Pink Floyd

Day 0: Arriving in Nepal

I've travelled from Heathrow to Kathmandu with Lilly, a twenty-six-year-old girl from Guernsey, with the most strikingly bright blue eyes and the kindest heart. It's a complete coincidence – our parents have known each other for years and we've known of each other for some of those years, but not closely, and we both booked the trip independently, neither of us at this stage quite sure who else will be joining us on the trek to Everest Base Camp and beyond.

We met a few times in Guernsey before we left. Lilly booked my flights, as she works in travel. We were delighted to be able to fly out together. It's funny because from the outset we've both been at ease in each other's company and, arriving here in Nepal, I'm just relieved she's on this trip with me and that I'm not arriving on my own.

According to the World Bank, the Kathmandu Valley is one of the fastest-growing metropolitan areas in South East Asia and the first region in Nepal to face the unprecedented challenges of rapid urbanisation and modernisation. It's also the main gateway to the country's tourism industry, so it is very busy and there is a sense of it being totally out of control.

We're both relieved when the minibus stops outside the gated compound of a modern-looking brick house, separated from other houses by a tall and protective metal fence. We're beyond the ring road here in a marginally quieter and residential part of town, nestled in the eastern suburbs, en route from Chabahil to Boudhanath, the largest stupa (a dome-shaped building erected as a Buddhist shrine) in Nepal and the holiest Tibetan Buddhist temple outside of Tibet.

Our host, a particularly short, smiley and very welcoming Sherpa (and practising Tibetan Buddhist) called Mingmar greets us at the minibus and leads us through the tall, heavy gates into the security of his home. We follow him into the cool, quiet and tall stone house and breathe a sigh of relief. It's dimly lit, but a sanctuary after the madness of the outside world we have witnessed on our journey here.

We follow Mingmar up two flights of wide stone stairs to the third floor of the house where we will be living while we are staying in Kathmandu. He explains that his family live on the first two floors and we will all live quite independently of one another. This comes as welcome news as it means we have the freedom to come and go as we choose.

Mingmar leads us into the light and airy bedroom, which Lilly and I will share. "No smoking here," Mingmar says, as he points to an impressive-looking, tall, dark-brown carved and polished wooden display unit housing a statue of Buddha and various Tibetan Buddhist paintings, with their beautifully bright primary colours and intricate detail.

Lilly and I look at each other. "No, no smoking in here," we assure him. (I have recently given up smoking…again… but I know Lilly smokes.) This makes me immediately aware of the significance of Tibetan Buddhism in this household, and I'm excited, as I know very little about this tradition, but am keen to learn about it.

Mingmar leaves us in our new room and Lilly and I start rummaging through our bags, not really sure what to do with the contents or indeed with ourselves. We're completely out of sorts with a combination of the jet lag and being in an alien environment. I take clothes out of my bag, shuffle them around and then put them back in again, so I'm pleased when Craig, a short, shaven-headed, friendly guy steps into the room and distracts me from this pointless task.

Craig and Lilly already know one another from the previous summer when they endured a particularly challenging six-day ascent of Mount Kenya and taught together for approximately six months in a Kenyan school. They are friends and keen to catch up, so I follow them out onto a large balcony on the side of the house that you access through two large wooden doors between our bedroom and the bedroom across the hallway, (both bedrooms have windows that look out onto the balcony), so that they can smoke and we can meet our fellow travellers.

It's a beautifully spacious balcony with views overlooking the surrounding area. The air is incredibly dusty, which makes it difficult to see far into the distance, although I have a sense that there are mountains, or hills at least, out there, beyond this crazy, overpopulated and ever-developing Kathmandu Valley, with its higgledy-piggledy buildings and the constant sound of horns.

Nepal is landlocked and has a strategic location between China and India. It contains eight of the world's ten highest peaks, including Mount Everest and Kanchenjunga – the world's tallest and third tallest peak – on the borders with China and India respectively. Nepal is among the poorest and least developed countries in the world, with almost one third of its population believed to be living below the poverty line. Agriculture is, at the moment at least, the mainstay of the economy, providing a livelihood for three-quarters of the population.

However, an increasing number of people are migrating from the rural areas of Nepal and moving to Kathmandu, the capital city, and the Kathmandu Valley, which surrounds it. The World Bank estimates that Nepal is urbanising rapidly, with urban population growth rates of up to 7% per year.

The Kathmandu valley is a region of 600 sq km in central Nepal and is home to three of the largest cities in Nepal, including Kathmandu itself. The valley lies at the crossroads of ancient civilisations of Asia and is said to have at least 130 important monuments, including several pilgrimage sites for Hindus and Buddhists. There are seven World Heritage sites within the valley.

Unplanned urban development in the Kathmandu Valley has led to rapid and uncontrolled sprawl; irregular, substandard and inaccessible housing development; loss of open space and decreased liveability. It has also increased vulnerability to disasters, making Kathmandu one of the most earthquake-vulnerable cities in the world (as we have since witnessed with the April 2015 earthquake).

When I look out from the balcony, I am fascinated by the urban landscape – it's so different to the urban environment in the West. At times, it really does seem that houses and buildings have just been built one on top of another in any old way, quite in contrast to the stringent planning and building controls at home in Guernsey.

Mingmar's home, also our home and base for the next two months, is set on its own to the side of a small, dusty road. There are houses across the road and when we are outside on the balcony, we are level with the flat roof of one of these neighbouring houses, where brightly coloured materials are hung on lines, drying in the warm and heavy air.

Another of the neighbouring houses is home to a wooden furniture-making business and we are aware of an angle grinder at work, its sound piercing our ears. In between the two buildings and stretching into the distance, we can see the dusty dirt road we've recently just been driven down, and I'm fascinated by the bamboo scaffolding that has been erected against one of the half-completed buildings lining the side of the road.

This area is filled with houses, many of them displaying brightly coloured red, white, yellow, blue and green Tibetan prayer flags on their balconies, indicating the Tibetan Buddhist families who live nestled throughout this predominantly Hindu neighbourhood. In the far distance, I can see the vague outline of hills that indicate a world beyond the Kathmandu Valley.

The landscape glows with reds, browns and oranges, earthy, as the hazy sun shines through the smog. My throat is coated with fumes and there's a taste in my mouth that I can't shift. But despite all this, there's a beauty to this place and I feel protected and safe on the balcony with the tall gate bolted and locked below us.

I'm so distracted by the views that it takes me a moment to notice that our fellow trekkers are also out here on the balcony, sitting around a large table laughing and chatting together. It takes me another moment to realise that they are all male and all much younger than my thirty-one years. I immediately feel shy.

On reflection, the fact that I am on an organised 'eight-week gap-year trip' should have given me a clue. However, I'm completely thrown because I hadn't expected to be spending the next eight weeks with actual gap-year students! I was so excited about doing this trip that I hadn't really thought of this finer detail. Anyhow, earlier this year I resolved to let go of expectation and accept situations and people as they are, so this has presented me with an opportunity for exactly that!

Craig is the closest in age to me, albeit he is five years younger at twenty-six. He likes to talk with a cigarette in his hand and he makes it clear that he knows best, certainly when it comes to volunteering. He's been doing so on and off for the last few years, as he feels passionate about helping to make a difference to children's lives in poor and underdeveloped regions of the world. He's particularly fond of Kenya and tells us that he hopes to return to the volunteer project there, after his time in Nepal

As it happens, he's only staying with us for a month to join us on the trek to Everest Base Camp and our subsequent volunteering in a rural Himalayan village, before returning to the UK and onwards from there. I don't warm to him initially; there's just something about our energies that are very different and, aside from finding ourselves together in Nepal, we don't seem to have a lot else in common. To be honest, I find him a little patronising.

Next in age is twenty-three-year-old Will, a bearded, rugged and attractive final-year Scottish medical student with a delightful accent and scruffy, dark-blonde hair. He'll be joining us on the trek before returning immediately to

Kathmandu to volunteer in the main teaching hospital here in the city as part of his medical studies. I'm a sucker for the rugged man and there is something about the fact he's training to be a doctor that warms my heart, but I'm soon aware that he has a slightly insecure edge to him, which can make him sarcastic and calculated.

We 'oldies' are joined by four gap-year students. Eighteen-year-old Ben is a friendly yet shy North Londoner with a slight athletic build and brown hair. He has a lovely disposition and reminds me of my brother at that age. I soon realise that although he likes to fool around, he is inherently sensible and caring. He'll make a lovely, devoted partner one day.

Ben is joined in Nepal by his friend and fellow gap-year travel companion, Matt. Nineteen-year-old Matt is also from North London and at 6ft 3in, he's all legs and arms with a big smiley face framed by floppy brown hair. He's a real gentle giant and it is clear the boys have a good friendship. They really seem to care about each other and intend to continue their travels to Thailand and beyond, after this trip, before starting university in the autumn.

Tim is another eighteen-year-old gap year student, from Devon, where he lives with his parents. He's another softy with the most incredible Egyptian green eyes and a heart-on-sleeve smile. I realise he's the serious one, he has his life planned out, knows what he wants, knows all about the trek because he studied the fine print and because he has an interest in outdoor pursuits. He has the proper gear and has everything budgeted. He's very independent, and another lovely guy, whom I'm drawn to. I quickly realise that because of his naivety at times, the boys find him an easy target for their jokes, but he laughs this off, his bright eyes twinkling, proving that he's the bigger guy.

And then there's Joe, the fourth and final eighteen-year-old gap student who, rather strangely, happens to live on Guernsey too! Even stranger, perhaps, is the fact that Joe's parents live about 100 metres as the crow flies from my own parents. Needless to say, we mix in different circles back home and I am intrigued how we all, Lilly, Joe and I (particularly), ended up on the same trip to Nepal. One thing is clear – I am going to struggle to achieve anonymity even up here in the Himalayas!

It becomes quickly apparent that Joe is used to having his mum look after him. This is his first time away from home and he is revelling in the freedom of it, with not a care in the world, and a lovely bank balance to support him. He's all floppy brown hair, which has been cut to fall on his face, so he's constantly sweeping it out of his eyes, or teasing the ends before sweeping these aside too. He's a film buff, loves quoting from films and is off to study film at university after the summer holidays.

We chat together on the balcony, excited about being in Nepal and about our approaching trek to Everest Base Camp. However, it immediately becomes apparent that other than Tim and Craig, none of us has the slightest idea what to expect in the mountains. We know very little about trekking in such an environment. The organisation quite rightly assumes a certain level of fitness, and while I made an effort to go for a few walks on the rugged, beautiful and demanding cliffs back home in Guernsey in preparation, I didn't get too carried away with training.

However, and as I mentioned earlier, I recently spent six weeks in Byron Bay visiting my brother, where he has also been undertaking his yoga teacher-training studies. There I practised maybe two to four hours of yoga each day and walked and cycled around town, but this was all at sea level and here in Kathmandu we're already at an elevation of 1,400 metres above sea level. Still, the yoga will have helped to strengthen my body and my lungs and I'm not too concerned; it's just a trek!

2

We live in a beautiful world,
yeah we do, yeah we do,
we live in a beautiful world.
"Don't Panic", Coldplay

Day 1: Kathmandu to Lukla to Phakding

It's 3.40am when my alarm goes off. Lilly has been coughing half the night and the dogs have been barking outside in sympathy. Mind you, the dogs bark incessantly in this country all the time. I've never known anything quite like it. I always travel with earplugs because I'm so used to backpacking and having to share rooms with others. Earplugs make it easier to sleep beyond the snores and the comings and goings. Still, I wasn't expecting to need to use them out here just because the dogs bark so loudly!

The night-time noise means that I'm feeling decidedly tired. However, like a creature of habit, I forgo an extra ten minutes in bed and squeeze in a cold shower and make myself a much-needed cup of masala tea to wake me a little. The boys simply roll out of bed and blink their way into their clothes; I don't know how they do it.

All of us rush around trying to pack last-minute stuff into our rucksacks. We've been told to keep the weight under 15kgs, not simply to conform to flight requirements, but also because porters are carrying our bags for us on this trek and we need to be considerate. I'm not sure I'd be able to do this trek if I had to carry my bag myself and I'm mindful to keep its weight to a minimum.

However, there are a few essentials I'm really attached to, even though I doubt they'd be classed essential by anyone else and certainly not by anyone about to embark on a trek up to Mount Everest Base Camp. So, I do my best to pack them as subtly as I can, although this is not so easy with the yoga mat, which has to be tied to the outside of my rucksack, but I manage to shove the angel cards and teddy bear into the main body of the bag without anyone else noticing. I take these 'essentials' with me whenever I travel. They've been around the world at least twice now!

There's an energy of both excitement and anticipation in the minibus that drives us to the airport in the pre-dawn darkness. Joe, especially, is struggling to wake up. We've only spent a few days together, but already we're getting a sense of one another. You don't need to be too sensitive to see that Joe likes to sleep. It's early even by my standards and I'm longing for another cup of tea. I'm really not sure what to expect in the couple of weeks ahead and I just hope that I've packed all I need for the trek, and if I haven't? Well it's too late now.

Soon at Kathmandu's airport, we grab our rucksacks from the back of the minibus and follow one another to the domestic terminal, where we have to queue at the door to put our bags through large X-ray machines to be checked by security staff. We're all half asleep and I'm also irrationally anxious that I've got something in my bag that shouldn't be in there. Fortunately, I don't have time to dwell on this as we're soon following Mingmar into the terminal.

Stepping inside, I'm immediately overwhelmed by all the noise and activity. The building itself is little more than a large, tall, open and functional concrete space with yellow-stained walls and a couple of birds swooping between the rafters high above. It seems so basic, little more than a warehouse really, and is full of activity, as lots of short Nepali porters shout to one another in Nepali, as they rush around carrying heavy luggage bags and trekking supplies.

There are lots of trekkers milling together in their groups with walking poles poking out of daysacks. Like us, they look a little startled to find themselves here in this hectic environment so early in the morning. This is certainly a new experience for me. I've never trekked anywhere in my life before. Making the Nepali Himalayas my first trek is definitely diving in at the deep end. Nepal is known for its serious trekking and I immediately feel ill-prepared.

Porters are soon fussing around us and Mingmar is shouting orders at them as they collect our bags and carry them two or three at a time to the large scales beside the basic check-in counters. From here, the porter weighs them, then shouts the weight out to the check-in staff, before the bags and supplies are piled high onto large, wooden trollies that are physically pulled through the airport before being attached to the back of the buses that drive passengers out to the planes.

The activity is still so overwhelming. It's a sensory overload for this time in the morning and I'm humoured to see birds flying overhead. I'm also struck by the sheer number of trekkers and porters who are being organised onto flights. For even though it may seem like bedlam, I am aware the Nepali porters and guides know what they are doing – there is order within the chaos! I'm just relieved to find that all our bags pass the weigh-in test.

Before we know it, Mingmar is shaking each of our hands in turn and wishing us good luck. It's at about this point in the proceedings, not quite able to get my bearings, and my mind in overdrive, that I start having strong words with myself about how precisely I now find myself in this situation. It's all very well listening to the heart, but maybe I should have given this a little more thought. I mean all sorts of things could go wrong, and am I really prepared for the Himalayas?

It really was one of those "Oh my good grief, this is really happening" moments that shall be forever etched on my memory, as all such moments are, real stomach-churning, heightened-awareness present moments. Those moments must get 'stuck' somewhere in the body because that moment is still there; whenever I think about it, I'm transported right back to that exact moment when time stood still and fear took hold.

As the Nepali frequently ask, often in a resigned way when discussing the state of the country, "What to do?" Well, that one's easy. I just follow the others, like a sheep, off into the unknown. Only that we cannot directly follow the boys because here in Nepal, in the domestic airport at least, the girls go through one line of security and the boys go through another. This segregation makes me laugh and fortunately the laughter calms me down.

Lilly goes ahead of me through security. When it's my turn, a rather gruff-voiced and scary-looking Nepali lady rummages through my rucksack, obsessed with finding knives and lighters that she can then confiscate. "Good grief, chill out, lady" is what I want to say. It's still dark outside and I feel like I'm being violated. Fortunately, I have neither, although I've only been in Nepal a few days and already I've started smoking the odd roll-up again so having a lighter wouldn't have been out of the question. It was inevitable; old habits die hard.

Relieved to survive the security woman, we enter the departure lounge, which consists of a much smaller open-plan and functional room filled with rows of plastic chairs. There's a small smoking room off to the side (this is Asia after all) and a small shop selling sweet Nepali tea and sugary snacks. The place is buzzing with Western trekkers, all chatting in a now more awake and excited "We are about to see Mount Everest" tone.

We sit to the side of the room and try and make ourselves comfortable on the plastic chairs. Tim is beaming with smiles and can't sit still. He's dreamt of this moment for weeks, maybe years, of actually getting up into the mountains and doing his outdoor-pursuits-trekking thing. His bright green eyes are twinkling as he talks non-stop to anyone who will listen.

Joe on the other hand is slumped in his chair, the hood of his faded red hoodie pulled over the black cap he's wearing as he tries to enjoy an extra few minutes of sleep. He's pulled his knees up to his chest and shares none of Tim's enthusiasm. The boys couldn't be more different. Joe doesn't come across as the kind of guy who you'd expect to want to trek to Everest Base Camp. He's more the kind of guy who you would expect to be hanging around on the beach, eyeing up the young ladies and charming them with his film quotes and twirling-hair skills. He's a sweetheart, really, a bit of a 'trust-fund boy', who's used to having everything done for him by his mum. Tim, however, is much more about the getting on with it and roughing it and then doing it for himself where he can. I can't imagine him lying around on a beach eyeing up the ladies.

I look around us and notice that we're surrounded by older people dressed in proper trekking wear. These people look like they know what they're doing, like they might actually be able to read a map and use walking poles. I can do neither. I might have a degree in geography, but I'm useless when it comes to reading maps. As for the walking poles, well, I have these with me, they're my mum's, but I've no idea how to use them.

The conversation is not soothing me. Tim talks about iodine tablets and he has a proper water filter on his water bottle. I have no idea what to do with an iodine tablet nor why you'd need one in the first place. I also have no idea what he means when he talks about Gamow bags or elevations and how this may affect us. I'm feeling incredibly naïve and yet comforted by the fact that Lilly has absolutely no idea about these things either.

Matt and Ben are laughing together as they've a tendency to do. They make me laugh, Matt especially, as he sits there wearing his black shorts and simple black T-shirt, seemingly oblivious to my concerns about us not looking like professional trekkers. There's Joe trying to sleep and Craig smoking a cigarette and our Scottish medical student, Will, drinking a small plastic cup of steaming-hot black instant coffee.

None of us has any idea of what to expect in the mountains, nor have any of us undertaken any specific training, other than Tim who is still talking about Gamow bags to whomever will listen. We really are novices and yet here we are, poised to trek up to Mount Everest Base Camp, classified by Lonely Planet's *Trekking in the Nepal Himalaya*, as medium to hard... Hmm, ah yes, that is right, medium to HARD. Fabulous!

Will, to whom incidentally, I'm still both simultaneously attracted and wary of, as he loathes hippies and I think he has me classed as one on account of the stud in my nose, my vegetarianism and my yoga, made a comment last night that keeps playing on my mind. The boys joke about getting out there into the Himalayas and doing the male-coming-of-age-kill-a-few-chickens-eat-them-to-survive thing until Will says that perhaps this trek is not going to provide the wilderness experience that they are expecting.

He is right of course, about expectations. Often our expectations are out of kilter with our reality. And even though I am trying to let go of expectations, or not create them in the first place, my mind is in overdrive and I can't help but do so. You see, I'm passionate about anything spiritual. I love the spirit in life, and mountains have traditionally been revered as places of sacred power and spiritual attainment – the Himalayas in particular.

The word *hima* in Sanskrit means snow and the word *alaya* means abode. However, the magnificent mountain range of the Himalayas is more than just an abode of the snow. It's without doubt Mother Earth's biggest miracle. The Himalayas are the roof of the world, overwhelming us with their sheer magnificence and size. They humble us by giving us a true perspective of how small and insignificant we human beings really are!

Geographically, the Himalayas span right across five nations: India, Pakistan, China, Bhutan and Nepal. This is perhaps a reflection of its wide-ranging influence on world religion and spirituality, with many pilgrimages taking place every year. A number of faiths right across the religious spectrum, but particularly Hindus and Buddhists, consider the Himalayan Mountains to be an epicentre of spirituality, and by visiting their amazing peaks, find spiritual guidance and divine inspiration.

There are several aspects of the Himalayan scope and the culture of the Himalayas, which are considered some of the most spiritually enlightening in the world. For example, the Buddhist faith believes that there is a mystical city hidden deep within the Himalayas called Shambala, which has never been seen by any living person.

I've heard it said that Shambhala is not a material entity which can be visited in a physical human body, but that you need to reach it through mental realms instead. It's mentioned in several ancient Buddhist scriptures, but it remains geographically obscure. Apparently, only those with sufficiently good karma are able to reach it within their mental state. Shambhala is said to be made up of a sacred civilisation of people who are enlightened.

In Hinduism, there is the Hindu triad or the Great Trinity, which comprises three deities responsible for the cosmic functions of creation, maintenance and destruction. These functions are personified by the forms of Brahma, the creator, Vishnu, the maintainer or preserver, and Shiva, the destroyer.

For many Hindus Mount Kailash, situated among the Himalayan range in Tibet, is considered to be of great spiritual importance, as Shiva is said to reside there. The mountain is universally known as an axis-mundi, a spiritually sacred point in the world at which North, East, South and West meet, opening up a portal of communication between the lower and higher realms.

Here in Nepal, Mount Everest is known as Chomolungma or 'Goddess Mother of the Land' to Tibetan speakers like the Sherpas, and has been long revered as an abode of the gods. Its slopes were considered off-limits to humans. Even now, the Sherpas regard the mountain as a holy place. All modern expeditions begin with a puja ceremony in which Sherpas and other team members leave offerings and pay homage to the gods of the mountain, hoping to remain in their favour throughout the climb.

So, you see, it is rather difficult not to have any expectation at all, as I've always been drawn to the spiritual in life and am keen to embark on my first pilgrimage into the Himalayas. Knowing how much others experience the spiritual in these mountains has made me keen to experience it for myself. That's not to say I'm seeking enlightenment (as if!), more so an experience of the lightness of divine energy (at least, that's how I imagine it to be), being that much closer to the heavens above.

It's very exciting actually, this idea of being in the real and actual Himalayas. I don't know anyone else who has travelled here – none of my friends, family or yoga students have been here. It's this idea of the energy that has drawn me, really, not the trekking, or even the volunteer work, but the opportunity for potential spiritual growth because my life feels stuck and I need to move it forward.

As a Reiki Master Teacher and a yoga practitioner and teacher, I am fascinated by energy and the idea of becoming lighter energetically. This awareness of energy has started to shape my life to a certain extent, as I am drawn to areas where the energy is lighter, such as Byron Bay, Glastonbury and Vancouver Island for example, and now here in the Nepali Himalayas.

There are seven main energy centres in the body and each one is called a chakra, which means wheel in Sanskrit, and is symbolised by a spinning wheel of light through which life force energy (known as prana, chi, ki etc) moves. You cannot actually see the chakras in your physical body because they are fields of energy which occupy the subtle body, although you can potentially feel them. Each one represents an important energetic centre of the body and mind, as well as a stage of spiritual development. The chakras are aligned from root to crown as a column of energy and they are both conduits of energy and generators of energy. Life-force energy flows through the chakras and the rest of the body along a network of channels known as nadis.

Our beautiful Mother Earth has also got many strong energy fields and chakras. Visiting these places, or energetically connecting with them long distance, can have a profound effect on our energy. The Himalayas are said to constitute the crown chakra of Mother Earth, broadcasting Mother Earth's purpose, or true will. Bringing this energy into our life is meant to help us become more in tune with our own true will, true purpose, or soul's blueprint. This has the potential to make us calmer and clearer and enables us to connect more fully to our intuition and our higher self, our soul.

It's this that I am keen to develop – to be able to connect more fully with my true self, to step into greater authenticity – to be me! It's very easy, I feel, to get caught up in how you think you should be, or what you think you should do to be spiritual, and deny aspects of the self in the process. I have certainly met people who have done this. For example, some become vegetarians because they feel that they need to be vegetarians to be perceived as truly spiritual, (nonsense by the way; there is no requirement to be a vegetarian to be spiritual), or dressing or looking a certain way.

I've been guilty of this as much as the rest. It's perhaps a process we all go through when we are sincere about the practice. In my own quest to be spiritual, I have gone through periods of denying myself some pleasure in life – not socialising or having fun with friends, being super-strict with my diet and locking myself away with early nights and early rises.

My primary focus these last few years has been on my yoga practice and becoming a more sincere practitioner (according to my perception of what that means). In the process, I have denied myself the richness and diversity of life. I've been incredibly controlling of myself. Looking back, I recognise that this has not been the way to go and I am now keen to find greater balance.

The gateway to the Everest Base Camp trekking route is Lukla, a small town in Eastern Nepal, 2,800m above sea level. It is from here that we will trek to Kala Pattar, a small peak at 5,545m above sea level, a little higher than Everest Base Camp, which is said to afford panoramic views of Everest and the surrounding mountains. (Apparently you can't actually see Mount Everest from Base Camp itself.) Now, I'm certainly no mathematician, but even I know that this is some hill we have to climb these next couple of weeks – if we survive the landing into Lukla of course!

You see, to get to Lukla in a timely manner we have to fly and Lukla's airport is commonly described as the world's most dangerous airport. Perhaps for many that's their spiritual experience – overcoming the fear that might otherwise prevent them from nestling into this magnificent mountain range, because I tell you what, there's some surrendering that needs to come with this, and trust – having huge trust in the pilot!

Admittedly, you don't have to fly. You could trek from the village of Jiri, which is a three-hour car journey or a ten-hour bus ride from Kathmandu and then a six- to eight-day trek through rugged terrain, depending upon your ability to acclimatise. However, the flight only takes 45 minutes, so it's a no-brainer for us and like everything else about this trek I haven't given it too much thought. I'm just going to get on that plane like everyone else and see what happens!

3

For here
am I sitting in a tin can.
Far above the world.
Planet Earth is blue.
And there's nothing I can do.
"Space Oddity", David Bowie

Day 1 Continued: Lukla to Phakding

A team supervised by Sir Edmund Hillary built the unique airstrip at Lukla in 1965 as part of a hospital project and it has been upgraded and expanded a few times since. It's built on a slope, high on the side of a mountain, so that there's an elevation difference of about 60m between the two ends of the runway which slows planes and helps them to stop before they continue into the mountain peaks that rise at the end of the 450m runway. We're told that there are no instruments or navigational aids of any kind, so the pilots have to use their eyes on their flight approach.

Sitting in the small twin-prop aeroplane flying towards the mountains, my mind goes into complete overdrive and I can feel the fear and anxiety rising within me. I distract myself from these unsettling feelings by entering into an internal dialogue about rather immaterial concerns, at least in the bigger picture of life: "Will they have green tea up in the mountains? Will I be able to eat the food? Will I have enough time to practice yoga each day, and what on earth am I going to do with my life when this trip is over?"

Thankfully, I am soon distracted from my thoughts by the sense of excitement that suddenly fills the aeroplane. Lo and behold, through the small windows of the plane, snow-capped peaks of the mountains can now be seen. There they are in all their majesty, poking through the thick and floaty white clouds below us and glinting as the rays of the sun reflect into the thin air, sparkling like diamonds. I quickly reach for my camera and capture my first glimpse of those awesome peaks. It's then that it hits me, and I feel an overwhelming sense of joy and excitement at the realisation that I am here, right in the heart of the incredible Himalayas. Wow!

Safely on the ground at Lukla Airport (phew!), we are greeted by our Nepali guide for this trek, Pemba, who has the most infectious smile and bright, scintillating eyes. He is a Sherpa, born in Solukumbu, the Everest district of the country, and he tells us that we will pass through his hometown on our trek. He now lives much of the year in America, where he has a work visa. Amazingly, he's a qualified lawyer by profession, but can only find work in a fast-food restaurant in America, yet he is very positive about the situation.

Pemba is a good friend of both Mingmar and the British chairman of the charity and visits the country each year to assist by guiding groups, like us, up to Everest Base Camp. The chairman of the charity has summited Everest a few times now and from what I gather both Mingmar and Pemba have been instrumental in helping him to achieve this and helping to advance his dream of making a difference to the Sherpas here in Nepal.

He does this in a number of ways, not least by providing an income to Pemba and Mingmar and their Sherpa families, but also by supporting a group of porters and their families back home in their rural village of Bupsa, a day's trek down the mountain from Lukla, on the trail to Jiri. Furthermore, he has helped with development projects in Bupsa and the neighbouring village, such as restoring the local gompa (temple) and establishing a hydroelectric plant to provide electricity to these villages and thus enabling them to have some light in their homes in the evening.

He also supports the local government school in Bupsa and it is here that we will go after the trek to help rebuild one of the classrooms and assist at the school itself. After that we will be volunteering in a boarding school in Kathmandu, where some of the Sherpa children board, including a few from Bupsa.

On this trek, Pemba is supported by a group of male porters who all live in Bupsa. This means that our trekking is helping to support these men and their families directly, as they will earn a wage carrying our bags up and down the mountain. There's a part of me that feels guilty that these men will have to carry my stuff for me, but at the same time I recognise that it provides them with an income. They're very gentle men and yet incredibly strong and waste no time in picking up our bags for us.

We're a jolly bunch as we leave the small airport on foot following Pemba, all of us delighted to have made it safely. It's incredibly different up here. Not only are we at a higher elevation, but the air is clean and it's so quiet, especially in contrast to the pollution and noise of Kathmandu. There are no vehicles in these mountains, the terrain does not allow it, so everything must be carried by foot, human or animal.

Lukla is a relatively busy hill town (compared to other hill towns) filled with a collection of lodges, airline travel agencies and shops selling trekking gear. There is the promise of some basic Internet access, although I've already realised that we're probably not going to be sending too many messages in the mountains. My mobile phone hasn't worked since we arrived in Nepal and we are a world away from Wi-Fi; it's an interesting concept, not having access to the outside world and therefore not being able to communicate with my family back at home in Guernsey and Australia.

We follow the porters from the small airport along the dirt road that leads us through the centre of the town, passing children playing in the mud at the side of the path. I've grown fond of the craziness of Kathmandu over the last few days, but it is refreshing to breathe clean and crisp air. I'm also joyful about the peace – it's beautifully quiet and I can now think a little more clearly without the constant beeping of cars and motorbikes, and the barking of dogs, that have been the predominant background noise in the city.

As we eat breakfast together in the restaurant of one of the many hotels in town, Pemba talks to us about the trek. He is keen to stress the fact that altitude is an overriding factor in the success rate of the Everest Base Camp route. He explains that virtually everyone trekking over 4,000m above sea level will experience some mild symptoms because at higher elevations there is less oxygen and lower atmospheric pressure. This combination can produce a variety of unpredictable effects on the body and, taken to an extreme, can even cause the brain to swell, fill the lungs with fluid, suppress the appetite and cause muscle tissue to waste away.

Altitude sickness is something I know very little about and it sounds scary! It's never been something I've thought about and I certainly hadn't considered it being a risk factor on this trek. Despite the whole no-expectation thing, in my head my vision of this trek centres around me practising yoga in the Himalayas with the mountains in the background, while I tap into the famed spiritual mountain energy and float around in a state of meditative bliss… There's no place for altitude sickness in this!

Pemba interrupts my thoughts to stress the fact that young people are particularly susceptible to altitude sickness and the simplest cure is to "Descend, descend, descend". He says it again to stress the point: "Descend, descend, descend", and he adds, "You must all tell me immediately if you start to feel ill. There's no time for the ego, not if you want to stay safe." It all sounds rather serious and I'm pleased when Joe pipes up with, "But we can just get a helicopter back down."

"Well, yes, there are helicopters," Pemba agrees, "but you don't often have the time to wait for one and you cannot always guarantee that the weather will permit a helicopter landing."

Good grief, I think to myself, this really is serious! I'd been thinking the same as Joe, that if things start to get really bad then surely we could just be winched off the mountain. There's usually always a way out – my mum has certainly worked many a miracle in my life when I needed a way out! But clearly it's not that easy, which makes me feel a little uncomfortable; there's no buying our way out of altitude sickness by the sound of it.

Joe laughs, "I liked the idea of getting a helicopter to come and take me back down the mountain. Imagine how cool that would be, especially if I got a photo of me in it", and the boys start giggling among themselves. The trouble is, Joe is on my wavelength with this one and semi-serious too. Perhaps it's a Guernsey thing, or perhaps it's due to the fact we both have very lovely parents who have always done what they can for us, but he too takes some comfort in the fact that there is always a way out of a situation, especially if your parents are involved, helicopter or no helicopter!

The reality is, however, that we are very far away from home in the mountains and we're very much at the mercy of our body's ability to cope with the altitude and the weather conditions along the trek. And right now, there's no way of predicting either, so it's just a case of wait and see. Still, we're here now and I'm joyful. It's not every day you find yourself in the Himalayas and I intend to make the most of it.

After breakfast, we rush around doing last-minute errands; Tim is on a mission to buy more iodine. "Why do we need iodine?" we ask him. "For your water," he tells us, as if we should know what he means. We don't. I have grapefruit-seed extract from the health food shop back at home to kill bad bacteria and I am hoping that this will suffice. The rest of the boys rush off to try and use the Internet, even though they only used it last night. It's the draw of Facebook (which is still lost on me; I don't even have an account at this point in my life) and I laugh because they want to show off to their friends by posting 'Here I am up in the Himalayas' photos even if it costs them triple what it would cost them to use the Internet in Kathmandu.

Lilly and I are more practical with our time and we make sure we have as much toilet roll and baby wipes as we can fit into our bags! We've a feeling both will become essential further up on the trek where supplies are in such short demand and, as we can't guarantee daily showers, the baby wipes may well come in handy. Furthermore, we're also aware of the necessity to constantly clean our hands in Nepal because even handling the money and then putting hands near mouths can cause sickness. I don't want to be sick regardless of where it is, but especially not on the trek.

When we've finished shopping, we sit on a stone ledge outside the hotel on the edge of the path smoking and watching the world go by. Huge yaks wander past us, their tinkling bells echoing down the dusty street. These wonderfully shaggy beasts are used to transport a plethora of goods from Lukla up the Everest Base Camp trail. We watch Sherpa porters half-run half-walk past us, carrying massive trekking bags. Supply porters pass us too carrying *dokos* – woven bamboo baskets that cause them to take on quite a stoop in their posture, the weight of the basket supported by their backs as much as the strap that loops around their foreheads. I'm immediately awestruck by the strength and agility of these men.

It's beautiful here in Lukla. As I mentioned earlier, not only does the air feel clean and crisp, but there's a certain energy that I can't explain; it's got a familiarity to it and makes me feel safe. Not only that, but there's a gentle rhythm to the pace and, aside from the porters who are clearly on a mission, the trekkers walking past are not hurrying, as they might do in Kathmandu. It's peaceful too, and I relish this moment of smoking, chatting and absorbing the morning atmosphere.

Despite all my best efforts to maintain my non-smoking status, I succumbed in Kathmandu and am back into the full swing of this dreadful habit. I did manage to stop smoking cigarettes after my first yoga trip to Byron Bay, the year after I started practising yoga and the year before I undertook my yoga teacher training. This was a huge relief, but back home in Guernsey, after I'd qualified as a yoga teacher and was trying to make a go of a more settled and less nomadic life, it didn't take too long for me to regress and start smoking roll-ups (which didn't feel as bad as smoking proper cigarettes!).

The desire to smoke drives me mad and I frequently wish that I had never first started all those years ago when I was at university and taught myself how to smoke (get that!) so I could experiment with hashish.

I grew to enjoy both, smoking cigarettes and joints, or at least I thought I enjoyed both, but both carry a price in terms of the guilt of knowing that neither are necessarily positive to my health. I was drawn to smoking hashish out of curiosity, really, but also because I had a sense that it might somehow expand my consciousness and aid my spiritual development. Perhaps there's some truth in this because certainly hashish, or charas, is widely smoked by Shaivite devotees, and cannabis itself is seen as a gift of Shiva to aid in sadhana (daily spiritual practice). However, it is illegal in much of the world and smoking and yoga are in conflict with one another.

Some of the boys were experimenting with hashish in Kathmandu and I couldn't resist joining in – like I say, old habits die hard. I wouldn't say it expanded my consciousness necessarily but it did result in me finding my conversations with Lilly even more hysterical than usual. Lilly has an infectious laugh and we've had so much fun together already – it seems that our friendship is further cemented by the fact we can smoke together (roll-ups for me, cigarettes for Lilly).

It's not ideal and I berate myself regularly for smoking – I'm a yoga teacher and Reiki master after all and I should know better. It doesn't feel right teaching others to breathe properly and to practise pranayama (breathing exercises), while clogging my own lungs with smoke. I know I'm not alone and that other yoga teachers and practitioners go through the same guilt process as me. Clearly there's still some healing work that needs to be done to heal the underlying reason for me feeling the need to smoke (creating a smoke screen in my life) in the first place. The trouble is, I love the ritual of it, of rolling tobacco and creating a roll-up, and I love the momentary time out that smoking creates.

After we've finished smoking, Lilly and I collect our belongings and meet with the boys for our 10am start. It's been a busy morning and I almost have to pinch myself because, again, it feels a little surreal to be here in the tranquillity of Solukhumbu in Nepal. I'm both delighted and nervous at the same time and I keep fretting about whether I need to go to the toilet, as I'm not quite sure where the next toilet will be (and what it will be like!).

Solukhumbu is one of seventy-five districts of Nepal, consisting of the subregions Solu and Khumbu, together covering an area of 3,312 sq km. Mount Everest is located in the north of the district within the Sagarmatha National Park. This is the highest national park in the world, home to three peaks higher than 8,000m, including Mount Everest. The park was formally opened to the public in 1976 and in terms of popularity among trekkers, this region ranks second after the Annapurna Range of Nepal.

The people of this district are known as Sherpas. The word 'Sherpa' originally meant 'people from the East' and before trekking became a popular pastime in the Himalayas, the term simply denoted a group of people who migrated to Nepal from Eastern Tibet before the two regions became separate countries. Sherpas therefore live in the upper regions of Solukhumbu. In the past they were traders and porters, trading with India, Tibet, China and beyond. The closure of the border between India and China undermined their economy, but fortunately they found their load-carrying ability could be put to good use helping mountaineering expeditions and trekkers, both on normal treks, like we're doing, and those at high altitudes.

The lead Sherpa's job is to set up camp, manage the porters, ensure that loads are evenly distributed and take responsibility for the group's safety. This is Pemba's job. He is supported by our four porters. These lovely men will carry our bags for us and go on ahead of us to ensure we have lodgings for the night.

The Sherpas are well known for their incredible strength, and I'm witnessing this for myself. I cannot believe the loads they can carry. It's unbelievable and puts me to shame, carrying just my daysack. Still, I appreciate that we are providing their livelihood and if I'm honest, I doubt very much I could carry my bag up any hills, so I'm grateful for the help!

With daysacks now on our backs and our porters already rushing off ahead of us, we're off, just like that. Every journey has to begin with the first step and we take ours... into the unknown of the Mount Everest trail, next stop the high mountains.

A minute into our trek and I have the sudden realisation that I have no idea what I'm doing. It sounds silly, but at what pace do I walk? Who do I talk to and about what? And how do I use my walking pole? On the latter, now I'm here, I just cannot remember what Mum told me about using them and it doesn't help that I'm only now using one pole as I've lent the other one to Lilly.

Fortunately, the terrain is fairly gentle initially, not that I notice too much of it as I'm head down, one foot in front of the other, caught in thought, wondering how the next few weeks will be, up in these mountains. I am soon aware, however, of the other people on the path, as I hadn't anticipated this – in my imagination, I thought we'd be the only ones here! Sadly not, and it feels busy to me, with many other trekkers also trying to get into their stride.

Busy or not, I'm very aware of the freedom of space. The path we're following is generous and there's room for us all. Thankfully, it's a relatively easy-going couple of hours, as we try to establish our pace. The time passes quickly as we walk through a dense forest, passing hamlets consisting of a few simple stone dwellings.

On we go, following the well-trodden path. We soon approach some Tibetan prayer wheels in the middle of the trail, and Pemba tells us that we must always pass these, together with temples and stupas, on the left-hand side. Tibetan prayer wheels fascinate me. They consist of cylindrical wheels on a spindle made from metal, wood, stone, leather or coarse cotton. Traditionally, the mantra *Om Mani Padme Hum* is written in Sanskrit on the outside of the wheel. At the core of each cylinder is a 'life tree'.

This is generally made of metal or wood and has relevant mantras wrapped around it or written upon it. Thousands and thousands (and sometimes millions depending on the size of the prayer wheel) of mantras can be wrapped around the life tree and sent out into the world with each turning (quite amazing!). Typically, large decorative versions of the syllables of the mantra are carved on the outside cover of the wheel too. They're very impressive and I love what they represent.

This mantra often translates as 'Hail to the jewel of the lotus' and is one of the most sacred Buddhist mantras used frequently in Tibet and in the surrounding countries like Nepal. Each syllable is said to have a secret power of producing a definite result, and when properly pronounced, it produces different results too. Tibetan Buddhists believe that saying this mantra out loud or silently to oneself invokes the powerful benevolent attention and blessings of Chenrezig, the embodiment of compassion. When a prayer wheel is spun, it sends prayers out into the Universe and is said to have the same positive effect as reciting the mantras and prayers.

Some ancient texts suggest that prayer wheels can be used to create and accumulate wisdom and good karma (merit) and in that way purify any bad karma being carried by an individual. The prayer wheels are spun clockwise as the direction in which the mantras are written is that of the movement of the sun across the sky.

Carrying on along the trail I delight in catching sight of brightly coloured Tibetan prayer flags tied between the branches of tall trees, their blue, white, red, green and yellow colours representing the five elements. They are woodblock-printed with sutras, mantras, prayers and sacred symbols. One of the most common symbols at the centre of prayer flags is the Wind Horse (Lung-ta), which represents good fortune and luck and is a symbol of basic goodness that is thought to possess powerful energy, while other central images include Buddha and Tara (an important figure in Tibetan Buddhism known as the 'Mother of Liberation').

Prayer flags date back thousands of years to healing ceremonies of the Bon tradition of pre-Buddhist Tibet. They are found, as they are here, strung along mountain ridges and peaks high in the Himalayas and at Buddhist stupas and temples. Nowadays you also see them adorning homes around the world – my parents have some fluttering in their garden in Guernsey, for example!

Tibetans believe that as the flags flutter, the wind catches the prayers, spreading goodwill and compassion into all-pervading space. They are said to bring happiness, long life and prosperity to those who are touched by their vibrations. It is my opinion that the whole world should be adorned with them!

I was especially fond of landscape geography at university and with, my spiritual perspective on all things, I am loving that the landscape is permeated by the energy of Tibetan Buddhism. As we walk on, we pass Mani stones too. These are large stones also covered with the Tibetan inscription, *Om Mani Padme Hum*, although sometimes they can consist of a mound of smaller stones, which people add to as they pass by, as a form of prayer.

It's incredible to think that we can bring mindfulness and compassionate and loving energy to the physical landscape through the use of mantra. The terrain itself demands a presence and the lack of access to Wi-Fi and other modern distractions certainly encourages one to be present too. However, the fact that you are also reminded to repeat the mantra and invoke the energy that this mantra contains, increasing compassion and wisdom for yourself while also spreading this energy out into the Himalayas and beyond, is mind-blowing and heart-opening all at the same time! This is a wisdom beyond all the technology and wealth of the West, and I'm keen to experience more of this spiritual landscape along the trail.

From time to time, I can also hear wind chimes, a gentle sound as the wind blows through the valley, adding to the esoteric and healing nature of this beautiful part of the world. I love that there is reverence for Mother Earth and an acknowledgment of the collective consciousness that permeates *all* life.

The terrain is still easy-going as we walk downhill for much of the morning. It's perhaps no surprise, therefore, that the trekkers we pass who are returning to Lukla, look like they'll be pleased to make it back to the hill town. It crosses my mind that we'll be those returning trekkers within the next two weeks (if all goes well) and I wonder what adventures lie ahead of us between now and then.

I'm delighted that for now we're being gently introduced to the mountains, although I'm surprised when we stop for an early lunch, after only an hour and a half or so of trekking – I've barely had the chance to get hungry!

Still, I haven't appreciated at this stage that the guesthouses (eateries) that you find along this trail are not like those I am used to visiting back at home. Not only is the one Pemba chooses little more than a wooden shack with small and basic windows looking out over the terrain, but it also takes a long time for our food to be cooked and for us to therefore eat.

The building itself contains simple wooden benches and tables and after taking a peek inside we decide that we might be better off sitting outside, so that we can be warmed by the late-morning sun. It's a novelty to us and we delight in reading the menu and ordering our first taste of mountain food. I choose a vegetable curry as this is the only thing on the menu that doesn't include the word 'fried' before it. Once our order has been taken we sit and wait.

And we sit and we wait a bit more. And then we sit and we wait even more. We're on mountain time, Nepali mountain time and, as I quickly realise, this means that things happen slowly, very slowly. Thus, we have plenty of time to sit back and go with the flow, however challenging we might find that, given the fact that we're used to a faster-paced life back home in the West.

The boys chatter noisily and joke among themselves, trying to outdo each other with their tales and I sigh with relief that Lilly is with me on this trip. It has already crossed my mind that if Lilly hadn't signed up, then I would have been here on my own, having to deal with these youngsters and their boyish ways. Don't get me wrong, they can be fun, but their youth means that there are lots of toilet humour jokes and taking the mickey out of each other, which can get rather tiresome.

While we continue to wait, I get to experience my first mountain toilet. The toilet itself is a Western-style one, although it's located in a rickety, old small shed, a short walk towards the river below. It's very smelly and doesn't flush like the toilets at home. Instead, there's a bucket of water to use to facilitate the flushing. There's no toilet roll and no sign of running water to wash hands afterwards either.

I quickly realise the reason they recommended we bring our own toilet roll and hand wipes on the trek and I'm pleased that Lilly and I have stocked up on both. It feels strange though, this lack of running water, and I can tell that it is going to take some time to adjust to mountain living. I'm slightly nervous of the toilet conditions ahead and I'm just grateful that I've recently finished menstruating!

Back at the table, Pemba laughs as Joe complains about the toilet, before telling us to make the most of it, because things aren't always so easy-going further up the trail. "This toilet here is good," he says, motioning in the direction of the toilet shed, a smile on his lips. "You have a Western toilet here," and with that he chuckles to himself.

I think we're all beginning to consider what might happen if we need the toilet while we are trekking and whether we will need to squat in a clearing. It crosses my mind that I don't have any way of digging a little hole should this be needed and I surmise that surely Tim must have made a provision for this. There are so many unknowns about this trip – clearly surrendering to the moment is one of the lessons out here for me, well, for us all, really.

I zone in and out of the boys' chatter, drinking fresh mint tea as I write in my journal. The weather has been overcast since we arrived into Lukla and yet warm enough that I haven't needed to wear my fleece over my T-shirt. However, sitting outside here at the café, the wind begins to pick up and I'm soon cold enough to put it on. This is the other thing about this trek, knowing or not knowing what to wear because I'm told that the weather can be changeable.

Here at these lower climes it is perhaps not such a concern. Aside from Tim, who is wearing shorts, the rest of us are in trousers. Well, I'm actually in leggings, but you get the gist. We also carry waterproofs in our daysacks, but our warmer clothes are packed in our large rucksacks, which are being carried by our porters who are already farther up the trail than we are. It's strange right now to think that we'll need warmer clothes because overall the weather is a pleasant springtime temperature.

Fortunately, our lunch finally arrives and distracts me from my thoughts. The boys wolf down their plates of fried food within seconds and I chuckle to myself about their lack of mindfulness, especially after the amount of time and effort it has clearly taken the Nepali staff to prepare and cook the food. This is more obvious to me just now than it might be ordinarily simply because, while I was recently based in Byron Bay, I also visited Govinda Valley, a Hare Krishna community near Sydney to help out on a yoga teacher-training course.

The Hare Krishnas infuse their vegetarian food with love, chanting various mantras as they prepare and cook the food, thus imbuing it with the loving energy of the heart and the positive energy contained within the mantra, let alone present mindfulness. You can tell the difference when dishes are prepared like this – quite a difference to the taste and quality of food cooked by someone with no loving interest or awareness, or even worse, fast-food or pre-packaged food.

The food feels lighter and more nourishing somehow – a little like when you eat home-cooked food made by someone who both cares about you and cares about quality and nourishing ingredients. The added bonus with the Hare Krishnas is the energy of the mantras, which also add a certain quality to the food – the proof is in the taste. I know my mum thinks I'm mad when I talk about this, but it's true! I love Vedic chanting and am very aware how chanting mantras changes how we feel, and thus the energy we put into something such as food preparation.

Moreover, we were positively encouraged to take our time eating the food, being mindful and appreciative, savouring the taste, chewing slowly and encouraging good digestion, as well as appreciating all the effort that went into its creation.

The vegetarian curry that I ordered for lunch is yummy and I'm heartened by this. I'm quite fussy, really, as I like healthy food and lots of vegetables, and I've been fretting about whether I'll be able to eat well on the trek. So far so good, and while I wouldn't normally eat a cooked lunch, I'm aware that we have a whole afternoon of trekking ahead of us so fuelling properly is vital.

We're soon on our way again and I walk on my own, enjoying a break from the constant chatter of the boys. I'm beginning to notice more of the landscape now that I'm finding my stride and not staring solely down at the ground. We pass tall pine trees and bright pink spring rhododendrons growing at the side of the path – the latter are an attraction for people to Nepal at this time of year, when they are in full bloom.

Below us the fast-flowing Dudh Kosi River runs through the valley and it is this that the path follows as we trek towards Phakding, where we are due to stay in a lodge for the night. It's invigorating to hear the water's roar and to watch it so full of life. There aren't any rivers in Guernsey, so being near one is always a welcome experience for me. This river drains all the water from the Khumbi area. The only downside of the river is the fact that we have to cross it from time to time and this can be a rather scary experience, as we soon discover.

Leaving the woods, we see ahead of us views of an upland plateau full of fields and scattered houses. There are green slopes all around and after a while we cross the first huge suspension bridge over the deep-sided valley. It seems like a really long bridge to me, a good 70 metres (not that I'm any good at estimating these things!), but certainly long enough to make me stop and stand in awe, wondering how on earth anyone managed to construct the bridge in the first place.

Nepal is famous for its suspension bridges, a major part of the infrastructure of rural life, which have helped to enhance the social and economic life of the countryside. Since Nepal has more than 6,000 small rivers, lying mostly in hilly and mountainous areas, bridges provide a vital link between villages and towns. Before the 1950s, they were constructed from wood, which caused a lot of deforestation. Later on, wood was replaced by steel, which is more durable.

This one ahead of us is made of steel, with a metal grid for a walkway and hurricane fencing along the sides. Faded prayer flags are tied to it, fluttering in the constant breeze that blows through this valley. Pemba stops us all and tells us that we must always wait for him before crossing any of these bridges on the trail. He explains that we must always look carefully before entering the bridge to check that there are no caravans of yaks, as they have absolute priority. These hybrid cows are used for cargo transportation and can pose a danger to us trekkers – they hate walking on the metal grids with the river rushing below them so can easily become agitated, which could pose a danger, especially as they have sharp horns.

We gingerly make our way across the swaying bridge. I hold the steel railing as if gripping on for dear life. I don't have a problem with heights ordinarily, but then I've never crossed one of these bridges before and I am a little freaked out by the thought of the bridge giving way and us falling to our peril, or of somehow slipping off the side, which is highly unlikely as the hurricane fencing provides some protection, but nonetheless my mind goes into overdrive.

I feel a little fear and have to consciously remind myself that this is essentially 'False Evidence Appearing Real', an acronym originated by actor Gary Busey. It's my mind that is creating the fear by running through different scenarios which are not real. The bridge is unlikely to give way and I am unlikely to fall from it, so I repeat 'False Evidence Appearing

Real' to myself as I cross the bridge, almost like a mantra, to remind myself of the fact the fear is just a story in my head.

Pemba follows at the back of the group and keeps shouting at us to walk slowly. The boys appear fearless and don't appreciate the hesitant nature with which Lilly and I cross the bridge. We attempt to chatter but it is difficult to hear each other, as I am walking in front of her and the wind carries my voice away from her and down the valley. All I can do is follow the boys, mindful of my step and trying not to look down too much, but this is difficult because my eyes are drawn down, both checking my step and being strangely curious of what lies below us.

It's a relief to make it to the other side of the riverbank though and continue on our way. I can still see the river: it looks so cold and powerful, studded as it is with huge boulders. Pemba tells me that its name translates as 'the milk river' and it certainly lives up to this, with its opaque milky and blue-white colour, due to the glacial silt and dissolved minerals in it.

We pass now a huge Mani stone, perhaps three metres or so in height, and carved with the mantra *Om Mani Padme Hum*, which is written in Sanskrit and has been painted in white to appear more prominent. It's huge in comparison to us and I marvel that someone took the time to create this, a work of art in the Himalayas, and spreading good energy for ever more. Amazing!

It's mid-afternoon when we arrive at our lodge at Phakding. Only a few hours' walk since lunch and 6.2km from Lukla where we began today, Phakding is a small mountain village in this Khumbu region, at an altitude of 2,610m and a UNESCO World Heritage Site. This is one of the main stopping points for trekkers at the beginning of the Everest trail and none of us can quite believe that we've finished our first day of trekking already. Apart from experiencing a slight burning in my thighs as I walked up the last few steps into this village, I feel absolutely fine, so does everyone else, and we're all pleasantly surprised.

Lilly and I share a basic room in the lodge and while it's certainly nothing to get excited about, at least it's clean. We manage to stash our rucksacks between the two simple wooden beds, before removing our shoes and testing out the mattresses. They're certainly thin, but not uncomfortable, and I unpack my sleeping bag from my rucksack to make it more cosy.

My main concern right now is the state of the shared bathroom and so I'm heartened to find it contains a proper Western toilet and a shower with hot water. Amazing! It seems so silly to get uptight about showering, but I love showering! I shower at least twice a day at home, if not more if I am teaching yoga or channelling Reiki. Not only does showering obviously clean the physical body, but equally, and if not more importantly at times, it also cleanses the body energetically, and it is this that makes me want to shower, certainly when I've been working with other people's energies, or as I am here, part of a group.

I unpack my travel clock and my 'altar' that I've brought with me, consisting of a little statue of Buddha, a few rose-quartz and amethyst crystals and my travel incense holder. I take these with me whenever I'm travelling, as they help to make me feel more at home; plus, I like to practise in front of my altar, as I feel that it deepens my connection to the Divine.

As there's nothing else to do, no shops to visit, no Internet to check emails, no TV to watch, I make the most of the opportunity to get on my yoga mat while the boys head out to investigate the Dudh Kosi River and Lilly is keen to relax. I've had a daily self-practice for many years now, having established one within weeks of discovering yoga, as I felt the benefits immediately, and was keen to expand my awareness of yoga. Furthermore, it just felt like coming home to myself and it is this I relish right now.

In my mind, I had imagined practising yoga in the Himalayas on the bank beside the river, with views of the mountains in the distance and me breathing in the fresh Himalayan air. However, reality finds me squashed into the dusty and ever so slightly cold corridor on the first floor of the lodge, squeezed between the paper-thin walls of the surrounding bedrooms. I can actually hear the muffled sound of people chattering in their rooms and they can probably hear me outside, wondering what on earth I'm doing.

Now I come to think about it, it's probably a little crazy and demonstrates my commitment, or indeed attachment splendidly! It doesn't cross my mind that I might be in anyone's way. Nope, I am hell-bent on practising yoga while tapping into the Himalayan energy and I'll do that whatever it takes. Really, I just want to stretch my body and ground and centre myself as it's been a bit of a whirlwind, since arriving in Nepal and adjusting to a new environment in Kathmandu and now here in the mountains where I am well and truly out of my comfort zone.

A little later, the boys return from their walk to find me covered in dust and sinking into pigeon pose. I look up at them and they seem surprised, as they've not seen me on my mat yet so it's new to them. I did practise yoga on the balcony in Kathmandu, but early in the morning before they were awake, plus they probably don't expect to find anyone in the corridor. Will breaks the momentary silence. "Ooh, you're doing yoga," he says in his lovely Scottish accent, surprised because it's one thing to talk about it and quite another to do it, and now he realises that I really do practise yoga, I don't just talk about it!

After yoga, Lilly and I walk along the trail further into the village and sit outside one of the basic 'cafés', and drink hot ginger tea. I'm pleasantly surprised that such a healthy drink exists up here. I'm not quite sure what I was expecting, but having been in Byron Bay, which is awash with organic, locally-grown produce and cafés selling very healthy foods, I figured I might have to lower my standards.

Fortunately, my evening meal is also healthy, as I order another curry, which is full of vegetables and tastes yummy, served with plain rice. As well as eating a vegetarian diet, I also try to follow Ayurvedic principles to support my constitution. Ayurveda is truly inspiring, the most ancient and authentically recorded health system in history – over 5,000 years old. It was created by yogis who spent their lives studying nature and the human condition.

Meaning 'the science of life', Ayurveda is exactly that, viewing health in four dimensions – physical, sensory, mental and spiritual – and centred on preventative medicine and bringing a person back to balance. It shows how an imbalance in one part of a person's being will affect them in another i.e. if a person isn't being true to their life path (dharma) then physical and mental illnesses can arise which cannot be effectively treated with modern medicines, but can be helped by Ayurveda.

Ayurveda uses elemental medicines, which means that they balance out earth, fire, water, air and ether in the body. These are divided into three doshas – vata, pitta and kapha – which are the basis of a person's constitution and also the factors that can create imbalances. Ayurveda places great emphasis on diet, lifestyle, yoga, meditation, massage and herbal medicines to bring a person back to health and keep them there. It's for this reason that I try to follow the Ayurvedic diet that supports my health and wellbeing.

The boys are fascinated by my vegetarianism, but are also quick to judge my choice and talk solely about the merits of eating meat. Will, the Scottish medic, is very much against the whole idea of vegetarianism, which is funny really when you consider some of the potential health benefits and him being a trainee doctor. I'm very aware that the whole concept of eating, and thus absorbing, the energetic fear imbedded in the flesh of the dead animal from the moment of death, is beyond discussion right now. After all, I respect the boys' choice to eat meat and wish that they would respect mine not to do so.

They are all determined to eat meat while they can because they've been told that there is a chance it will become harder to source further up in the mountains. Will is already concerned about this prospect, particularly as this means that he too will be eating a vegetarian diet. I really don't understand the big deal, but then I'm used to eating this way, as I have been a vegetarian on and off since I was thirteen years old. Initially I stopped eating meat because I didn't like the texture and taste of it, and then I became concerned about the ethics, and am now also mindful of the energetics of food and the impact this has on how we feel energetically, emotionally, mentally, physically and spiritually.

Yoga students have asked me whether they should become vegetarians now that they practise yoga and I'm always keen to stress that vegetarianism is not a requirement for someone following the yogic path. It's all about being true to ourselves. If we want to eat meat, then we eat meat; if we don't want to eat meat, then we don't eat meat. When someone regularly practises yoga, or perhaps brings something like Reiki into their life, then that person may find that their sensitivities change and with that they experience a shifting awareness of all aspects of life, including the food that they eat. But it should arise naturally, not be forced.

I'm aware that one of my challenges on this trek is to not be affected by the boys being unkind about my life choices, simply because they have a different perspective on life. Another challenge is the fact it's 8.15pm and it's bedtime! I haven't gone to bed this early for a long time now, but there's nothing else to do. We have access to a very faint electric light in our room, but this barely provides enough to read easily. It's little things like this that are a novelty. We're so used to a constant supply of electricity at home that it's taking some adjustment. The process began in Kathmandu, where there's load-shedding for up to eighteen hours a day. This means that each area of the sprawling city has a timetable of the days and times each week when the residents should, in theory, have access to electricity. It was a bizarre concept for us, that the electricity wouldn't work at certain times of certain days, meaning the fridge would go off and we would lose light. It seems so alien to us because if there is a relatively short power cut back home in Guernsey, then there's an uproar. Nothing works. You can't get any light, you can't cook any food, the TV doesn't work, the Internet doesn't work, you can't do any washing, your computer is silent, and the fridge and freezer stop. It's certainly an inconvenience.

Here in Nepal there's very little consistent electricity and the people have had to adapt. In the house in Kathmandu there is a gas oven, so that we can continue to cook without electricity, and torches and candles are stashed all around the house so that we can access these during the evening and be able to see in the dark. Furthermore, without a fridge to rely on, we are forced to buy food daily and use it in a more mindful way than we may have done back at home in the West. Plus, of course, one has to be aware of food poisoning which may result from food repeatedly being cooled and warmed in fridges and freezers that don't operate consistently.

Still, it's part of the experience and here we are now, Lilly and I both lying in bed wrapped in our sleeping bags, wearing small travel head torches on our foreheads (connected by elastic, wrapped around our heads) to enable us to read our books. We laugh to one another, shining the light in our respective faces, as we comment on the simplicity of our Nepali mountain life and our early bedtime. How times change! Mind you, I enjoy the novelty of living more in touch with nature and moving with the natural cycles of day and night, even if it does feel a little strange right now.

4

We're surfing in the air.
We're swimming in the frozen sky.
We're drifting over icy mountains floating by.
"Walking in the Air", Howard Blake

Day 2: Phakding to Namche Bazaar

Arghhhhhhhhhhhhhhhhhhhhh.
I hate trekking.
Trekking is hard, hard work.
So much for a gentle climb; if someone had told me it would be this difficult then maybe I might have taken a few minutes to actually consider whether I really wanted to put myself through this whole ridiculous experience.

So much for non-expectation – I can't believe I was expecting a gentle climb. I'm properly mad. It's only now I realise that I'm not in the slightest, not even the teeniest little bit prepared for the enormity of this trek.

I am up at 6.11am, so there is no time for a yoga practice, which is probably just as well as I need every ounce of energy just to get up the ridiculous and rather endless steps today. However, I do manage to squeeze in a quick shower as someone has accidentally left the hot water turned on, and I make the most of the sneaky opportunity to be super-clean and awake. I was the only person to take a shower last night too. Clearly, I am utterly obsessed with the need to be clean.

We all meet in the small dining room at 7am to eat breakfast, which sadly consists of tasteless porridge, *yuck*, washed down with hot lemon squash (at Pemba's recommendation). I don't usually eat breakfast so this alone is a major change for me, so too is having to converse with others so early. I've become increasingly aware throughout my travels that I'm someone who needs space in the morning and I've learned to take myself off first thing for a time of contemplation, but there is no such time available to me today.

Pemba tells us we need to eat a full breakfast, tasteless or not, as we will need lots of energy, for the long day ahead. We're all upbeat because, let's face it, we don't really know what's ahead of us, and the trekking yesterday was so gentle that I suspect we're all thinking it will be the same today. It doesn't take us long to pack up our bags, as we had barely unpacked the night before, and I'm aware this will feel like second nature soon, rolling up my sleeping bag and stashing this back in my bag, together with my little altar and my basic toiletries. Thus, we're all packed and ready to go by 7.30am.

Outside, the sun is already rising and the sounds of the river and the morning birdsong are beautiful. I begin walking alongside Will, Tim and the deputy Sherpa guide, a small, yet incredibly strong and quick-walking man called Dawa, up at the front of the group. Mother Earth is truly stunning along this section of the trail, as we follow the Dudh Kosi Valley further north, staying 100m or so above the river below.

Until this point, I've never given too much notice to the changing spring season other than to recognise that summer is on its way, but here, it's a joyful encounter and I feel almost an awakening. The energy of new life fills the air, making the whole world feel full of potential and new beginnings and I notice how this makes me feel more alive, filling me with energy. We pass through small mountain villages and witness more signs of spring – cherry blossom and chicks in upturned wicker baskets, so small and cute, and baby goats bleating for their mum's milk.

We climb up onto a ridge overlooking the next section of the valley and pass three young Nepali children sitting on a wooden platform, singing their hearts out, seemingly oblivious to us. They're each wearing mismatched clothing and there's a stream of snot congealing under their respective noses. I feel an urge to wipe their faces, and I laugh at myself, for the children are utterly oblivious, totally caught in the moment, contented and happy, singing away together. It's a beautiful scene and reminds me of the simplicity of this mountain environment and of the potential simplicity of life generally.

The views from the ridge are stunning. Tall snow-capped mountains appear in the distance, making us very aware that, yes, we've made it into the Himalayas. I almost need to pinch myself. Below us terraced land stretches as far as the eye can see, giving a true sense of the mountainous nature of Nepal – so much of life lived on steep terraced land. It's still very green at this height and filled with the vibrancy of new growth.

I find this kind of landscape truly spectacular and already I'm loving the rugged alpine terrain and the still, fresh air and the simple villages and beautiful people. This is the reason I've always had a passion for geography – people and places fascinate me. The word 'simplicity' frequently comes to mind, because life here is, well, simple, certainly compared to home, and there is a joy in this. I love the fact that the landscape doesn't allow vehicular access and, thus far, there have been no aeroplanes flying overhead; there's just us and nature, Mother Earth.

It is customary here to say "Namaste" to those you pass. It's a form of greeting and gesture of respect. Essentially it means, 'The love and light in me recognises the love and light in you', and it's a term that we commonly use at the end of yoga classes too, with our hands held together in prayer position, in front of the heart. I thoroughly love the fact that on this trek we frequently acknowledge those we pass, coming from the opposite direction, with a "Namaste".

Thus, I am frequently saying "Namaste" to Nepali porters, villagers or other (on the whole) Western trekkers like us. Often the children in the villages – those who aren't absorbed by their play – love to call out "Namaste" to us, while others gesture for something from us, as if begging, or stare at us as if they've never seen trekkers before.

The whole children-begging-on-the-trail thing fascinates me. From what I gather, historically, trekkers have brought sweets with them to hand to the children, thinking that they were being kind in treating the children to the sweets. However, without access to proper dental care in the mountains, a reality faced by many Nepali, the sugar from the sweets inevitably rots the children's teeth, which obviously wasn't the intention, but has become the reality. So giving sweets to children is now discouraged and trekkers are encouraged to bring school supplies instead.

The charity suggested that we might like to bring school supplies with us to take to the village where we will volunteer after the trek. However, I've also brought extra pencils with me to hand out to children we pass along the trail, but I haven't thought to keep them to hand in my daysack. They're in my bag being carried further up the trail by one of the porters. Still, now that I'm here, I'm questioning (as others do) whether even handing out pencils is a good thing because essentially it still encourages the children to beg, and I'm not sure that I feel comfortable about this. It's a tough one!

We follow the path down towards the river below and in the direction of another scary-looking steel suspension bridge which we need to cross to reach the east bank of the Dudh Kosi. The wind whistles through the valley and with the Dudh Kosi River flowing far below us, I feel a sense of trepidation as I slowly follow the boys towards the swaying suspension bridge covered in fading Tibetan prayer flags. Lilly is equally concerned because these bridges are still an unknown to us and the fear takes hold of me very easily, despite knowing that I have to cross them regardless – there's no going back now!

It doesn't help that I can see evidence of a settlement on the steep hillside ahead of me and off to the side, and I surmise that we must need to trek up there next, which looks like it might be a challenge in comparison to trekking at lower elevations. Lilly and I stand together both feeling a little anxious as we try to build up the confidence to step onto the swaying bridge.

The situation isn't helped by Joe and Will who both find it hilarious to jump up and down on the metal grids, so that the bridge moves more than it would do ordinarily. I step onto the bridge and try to focus on my breath. Lilly is behind me holding on to the steel rail as if her life depended on it. The boys jump up and down again and Lilly screams. I bend my knees trying to establish a solid foundation through my feet as the bridge sways a little from side to side. It's the strangest sensation trying to trek across a bridge that moves. No wonder the yaks get freaked out by it!

We're almost safely to the end of the bridge, when Joe and Will, who are quickly becoming partners in crime, jump up and down again, prompting more screaming from Lilly, and we both hold on to the steel ropes, half-running, half-walking to solid ground, trying not to get our respective walking poles caught in the wire forming the protective edge to the sides of the bridge, in the process. What a drama! Lilly and I laugh with the relief. We made it! I'm in awe of whoever managed to construct the bridge in the first place. What a feat!

I'm not, however, in awe of Joe and Will. I just can't be doing with their juvenile behaviour. It's not something that I usually invite into my life and, really, I haven't consciously invited it in now, but clearly there are lessons that need to be learned from finding myself in this group. I'm a loner, really, quite at peace in my own company, and I struggle with group energies and the pressure they bring in terms of trying to fit in, or being singled out. I also don't like having to watch my back, wondering when I'll be on the receiving end of the next joke.

Fortunately, I'm not alone. Tim is also someone who is very much at peace in his own company and he is also tiring of Will and Joe's joking and constant need to be noticed. Joe quotes from films at every available opportunity and Will is a know-it-all and appears to have placed himself on a pedestal on account of being older than the four gap-year students and already studying at university.

Ben and Matt stick together mainly, sometimes walking up ahead, while Craig hangs back with Lilly and Pemba who often form the back of the group. I find myself walking beside Tim for much of the trail, sometimes talking, sometimes not. It's funny the things you talk about, given the age difference.

We talk a lot about him going to university in September and about his life in Devon with his family.

I have my iPod with me so sometimes I listen to music, although I'm aware that there is limited access to electricity to charge it. Other times I enjoy walking on my own in silence. It's all a novelty for now and I'm contented taking in the scenery. This is a beautiful part of the trek as we pass villages interspersed with magnificent forests of rhododendron, magnolia and fir.

Soon it starts to get challenging though, with a steep climb up to the village of Monjo, which has a pretty setting beside the river, the Dudh Kosi. The path can get uneven underfoot, so you have to be mindful of your footing, which means that it is not always easy to take in the views, as you have to look down to avoid tripping.

Still, I'm intrigued by life here, as we pass through Monjo, which consists of a number of mainly stone-built lodges and houses set either side of the slim path. Their brightly coloured roofs in reds, blues and greens create a pretty scene, especially with the bright blue sky above and a mountaintop coming into view in the distance. Let us not forget the plentiful Tibetan prayer flags, hung between buildings, which further brighten the landscape with colour and sacred mantra.

Just above Monjo, there's the entrance checkpoint for the Sagarmatha National Park, designated as such in 1976 to protect a 1,148 sq km area surrounding Mount Everest (called Sagarmatha by the Nepalis), which was declared a UNESCO World Heritage Site in 1979. It's busy here, as people queue to pay their entry fees to obtain the relevant permit and log their arrival in the record book. Pemba is sorting permits and payments for us, so I'm a little oblivious to the technicalities, but from what I gather, we each have a Trekkers Information Management System (TIMS Card), which was obtained in Kathmandu, and now a permit to enter Sagarmatha National Park.

As we mill around together in the bright sunshine, waiting, I notice familiar faces from the trail yesterday.

I really hadn't expected it to be so busy, but I'm told that all trails headed to Everest come through here and I feel a sense of excitement in the air; we are on our way to Everest! We enter the park and make a steep, rocky descent, my walking pole helping me to navigate the terrain, before we cross another steel suspension bridge covered in yet more fading Tibetan prayer flags, this one 120m in length; that's long! The boys play their usual game of trying to scare us, but we're becoming more confident now and don't rise to the bait.

On the path goes, the air is clear and bright and we're wearing our fleeces to keep warm from the morning chill, but I expect that the combination of the heat of the sun and the demanding nature of the uphill climb will find us in T-shirts soon. I'm forming emails in my head now to my family back home, detailing the trek thus far. I'm keen to try to remember what I can of it and I stop to take the occasional photo with my camera. (This is in the days before mobile telephones had cameras built in.)

By the time we stop for lunch in a 'restaurant' that resembles a wooden shack on the side of the path, we're all really hungry. Trekking in this mountainous and hilly terrain certainly takes it out of you and we're impatient to eat, but as we've already experienced, we have to wait for our food to be prepared and cooked first.

Pemba has ordered Sherpa stew for all of us to eat because he believes it will provide much-needed energy for the afternoon ahead. It's a thick stew with dumplings and, much to my dismay, I quickly realise that it contains bits of meat. I almost spit my mouthful out in horror. What on earth is Pemba doing ordering me something with meat in it? I can't eat it, not least because it has meat in it, but also because it tastes revolting. I'm extremely disappointed as I'm very hungry. The boys laugh at me; they think it's hilarious that the stew has meat in it. I don't find it funny at all, and sulk, sitting back from the simple wooden table, and eating my muesli bar instead. I'm just hopeful that this, and the black tea I drink, will give me sufficient energy for the afternoon ahead.

It's the first time that I've properly thought about home and about my on-off boyfriend, B, whom I have left behind in Guernsey. He was a bit like my knight in shining armour, as he came into my life and picked me up when I was feeling low and lost. We're the best of friends, which is partly the reason for us having an on-off relationship these past four years, as it is difficult to let go of your best friend. We've known each other since primary school, growing up within about 200 metres as the crow flies from our respective family homes.

I enjoy his company, and our chatter, and the manner in which he makes me feel safe. This is quite in contrast to how I feel now because there's something about the energy of Will that bothers me and on top of that I'm really not someone who thrives in a group environment. I'm emotional just thinking about home and being here out of my comfort zone and not having a proper meal to prepare me for the afternoon.

Back on the trail, it soon becomes apparent that I should have eaten something more substantial than a muesli bar, and I berate myself for allowing Pemba to order food for me – I won't let that happen again. Pemba is right about one thing though. We need every ounce of energy available to us because the afternoon trekking is mainly uphill and it is extremely hard work.

We begin by crossing the river again on yet another suspension bridge. I'm getting used to these bridges now but I'm slightly challenged by views of a flood-damaged bridge just upstream, which makes me question the fragility of life in this mountain range where nature often takes control of things.

Initially, we are led into a false sense of security about what lies ahead because the trail follows the riverbank along the base of the valley itself, so we're not having to do any uphill climbing just yet. If anything, it's rather lovely being so close to the river as I find its energy cleansing and soothing for the soul. We just need to be mindful of not tripping over the gravel and pebbles underfoot.

In the distance, I can see a group of porters sitting on pebbles, under the shade of the trees, against the far riverbank, boiling tea in a pan set over a roaring flame. This way of life is a world away from the world I inhabit in Guernsey. It's much slower and more in touch with nature and brings with it a certain feeling of freedom. I could sigh with the relief of it, rooted as it is in survival and getting through each day safely.

Soon we reach the confluence of the Bhote Kosi and Dudh Kosi Rivers, and here I follow Dawa and Tim onto the trail, which I am told will take us to Namche Bazaar, our resting place for the next two nights. We're substantially increasing altitude today so it is essential that we take the time necessary to acclimatise to this. I'm told that the majority of people spend two nights at Namche for this very reason. The theory is that staying at this height for some time will help to adjust to this altitude. Already, I'm looking forward to having the time to chill out.

I have a sense that it is now time to grit our teeth and dig deep and I'm not wrong. I've heard it said that we go through both heaven and hell in our lifetime on this earth, and the next few hours are hell, in every sense of my understanding of the word, as we climb the endlessly-steep hill to Namche Bazaar. It is this 'hill' that takes us from a safe altitude to one where altitude sickness is a danger. Not that I realise this at the time. I'm ill-prepared, let's not forget. Perhaps ignorance is bliss, who knows, but that 'hill' will be forever more a mental obstacle to my returning to Everest Base Camp again!

Needless to say, it's a tortuous and painful few hours ascent as we zigzag through dense pine forests. The sun shines brightly and I'm grateful that the trees offer some shade because I'm increasingly warm with the effort involved in going uphill. I'm also now tiring. It's a struggle, step after step, up the really dusty path, so much so that the dust fills my nose and sticks to my sunglasses. I now struggle to breathe, let alone say "Namaste" to the people I pass going in the opposite direction. There is a huge part of me that wishes I could join them right now as they walk eagerly down the steep hill, full of smiles and energy with the increasing levels of oxygen in their lungs.

We switch back and forth on ourselves, up one steep and dusty path and then back on ourselves up another, zigzagging. It's really busy on the path and people continually stop at the side of the trail to lean over their walking poles and catch their breath, resting their hearts and legs, before carrying on up the trail. We keep passing the same trekkers, who then pass us when we are also stationary, trying to catch our breath, the pain and effort etched on all our red and sweating faces.

For the first time on this trip, I begin to feel miserable, really miserable. I hate every minute of the afternoon, trekking up the endless and relentless hill. It's monotonous and hard work. There's nothing but steep uphill and dust filling my nose as I struggle to breathe enough oxygen, then more steep uphill and sweating, and right now, it's exhausting and tiresome.

I don't do myself any favours, as my body knows only one speed – its mission is to make it to the top as fast as possible. This is a reflection of the way I live my life and the impact this is having on my body is not lost on me, but still this awareness doesn't encourage me to go any slower. I'm determined to make it to the top. I want this exhausting experience to end. All I want to do is reach the top and sit down.

The trouble is, I don't have the energy to keep going at the same fast pace so I have to stop to rest from time to time, squatting on the earth and collapsing my head onto my arms, supporting and balancing myself with my walking pole. I've never been quite so physically and mentally challenged in all my life; it would be humbling if only I could see beyond the anger and fury rising inside me.

I try and distract myself from the physical pain and mental unease that accompanies this by going off into my head, trying to find a way to distract myself from my current reality. I ran the London Marathon back in 2003. It was running this that led me to yoga, as my body was in such a mess afterwards and my depression returned (more on that later). During my training, I developed a way of dealing with the physically and mentally demanding nature of long runs by setting myself little goals, "From here to here, I'm running to Mum's for a cup of tea", and then I would spend that distance visualising what I'd be doing at my parents' house when I got there. Then, when I reached that goal in distance terms, I'd set another one, "So now I'm running to work", and in my head I'd spend the next distance visualising what would happen at work.

I employ this approach now, visualising (or trying to visualise, as I've never been here before), what will happen when I reach the hotel in Namche Bazaar, imagining myself enjoying a lovely cup of Nepali tea and smoking a roll-up as a way of congratulating myself for all my efforts in getting there. This is the irony of smoking – I can't breathe very easily on account of the steep incline and the reducing oxygen in the air, and yet all I want is a roll-up!

When I exhaust that coping technique, I create yoga sequences in my mind. This is something I do a lot, if ever I'm cycling up challenging hills, or on long car journeys, or having trouble falling asleep, then I mentally run through yoga classes, visualising the flow of a sequence and imagining what it might feel like. I teach a flowing form of Hatha yoga, linking breath with movement, so that classes become a creative expression, both a dance and a journey, with a beginning, a middle and an end.

After that, I find myself considering the recipes I'll cook when we finally return to Kathmandu. How do I steam rice? I've forgotten, and I make a mental note to email my brother at the next available opportunity because for some reason, right now, as I climb endlessly uphill, it feels very important that I know how to steam rice properly, exactly as he does. He is, after all, my rice expert. How does he do it, again?

I then start chanting the Hare Krishna mantra silently to myself: *Hare Krishna, Hare Krishna, Krishna Krishna, Hare Hare, Hare Rama, Hare Rama, Rama Rama, Hare Hare.*

I chant it over and over again. I'm not a disciple of the Hare Krishna faith, nor do I have the intention of becoming one either, but I love their energy and right now, I would love to experience the same peace of mind that I experienced when I was chanting with them each morning and evening while staying at the Govinda Valley Retreat Centre. There I also enjoyed karma and bhakti yoga, the latter being the yoga of devotion and of the heart, which I found utterly blissful and enlightening.

Life is far from blissful right now. Instead, I'm just downright angry. I can feel it seeping through my pores. I hate these steps. I hate this trek. I hate it all. If only I could find a way to step back and witness myself then I'd probably have a good old laugh because here I am, a lucky yogini on the adventure of a lifetime, about to see Mount Everest with her own eyes, experiencing Tibetan Buddhism in the Himalayas, and all I can do is complain.

The irony is not lost on me. I'm very aware that all the yoga and meditation that I do have been leading me to this moment, to be able to put the practice into practice, being able to stay present to what's happening and be OK with that, however challenging. But you know what, I'm angry with the practice, I'm furious that it hasn't made it any easier for me, that if anything it's helped me to be even more aware of my reaction, which just makes it doubly challenging. I'm so angry I want everyone to know about it and I wear an angry scowl on my face in defiance, my body speaking my mind: "I hate this trek!"

An inspiring Scottish yoga teacher once told me that anger arises when there is uncertainty inside. *He's right!* I'm feeling really uncertain right now, uncertain if I can complete the trek, uncertain about the terrain ahead, uncertain about the future course of my life. Uncertainty is enveloping me in its stickiness. My Ayurvedic doctor would say that anger is a result of a pitta imbalance, too much fire. Yep, right now, the fire is all-consuming, red and hot and most definitely providing me with the energy and motivation to keep moving, if nothing else!

5

At the foot of the mountain
Such a long way to climb.
How will I ever get up there?
Though I know I must try.
"Foot of the Mountain", Paul Weller

Day 2 continued: Up the hill to Namche Bazaar

It is a relentless uphill climb; there doesn't seem to be any respite and no end, step after step, zigzag after zigzag, continually and constantly uphill. I'm no longer aware of my surroundings beyond the dust that keeps blowing up into my face and the unrelenting incline of the terrain. I'm hot and feeling really weak now, so I stop to rest and to drink some water. As soon as I do, I'm concerned whether I'll be able to start again. It's an effort simply to remove my rucksack and reach for my drink. I crouch down, low to the earth, giving my legs a break. When will it end?

With water drunk I'm off again, traipsing after Tim and Will with Ben and Matt ahead of them. I've lost sight of Lilly behind me. She's walking with Pemba, who keeps pace with her, leading the back of the group together. None of us at the front of the group has the energy to talk to one another and we keep passing each other as we frequently stop to catch our breath and to sip our water, trying to stay hydrated.

I'm gaining a good insight into the nature of suffering. I feel like I'm suffering and yet I'm very aware that it is of my own making. I chose to trek in the Himalayas, no one forced me to be here. Furthermore, I am also the one choosing the thoughts to which I give my energy and attention, so in many respects, my mind is creating my suffering by fixating on it.

I've heard it said that when one's own suffering is fully experienced, when you can absolutely be with it, it manifests as a blessing. I'm not doing so well at being present to my suffering because I'm still so angry and in many respects, resisting it. I want to blame someone or something for my suffering and I silently berate the terrain for being so challenging.

I am reminded how this suffering can show up in our yoga practice when we are practising a posture that we find really challenging. As I mentioned earlier I sought yoga back in 2003 because my body was a mess from running the London Marathon and I was suffering a bout of depression again. Depression was a theme running throughout my twenties, and I was keen to try to do something about it because I was tired of being unhappy and suffering bouts of anxiety and paranoia too.

Someone mentioned that I should try yoga, so I went along to my first class with Vanessa Lasenby in an old parish hall in Guernsey with my younger brother, Ross, in September 2003. To be honest, if he hadn't accompanied me then I doubt very much I would have gone through the door and entered the room. I'm pleased I did (and shall be forever grateful to Ross for giving me the courage) because yoga has been life-changing for me. It was through yoga that I met my Reiki master, Alyssa Burns-Hill, and Reiki came into my life, which has also been hugely healing and life-changing. The two modalities have certainly saved me.

Within weeks of starting yoga, I began attending Ashtanga-inspired yoga classes twice a week and then with the help of Katy Appleton's marvellous book, *Yoga in Practice*, I established my own daily self-practice. After a couple of months, I was practising yoga six days a week and taking my yoga mat on trips abroad. I wasn't aware of it at the time, but subtly my whole lifestyle was changing too. I read up on nutrition and started eating a more balanced and healthy diet.

It is a recognised fact that regularly practising yoga will naturally draw you towards lifestyle choices that nourish your well-being and anything which is no longer nourishing you will drop away effortlessly. But these were difficult times. The mind has a tendency to be preoccupied with the external world – we often guide our lives by the wishes of our ego. We accept things that feed the ego and reject those which challenge it (we alternate between desire and fear). We continue wanting and desiring under the illusion that if we attain our desires, our problems will be solved, for example, acquiring an expensive car or the newest mobile telephone.

Like many, I had been deluded by a material existence for some time, spending so much of my energy chasing after what I thought I wanted rather than what I actually needed. Times were changing. Yoga brings self-awareness, enabling you to analyse the motivating factors behind your actions. You are also more likely to be able to observe your desires and fears and see them for what they are. I became more aware than ever of how unhappy my lifestyle was making me – and I realised that the only person who could do anything about it was me. It was time to stop blaming other people, or situations, and take responsibility.

For a long time, I had talked of pursuing a career in writing, but the substantial drop in salary compared to working as a professionally-qualified company secretary in the offshore finance industry had always prevented me from doing so. But all of a sudden, in June 2004, following a few months of dedicated yoga practice and a course of intuitive life-coaching sessions using Reiki, money didn't seem so important anymore. I resigned from my permanent job as a professional company secretary managing a team of administrators and secured a three-month contract position to provide me with the flexibility I needed to investigate my career options. A few weeks after starting my contract job, my brother, with whom I co-owned a house at the time, confirmed he was going travelling for a few months before moving to the UK. Yet more change. We decided to sell our house; neither of us wanting the responsibility and burden of covering the mortgage payments each month.

Thankfully, my parents were very accommodating and agreed that I could move back to the family home with my cats, while I decided what I actually wanted to do with my life – and bless them, I'm still living with them four years later (well, in between my bouts of travelling)!

Selling the house released a massive weight from my shoulders. Initially, I was concerned about losing my independence by moving back home but, if anything, I actually felt freer than I had done for a long time. My only responsibility was the cats, but they settled very quickly and my parents were soon charmed and they are still living with them to this day.

I applied for a magazine journalism course in Portsmouth, but as I waited to hear whether I would be called for an interview, I began to have doubts. Was this really what I wanted to do? It was time to start listening to what I really *felt* in my heart, not what my mind *thought* I should be doing. This was quite a frustrating process and it wasn't until I was moaning to a friend about my predicament that I finally came across the answer.

I mentioned that all I really wanted to do was go travelling and do yoga. Hey presto. It was July 2004 by then and I had been practising yoga for almost a year and was utterly hooked. There it was, yoga was calling me! I didn't even realise what I had said until my friend pointed it out to me. My immediate reaction was to deny that this was even an option. After all, at the age of twenty-nine shouldn't one be thinking of settling down and giving consideration to the pension? (That's what I kept being told.) Well no, at that moment, for me, this was simply not going to bring happiness. So what to do, where to go and how to tell my parents?

I played around with a few ideas, but strangely, I already knew where I wanted to go – Byron Bay, Australia. Aside from that, I wasn't too concerned. So after an hour on the telephone to a Travelbag representative, it was all booked.

I was intending to stay in Byron for two weeks, but I ended up staying six weeks. While I didn't realise it initially, Byron is renowned for its healing energy, which attracts people and holds them until they are ready to leave. (There is a need to recognise when it's time to leave, otherwise you might never leave!) Discovered in the 1960s by those seeking an alternative lifestyle, Byron, at least when I visited, was a place of surfers, hippies, writers, travellers and yogis. It's become an increasingly busy small town today set beside the main beach – a long strip of white powdery sand – where fast-food chains have been banned by the local community and strict height limits have been imposed on buildings. It is my kind of utopia.

By coincidence (not that I believe in coincidence per se!) I was staying in a laid-back hostel, 20 minutes' walk out of town and almost next door to Byron Yoga Centre (as it was at the time) and the inspirational figure of John Ogilvie.

Bizarrely, John, who had been practising yoga for 25 years at that time, was married to a Guernsey girl and had actually taught yoga on the island many years ago. For me at that time, I found John inspirational. His dynamic and energetic approach encouraged confidence and increased my enthusiasm for yoga. Primarily integrating the different yoga styles of Ashtanga and Iyengar, the classes with John were challenging yet fun and joyful. After one class, I was hooked.

By coincidence (there it is again), I was fortunate to meet Frida Lezius, a yoga teacher and a wonderful massage therapist, at the first class I attended. Frida concentrates on clearing physical and emotional blockages within the body, enabling a deeper recognition of oneself and dissolving hardened old defences. While the massages themselves were brutal, Frida taught me much about the breath and the effect this has on the body. Before I met her, I had never realised the extent to which our emotions manifest themselves physically within the body; with this awareness, things started to make a bit more sense.

Another lucky meeting was with Lance Schuler, who was thankfully in town at the same time as me. Having taught yoga for around the world for over 20 years at that time, he is another truly inspirational figure and again taught me much about yoga, the mind and the body. Like John's classes, Lance's classes were dynamic, incorporating Ashtanga and Iyengar, encouraging and enhancing vitality, flexibility, strength, stamina and bringing greater balance to the body and the mind.

Because I was doing so much yoga in Byron – sometimes six hours a day – I went through a period of feeling like I was on an emotional roller coaster. I didn't realise this until much later, but all the yoga was well and truly opening up my body and clearing away years of embedded emotions. This is not unusual. The hips, for example, are renowned for holding emotions like anger and frustration and when these are encouraged to open, you can find yourself in tears or feeling particularly angry; not from the pain as such (although it can be very painful physically, mentally and emotionally), but from the releasing emotions, which may have been trapped for many years.

I would go through periods of insomnia and then be plagued by really vivid dreams featuring people and situations I had not thought about for years. It was like my mind was cleansing as much as my body. It wasn't always an easy process, as I became increasingly aware of my suffering and the manner in which I had been in denial of much of this, self-medicating back at home with alcohol and hashish, anything which might numb those intense feelings.

A year later, in September 2005, (two years since I had started practising yoga), I returned to Byron to undertake an intensive six-week (240 hours) yoga teacher-training course with Lance Schuler at Inspya Yoga. Here we started the day with an hour of pranayama and meditation, before two hours of asana, mainly a strong vinyasa class with awareness of alignment. It was during these asana classes that I became very aware of suffering and the manner in which it can shift if we sit with the feeling.

I'll never forget being encouraged to settle into Gomukhasana (cow face pose) for a significant length of time. This seated posture encourages an intense stretch to the hips and outer thighs as you place one knee on top of the other with the right foot on the floor placed by the left hip and the left foot on the floor placed by the right hip. For me, it was a very challenging pose and one that definitely brought suffering to the surface. I wasn't in it for too long when the urge to run away became all-consuming. I found this fascinating. Here I was suffering and all I wanted to do was run away from it. They say that what arises on our mat is a reflection of what arises in our life generally, and it didn't take me long to realise the correlation – when life got challenging, I would run away, whether that be physically running away, going on a trip, or whatever it might be, but also taking a part of myself away from my reality, numbing out, whether through alcohol, drugs or food.

During this session though, I couldn't run away. Instead, I was encouraged to sit with my suffering and breathe into the sensation. This too was fascinating. The feeling was decidedly unpleasant and edgy. I felt sick to the pit of my stomach and then very angry, then frustrated and then resigned and then all of a sudden, I started crying. I couldn't associate the tears with an emotion as such, it was just a general release and it surprised me as they popped up from nowhere, cleansing and releasing.

The longer I sat there, the more I realised the extent to which we create our suffering from our thoughts and our stories, and the manner in which we attach ourselves to things we like and run away from things we don't like, and how, actually, if we can just allow ourselves to be truly present to our suffering, it loses its control over us and provides us with an opportunity to enter a more peaceful and indeed resourceful state of being. This is the blessing.

I can't imagine a blessing arising right now though, because I'm well and truly stuck in my suffering and am keen to blame anyone but myself for it! I blame the hills mainly. I hate these awful hills. Why would anyone choose to trek in these mountains for pleasure? What was I thinking signing up for this trek?

I'm in my story now, my suffering, poor me. It all comes up, all the stuff that's wrong in my life in this moment. What a terrible life I lead… or so I think as the self-pity creeps in. It's far from the truth as it happens but, my gosh, like sitting in Gomukhasana for too long, this part of the trek is massively challenging me. Then a blessing arises to distract me from my suffering because all of a sudden I catch sight of Mount Everest.

Mount Everest.

Right there, peeking over the ridge of Nuptse (7,879m) in the far distance, I glimpse the tallest mountain in the world with my very own eyes; beautiful Mount Everest.

As soon as the blessing arrives, it passes, because I am just too tired to jostle with the other trekkers for a front-line view. For many, this is their final destination on the trekking route. They simply walk to this point on the trail to see Mount Everest with their own eyes, take a few photos, and then turn around and trek back down to Lukla again. Many of them manage to do this in one day from Lukla to Namche and back down again to Lukla. We've taken two days to get here and I'm pleased about that. I can't imagine how tiring it must be to do a day trip.

I crouch to the side of the path and rummage through my daysack for my camera to take the obligatory photo. However, when I find my camera, I'm distressed to find that it no longer works. *Good grief, what's going on?* My mood is foul already, but now I have that feeling that the whole world is against me, that the angels have deserted me and I'm out of favour with the Universe.

I could cry, only that I'm actually too angry and enraged to even do this. I'm so wrapped up in my frustration and anger and bad mood that I don't have the clarity or the ability to consider that not having a camera may actually be a blessing in disguise. I can't see that sometimes things happen for a reason, that one is better to go with the flow of things and trust in the process than fight what is reality.

It reminds me of something a practising Buddhist yoga teacher said about cultivating a sense of equanimity. "Can you be with what is happening without wishing it were different or without trying to change it?" Um, well no, right now, I can't. Right now, I feel zero equanimity. I have an internal war going on because I want things to be very different than they are. I'm not feeling stable or calm or any of those other qualities which may arise if only I could accept what is happening in this moment.

This moment brings with it yet more uphill ahead and a mind consumed with thinking about a broken camera. I just can't let it go. My mind is totally and utterly obsessed with the irritation of the broken camera and the fact I won't be able to visually record my trip in the Himalayas. Years later I will come to laugh at this, the weakness of my mind in allowing the thoughts to consume me in such a way and affect my mood and increase my stress levels in the process (the mind and body being so intrinsically related).

The mind is a tricky thing. And this is where yoga and meditation really come into their own. These modalities can help us to become a little more familiar with the workings of our mind, so that we are able (perhaps) to identify the negative behaviour patterns and tendencies that do not always support a happy and healthy way of being. Of course, it takes practice, commitment and an openness to what we might find, because it isn't always pretty!

I've seen this show up a lot over the years. People know that they need to make changes in their lives, so they come along to practise yoga because they've been told it's good for their health and well-being, but often it brings them face to face with themselves in a way that they hadn't anticipated. Perhaps they begin to realise that they are very unfit or out of shape, or they realise how tight their body has become, or perhaps they find that their mind is so restless that it is difficult to relax or to focus on what is going on.

They can't escape so easily from themselves on a mat and for many it's a confrontational experience they can't handle. They'd rather stay in denial and pretend that everything's OK than delve into the darkness and see what's going on in there. Many stop practising as soon as they've started, deciding that yoga's not for them. They'll try a different approach instead, perhaps a diet or a gym workout, something that keeps them from introspection and delving deeper (into the denial).

It's a shame because, like with sitting in Gomukhasana for me during the yoga teacher training, I've come to recognise that the more we can sit with our pain and discomfort in life generally, be present with all the 'stuff' going on inside, the more we can befriend it. This isn't easy, of course. We have to recognise it for a start and remind ourselves to sit with it, whatever it may be, rather than turning away from it and adopting our usual coping mechanism or tendency, and we need to have the courage to bring light into the darkness and deal with whatever it reveals. The more we do this, the more we can heal and transform so that things begin to shift, not only internally, but externally too.

I know the theory but here in this moment, I'm incandescent. I'm no longer here and I'm no longer there, lost in my head, consumed by the same continuous thoughts about my broken camera. How am I to take photos of this trip, further up into the Himalayas, without my camera? And why isn't it working? What has happened to it in the space of a few hours?

My legs are burning with the effort of all the uphill trekking and I just want to lash out at someone, but there's no one to lash out at, so I lash out at myself. *I'm useless, things just keep going wrong.* There we go, I said it. With that voiced, I drop back, no longer feeling the need to keep up with the boys. In any case, I can't keep up with the boys. I've literally run out of energy. Even Lilly's now catching me up, with Pemba almost pushing her up the final stages of this seemingly never-ending hill.

I am really struggling to put one foot in front of the other, my blood sugar levels are extremely low, the altitude has kicked in and I actually worry now that I may never make it to the top of the hill. This is the first time I've even considered that maybe I really can't make it, maybe I really can't do this, maybe I'll fail. That's not a concept that crops up in my life too much.

Right now, I'm so tired, so very tired that I just want to lie down. I just want it all to be over. I don't care about anything anymore. I am now resigned to failure – lost in the dark recesses of my mind, pushed to the edge. I have no humour to laugh at myself. I'm feeling dejected, rejected, inadequate and still so irritated by my lack of a working camera – it's funny the things that can push you to your limit.

I feel the tears arising. All of a sudden, they start running down my face. It's almost a relief, a letting go. Nothing really seems important anymore, aside from making it to Namche Bazaar in one piece. I keep my head down, drying my eyes and not wanting anyone else to see that I'm emotional. Still, I feel a little calmer; sometimes you need to drop into the darkness to find the light.

I stumble on, accompanied by Craig and Lilly. I'm now with them at the back of the group, my head pounding. "How much longer?" we keep asking Pemba, who mutters a response that we don't want to hear. "A little further, a little further." "Bistari, bistari," he adds. This means, "Slowly, slowly" in Nepali, and it is something that he keeps repeating. We sigh to one another. We're all feeling sick of it now. When will we ever make it to the village, our resting point for the next two nights?

Namche Bazaar.

At last, and with all of us flagging spectacularly, we approach the welcome cobbled streets of Namche Bazaar, an incredible trading village set 3,420m above sea level. That's quite some height, especially for an island-living girl, and it means that we've climbed almost 1,000m today alone. Wow! Pemba tells us that this is the largest ascent in any single day on this trek. I could cry with the relief. It's done, we've made it!

However, we're not quite there yet. Namche Bazaar is a steep village set in a horseshoe-shaped bowl, like a natural amphitheatre, looking directly out at the sheer face of Kongde Ri (6,187m), and consisting of layer upon layer of terraced land. This means that we still have to walk a little further uphill, consciously lifting one foot after another, our leg muscles protesting and aching now, up yet more steep stone steps.

I was told that Namche Bazaar is one of the most attractive settlements in the Khumbu region and my first impression certainly confirms this. It's often described as a village and yet it feels like a town as we follow Pemba through the tight tangle of small and narrow cobbled streets, navigating our way past other trekkers and porters. It's a hive of activity, quite an amazing place, if only I could see beyond my weariness and thumping headache, let alone breathe this now thin air.

Historically, Namche was an important staging point for trading expeditions across the Nangpa La into Tibet, but today the village makes most of its money from the hundreds of trekkers (and climbers) like us who arrive every day en route to Base Camp or from Lukla during the two trekking/climbing seasons. There's a plethora of lodges and shops selling all sorts of things from trekking supplies to books and seemingly essential food supplies like Mars bars and cans of Coke. There's a couple of German bakeries too – I'm quickly learning that these are a popular feature in Nepal. There's Internet up here too, as well as a dentist and a doctor, should you be feeling the effects of the altitude or experiencing any other form of illness.

I find a sense of comfort from this normality and the fact that we could, should we choose, make contact with the outside world. It almost gives me the extra energy I need to push on to the lodge where we will be staying for our acclimatisation day.

Finally, we make it to the lodge and Lilly and I could cry with the reprieve of sitting down and resting our weary legs. I've never walked so hard in my life, the cliffs at home seem a breeze in comparison! It's a dream lodge, really, bigger and a lot more comfortable than the one we stayed in when we were in Phakding.

The stone walls have been painted an off-white colour and it has large windows, the double frames of which are painted white and burgundy. Outside the main entrance is a lovely low stone wall, which has small rugs placed on top of it so that we can comfortably sit outside. Mind you, the weather has deteriorated and it's a little fresh now, but Lilly and I are keen to celebrate our arrival (it was my dream further down the trail) with a pot of Nepali tea (milk tea) and a roll-up!

The combination of caffeine and nicotine provide both an invigorating hit and welcome boost to our flagging bodies, while we look out at the views. Both our heads are pounding with the change in altitude and this makes us feel a little out of sorts and now lightheaded from the nicotine. (Why, oh why, do we do it?). But what a joy to be here, to look down on all the lodges below and across the valley and notice the Tibetan prayer flags brightening the landscape.

We get a real sense of height from the lodge and we marvel at how far we've climbed throughout the day. Namche certainly looks like a lovely place to stop for a day and I'm keen to investigate. However, I'm just hopeful that a good night's sleep will leave me feeling decidedly better than I do right now. I wasn't anticipating such a demanding day of trekking and I really feel physically, mentally and emotionally drained.

Lilly and I share a room, which is set at the back of the accommodation block, accessed through a separate door to the main lodge itself, away from the rest of the group, away from everyone in fact. It's cold and basic but clean and spacious with views across the valley. We share a communal bathroom with others; this just contains a toilet and a sink. Hot showers are available in another part of the lodge.

We've both begun to voice our doubts about our ability to do the trek. Lilly, in particular, is haunted by her bad memories of summiting Mount Kenya and doesn't know if she can put herself through that again up here on the Everest trail.

"I just don't think I can do it," she says.

"I think you can," I tell her, knowing that she's stronger than she thinks.

But she's adamant. "I really don't know that I can keep going. My head's hurting and I'm extremely tired."

"I know," I tell her. "I feel the same, but it will get easier. Pemba said that that's the hardest day done now." I try to reassure myself as much as Lilly, as I too am concerned about going through another afternoon like today.

"But we're just going higher and higher and the altitude will become increasingly challenging," she adds, knowing much more about this than I do. I'm still naïve to this whole altitude thing.

"I might just wait for you here," she says, "or trek back down to Lukla and wait there, or go back to Kathmandu." She plays around with ideas in her head, forming her get-out plan.

Deep down, I know that I want to carry on with the trek, having made it this far, but I'm feeling so rotten and fearful that the thought of going back to Kathmandu with Lilly sounds very appealing right now. It's like being attracted to the bright lights of the city, where all will be well. There's yoga and lassis and Wi-Fi, but I know that the novelty would wear off very quickly and I would be forever wondering, "What if?"

Pemba checks on us and Lilly tells him that she doesn't feel very well and worries that she may not be able to continue. He assures her that she will be fine. "You just need to keep drinking water and resting now," he says. I reassure her too. She'll be fine, we just need a good night's sleep and time to adjust.

The other part of my 'arriving at Namche dream' was to have a hot shower, so that's what we do next. You have to pay extra for showers in the mountains on account of the cost to the lodge of providing hot water. Here, at this lodge, it costs us the equivalent of £1.50 each, but I would pay almost anything given the way I feel; there is nothing quite so lovely as a hot shower after a long day of trekking!

As we have a rest day tomorrow, Lilly and I also arrange for our clothes to be hand-washed by the hotel staff. The boys think we're mad, and probably we are, but we're still in Western mindset and want some clean socks! Tim and Joe are more concerned about updating their Facebook profiles than washing themselves; I'm just amazed that you can access the Internet all the way up here, albeit at a cost.

After showering and therefore feeling lovely and clean, Lilly and I lie around on our beds chatting and trying to keep our spirits positive. We've only started getting to know each other properly since travelling to Nepal together, but I feel like we've been friends for years. We're different in age and have different friendship groups and ways of life back home in Guernsey, but there's something about Lilly that resonates, as if we are kindred souls.

She too wears her heart on her sleeve and is very open and honest about how she feels. She loves to travel and has travelled a lot for work, but has also taken time out to travel by herself, seeing the world and experiencing different cultures and ways of living, as I have done too. Perhaps it is this mutual love of travel and trying to live life a little out of the box that binds us both and the fact that we can talk together so openly about our hopes and fears for the future.

As I've mentioned earlier, I've been in an on and off relationship with B for four years now. I know it's not for the long term, but being best of friends makes it so very difficult to break apart from one another and this is my quandary. I feel stuck. Lilly has awareness of this kind of relationship, so knows only too well the challenges that this presents.

"I just want someone to appear in my life and whisk me off my feet," I tell her. "That will sort the quandary for me, as I will then have to separate from B."

"It would be lovely, wouldn't it?" she agrees. "Perhaps he'll appear on this trek!" she adds.

At that, we both giggle, because it has crossed my mind as I know it has crossed her mind too, but at the same time, we're both so fiercely independent that probably neither of us are ready for the commitment of a long-term relationship!

That evening we join together in the busy restaurant of the lodge, where it is warm and cosy and full of noise and laughter. There's a team of British men at one of the tables who look like professional trekkers and extremely happy to be descending the mountain. They're drinking Nepali beer and their laughter fills the room as they celebrate a safe trip up to, and return from, Everest Base Camp. Their energy is infectious and I can't help thinking what a wonderful feeling it must be to have made it to the top and to be descending right now. We still have so far to go!

The menus in the restaurants and cafés along the Everest trail are almost identical in their offerings and the boys have taken a liking to the fried noodles, ordering them at every occasion. However, this evening, Pemba is keen for us all to eat dal bhat, which is the staple meal eaten by Nepalis twice a day, every day of the year, consisting of plain rice, a vegetable curry, dal (lentils), curd and some spicy relish. To me, it sounds heavenly but there is resistance in the ranks and Pemba has his work cut out convincing the boys that this is exactly what they need to eat after our hard day.

It's not so much that they want to eat meat, although this is a consideration, the boys are just keen to avoid anything authentically Nepali and stick with the fried stuff instead. Being a vegetarian in Nepal is easy. Nepal is a secular state, but just over 80% of its people are Hindu and it is illegal to kill cows here (penalties are similar to those for manslaughter). The majority of the population, therefore, eats a primarily vegetarian diet, which, more often than not, consists of dal bhat.

There is a routine to meal times too. We order and then sit around and wait, maybe reading our books, chatting, or the boys playing cards to pass the time. Once ready, our food is served to us by our porters, which has challenged me a little. Not only have these gentle and kind men carried our bags up the mountain for us today but now they have to serve us our food and wait for us to finish eating before they can eat their own meals. It is the custom here, and I realise that there are lots of customs that I have yet to learn in Nepal.

Apart from Lilly, we're all really hungry and the meal is so yummy and filling that I resolve dal bhat will be my meal of choice from now on. The boys aren't convinced.

"Lentils? Who wants to eat lentils? Yuck," says Will.

"But they're good for you," I say.

"They're not good for you. Give me meat," responds Will.

"A big pizza," adds Joe.

"Pizza? Up here?" I laugh. "Really?"

"Pizza with lots of meat," adds Will, at which he and Joe burst into giggles.

Pemba encourages us to eat dessert and the boys become increasingly excited about ordering deep-fried Mars bars, which appear on the menu. Sure enough, when the dish arrives, we find that that they are, indeed, deep-fried Mars bars, and more giggles follow about indulging in such a guilty pleasure. To my eye, they look revolting, but the boys can't get enough of them and clearly need to eat a lot of calories on this trek. The deep-fried Mars bars are followed by yet more chocolate bars, washed down with cans of Coke – fizzy pop gets everywhere, even up here in the Himalayas.

The boys have a teenage-boy banter going on, where they try and joke with one another and win points all the time. I recognise that in all my efforts to be open-minded, accepting and non-judgmental, I'm exactly none of those things where the boys are concerned, simply because I find the banter and one-upmanship exhausting and childish, which makes me question if I've become too serious in my older age. I find myself trying to support the underdog, Tim, who is the butt of many of the jokes on account of his seriousness.

I can't stop thinking about whether Lilly and I really will be able to complete this trek and I'm already worrying about what I'm going to do when we've finished all our volunteering work. It's funny how you can be in one place and yet your mind is somewhere else, planning the future, or reflecting on the past so that you're not really in the present, and you start worrying and feeling out of control and before you know it you're anxious and stressed.

The crazy thing is that I know all this. I teach people techniques to help them get out of these pointless and exhaustive states of being. I also try and teach them how to avoid getting into this state of mind in the first place. But it's all a work in progress and at least there's an awareness that worrying and stressing are a complete waste of energy, as they change nothing, aside from your physiology and health. The trouble is, in the mountains there's too much time to think, there's not the same opportunity to numb out as there may be at home with TV, work, alcohol, or any of the other myriad of things that people (including me) do each day to fill their time.

In the absence of TV and the Internet in the hotel, or any other form of entertainment, we all have an early night. We're physically exhausted and the lowered level of oxygen in the air means our heads are still pounding, which means that even reading is a challenge. With the lights off, it is eerily quiet and dark and I'm pleased I'm sharing the room with Lilly, even if I am paranoid about snoring and keeping her awake. It's been a strange day and I'm feeling decidedly out of sorts and keen for sleep.

6

Day 3: Namche Bazaar acclimatisation day

I awake to find that my head is still pounding and I promptly burst into tears, feeling decidedly vulnerable and not quite myself. I'm not used to suffering from headaches and there is very little I can do to ease the pain, which concerns me as this is yet another unknown: what does it mean to have a continuous headache like this?

Lilly has been squatting over the basic and rather filthy communal toilet all night suffering from diarrhoea.

I'm sick of the trek already and am questioning again what I'm doing here. I can't believe I thought this would be a gentle climb. And as for my camera, I still can't let that go, my mind just keeps going over and over it, wondering how I'll be able to capture my experience in Nepal to share with family and friends back home in Guernsey.

Spiritually, I'm feeling totally out of touch with the Divine, with that sense of something greater than me, which usually provides so much comfort to me in my day to day life. This lack of connection throws me a little, as I had hoped that my connection would be strengthened in the mountains, closer to the gods, but I feel almost as if I've fallen out of favour. Here I am adrift and totally out of my comfort zone.

Lilly and I dress quickly before joining the boys for breakfast in the warm and bustling dining room. There's an energy of trepidation in the air as people fuel for the day ahead. We eat warm porridge mixed with a few bits of peeled and chopped apple and wash this down with tea. I'm still not used to eating breakfast, but I'm becoming increasingly aware that in these mountains it's essential to fuel properly throughout the day.

Pemba is keen to guide us on a walk further up the hill to help us adapt to the increased altitude, but Lilly's not feeling very well, so after some negotiating Pemba agrees that she can stay at the lodge. I'm envious because I don't really want to do any walking today either and I sulk as I traipse after the boys out of the lodge.

Apart from Tim, the other boys aren't into it either. Every one of us is feeling challenged by the change in altitude and, like me, Joe is sulking too, moaning to Pemba that he wants to stay back at the lodge, that his legs are tired from the day before. Ben and Matt are more subdued than usual and we are all conscious of the effort involved in trying to breathe the thin air. It doesn't help that it's windy and cold today too and we need to wear lots of layers to keep warm.

I focus all my efforts on following on the heels of Tim who is walking in front of me, the wind whistling in my ears and still, the relentless pounding in my head. I question over and over again in my mind whether I'll be able to continue, and long for reassurance. The trouble is, we're all going through our own challenges. The only reason we're out here is because Pemba has told us in no uncertain terms that it will help us to acclimatise. Given the choice, we'd probably be much happier relaxing at the lodge, although the relentless headache might not make that pleasurable either.

Traipsing after Pemba, we go up to the Sagarmatha National Park headquarters, home to a visitor's centre and police headquarters. It's exposed to the elements and the wind is so relentless now that we can't hear each other to chat. That suits me fine. I'm happy to withdraw from the world and revel in my own self-pity. I know it's ridiculous, but I can't help myself!

We continue further on across the flat area in front of the visitor's centre and Pemba leads us up and out to the far ridge. He points in the direction of the mountains that are now in view in the distance and says, "Mount Everest." The boys quieten their moaning and everyone looks to where he is pointing. "Which one?" I ask, for there is more than one mountain peak in the distance. Tim tries to explain the difference to me as he points out the eye-watering panorama of Himalayan peaks, from Nuptse (7,861m) and Mount Everest (8,848m) to Ama Dablam (6,856m) and Thamserku (6,608m).

Mount Everest is a rock peak sprinkled with snow and is the tallest mountain in the world, with sharp peaks and ridges. There are two routes to the summit and it is known as the roof of the world. It's impressive, I have to say, especially as you can clearly see snow blowing from it, even from where we are standing, indicating the strength of the wind. Witnessing this magnificent mountain in all its glory, I struggle to get my head around the fact that I'm meant to be trekking all the way to the base of it, because it looks so far away.

Tim interrupts my thoughts. "You know, Mount Everest is 8,848m above sea level at its peak. It sits right on the edge of the Tibetan Plateau on the border of Nepal and what was Tibet until the Chinese invaded it."

"It's pretty incredible," I respond.

"It's the tallest mountain in the world," he adds with excitement in his voice, desperate to get that bit closer to it over the next week. "You know, the mountain was sculpted by the erosive power of the glacial ice into three massive faces and three major ridges, which soar to the summit from the north, south and west, and separate the glaciers."

Pemba joins our conversation. "At this time of year the moisture-laden air rises from the south slopes of the Himalayas and condenses into a white, pennant-shaped cloud pointing east, known as the 'flag cloud'. See?" he says, as he points towards Mount Everest. "Today the flag cloud is almost at a right angle to the peak," he adds. "You know, the winds up on the summit can often reach 80 kilometres per hour!"

It's at that point that I am reminded how little I know about this incredibly hostile environment and what lays ahead for us. I can't even begin to imagine how people manage to summit it, or why they would want to do so in the first place. How do they escape from the effect of altitude, let alone protect themselves from those winds and the cold temperatures? It's a mystery to me.

I've borrowed Lilly's camera and the boys and I take photos of each other with views of Mount Everest and the other majestic Himalayan mountains in the background, before standing together for a group photo. Joe and Matt pull faces, which makes us all laugh and lightens the energy. It also helps to distract us from the pounding in our heads, and the whingeing and moaning stops as we begin to get excited instead – there's Mount Everest standing proud ahead!

The boys are keen to rush off to the very expensive Internet café that they have found to share their photos on Facebook! However, before they can do that Pemba insists we go to the small visitor's centre. We're all a little resistant, but once we're there we find that it is actually quite interesting. I hadn't realised, for example, that the Himalayas are considered young and are still growing, rising a few millimetres a year through geological formation.

From the visitor's centre, we venture out to the remains of a crashed helicopter up on the plateau, where the wind is certainly challenging. The boys embrace the moment by pretending to be helicopter pilots, examining the wreckage and running around pretend-fighting and making us all laugh again – they do have their benefits at times!

Pemba wants us to see a little bit more of the town, so we follow him down the steep incline and along a path on the ridge above Namche Bazaar. It's a beautiful sight as I look down on the stunning village – a hundred or so stone buildings with a combination of blue, red and green roofs built close together on the slopes. Prayer flags fly from rocks in the distance, brightening the scene further, while the wind continues to whistle around us. Sadly, the sun is hidden by clouds.

Still following Pemba, he leads us up the path to the large Namche Gompa, a humble Buddhist monastery positioned at the top of the hill. Along the way, we pass more Mani stones set off to the side of the path. We really are in the heart of the Tibetan Buddhist landscape here and this delights me – the boys, however, do not share my enthusiasm and are desperate to go off and do their own thing.

The Gompa is a small monastery from the Nyingma tradition of Tibetan Buddhism built in stone and painted red, with blue and green wooden window frames and yellow shutters, creating a bright and pretty scene. There are even white window boxes to compliment the Tibetan colour theme. Prayer wheels line the path and Joe, especially, takes great delight in running his hand along the cylinders as he walks past, encouraging them to revolve. I doubt very much he realises that in the process he is sending prayers out into the Universe and beyond.

At the entrance to the Gompa we remove our shoes and set these off to the side, before climbing the steps up into the monastery. Here, the head monk greets us with a welcoming smile, his hands held together in prayer position. "Namaste," he says. "Namaste," I happily respond, with my hands held together in prayer position too, feeling my heart warmed by his gentle presence.

The smell of Tibetan incense permeates the dark room and I admire the wonderfully bright *thangkas* (Tibetan pictures) that adorn the walls and surround the altar where there's a large statue of Guru Rinpoche (also known as Padmasambhava, an eighth-century Indian Buddhist monk considered by the Nyingma school to be founder of their tradition).

I sit cross-legged on a rug placed on the main bench facing the statue of Guru Rinpoche and soon notice a rat scuttling across the floor to my side – I'm pleased that my feet are off the ground! It's very cold and a little damp in the room and I hug myself, trying to keep warm. I take a deep breath in and out, and for the first time on this trek, I feel a refreshing sense of peace that I have not felt since I've been in the mountains. There is something very comforting about the energy of this Tibetan Buddhist monastery and for the first time today, I forget about my headache. I bow my head and I pray.

I'm praying for a safe passage up to Everest Base Camp and I'm praying for clarity about what lies ahead for me after this trip. It's crazy because I know that I need to be present for this experience, but I also feel a need to have certainty about my plans for the months ahead. I know that I'll be staying in Nepal for two months, but after then I have no plans. Lilly and I have already talked about travelling in India together, but while she obtained her Indian visa before our trip, I didn't, as I wasn't sure whether it would be needed.

Already this seems to be the focus of many of our conversations with the boys: Who is doing what next? Will is booked to return to Kathmandu immediately after the trek where he will undertake six weeks of voluntary work at the main hospital in Kathmandu before returning to the UK. Matt and Ben are joining Craig, Tim, Joe, Lilly and me in Bupsa, the rural village, for two weeks of volunteering before leaving Nepal and continuing their travels together into Thailand. Craig will also leave Nepal after Bupsa to return to the UK, before travelling on to Kenya to undertake further voluntary work.

Joe, Lilly, Tim and I will return to Kathmandu to volunteer at a boarding school. There is chatter about the four of us then travelling into India together, as we are getting along well. I like the idea of travelling in India, but I'm aware that Lilly only has a month of freedom before she has to return to Guernsey to work. I, on the other hand, have absolutely no commitments, which is a strange feeling, like I've uprooted myself and am adrift. The lack of clarity means that I'm seeking some form of divine inspiration to make it clearer.

The last few years have been unsettled. After I qualified as a yoga teacher, I returned to Guernsey and established my own business called 'Beinspired', teaching yoga and offering Reiki treatments. I worked part-time in the Guernsey finance industry to supplement my income and afford me the opportunity to continue travelling and training.

I carried on living with my parents and cats when on Guernsey and revived my on-off relationship with B (on when in Guernsey; off when away). I've grown weary of this way of life though and I'm desperate to meet my life partner and soulmate. (Even though B is my best friend and a soulmate of sorts, I know deep down that he is not my life partner.) I really want to have children too, and at the age of thirty-one, I know I need to make changes to move in that direction.

It's one thing to know this, however, and quite another thing to know what to do about it. It's not like you can just order yourself a life partner and soulmate – believe me, if I could, I would have done it by now. It's a really horrible situation and I know that I'm not alone because I have friends who are also keen to have children and to meet the person who will provide them with this opportunity.

I have a sense that it is all about timing and being in alignment. So all I can do – or so I believe, but I'm certainly no expert – is continue to listen to, and follow, my heart, however tricky that might be, and trust that the Divine will work magic in my life to help me to create the life of my dreams.

It's not easy following one's heart, however, because it seems to me that following the heart usually means living a life that's outside the box. And this involves courage; courage to live differently to the norm and to be able to stand strong in one's truth (and connection to self) when others question your decisions (especially well-meaning parents) because your way of living and the decisions you make don't make sense to them (any more than the mainstream approach makes sense to me at this stage in my life).

The other issue is the need to create a vacuum in terms of properly ending the relationship with B because energetically this prevents anyone else from entering. I'm very aware that the on-off nature of our relationship is preventing either of us from moving on with our lives independently of each other.

As I mentioned earlier, I think of B as my knight in shining armour for good reason. He was the person who stepped into my life and helped to rescue me when I was at a low point, albeit I was trying to move my life forward (or run my life forward) by training for the London Marathon. It's funny, as he arrived in my life a few weeks before, I bought two British Blue kittens and I later realised that the arrival of all three of them was divinely guided and timed. The three of them were gifts from the angels and yet angels themselves: Grace.

Life changed. Grace is powerful when it enters your life. It makes the seemingly impossible possible as new doors open and opportunities present themselves to you. I ran the London Marathon, which led me to yoga, which led me to Reiki, which led me to crystals, which led me to the concept of energy and true potential and realising our dreams. It also helped me to realise that we have a choice, even though it doesn't always feel like it at the time.

I was living a life that had presented itself to me. On some level, I was obviously making choices, but more often than not they were well-considered intellectual choices that were based on other people's opinions and dreams for me. They were not heart-felt choices. The concept of the heart and listening to it was lost on me. I was lacking in both self-confidence and self-belief and I didn't feel I was worthy of living my dreams and these lay hidden, so it took some work to realise what they were in the first place.

Through intuitive life-coaching, using Reiki, I realised that my greatest dream, other than to meet my soulmate and have children, was to become a writer, but I certainly didn't believe in it. I was living a life that seemed a million miles away from the one of writing, and intellectually I couldn't work out how I could make the change. At the time, I was trapped by a mortgage and monthly expenditures that required a secure and safe job in finance. There was no way out.

B thought otherwise however and initially he gifted me a fountain pen and journal with the idea that I actually start writing. Another time he gifted me a mini-word processor, so that I could write more easily while travelling. I still felt that it might never happen, but it helped enormously that someone believed in me and essentially empowered me. Not to say that my parents didn't believe in me, they just worried about my long-term future and security.

When I initially made the decision to sell the house with my brother and take off travelling, I also determined that I could no longer be in a relationship with B; that I needed to be free. However, even then, I called him when I initially arrived in Byron Bay and speaking to him helped to calm me down and feel at ease in my new environment. Inevitably, every time I've returned home to Guernsey, he's been the person I spend my time with (other than my parents). We're best friends and it is very difficult to make a clean break.

The trouble is, as I alluded to earlier, it means that we're actually preventing each other from properly moving on. On some level we (I especially) have become dependent on one another. Here, with little distraction, it plays on my mind relentlessly. I know we're not meant to be together, I don't feel passionate about him, but I don't know what to do about it, and I long for the angels to intervene, and make the transition painless for both of us. I also know that this is unlikely!

This continues to play on my mind, as we walk through the narrow and cobbled streets of Namche, pleased that we're now free to spend the rest of the day doing what we choose.

Back at the lodge, feeling a little inspired by my visit to the monastery and yet still a little out of sorts, I decide to practise yoga to see whether this will relieve the pain in my head and settle my over-active mind. I practise outside, hidden away from the rest of the hotel guests, in front of the mountains that are standing tall and glistening in the distance, and with the sun now shining brightly overhead. This spot provides a stunning view west across the valley of the Bhote Kosi to the knife-edge ridge of Kongde Ri and east across the valley of the Dudh Kosi to the snow-dusted peaks of Thamserku (6,608m) and Kantega (6,685m).

I lay down my mat, just as I have imagined doing in the Himalayas, outside and in view of mountains and play some

Hare Krishna morning prayers on my iPod, before moving my body through a sequence of yoga postures, breathing in the light air.

I'm halfway through my practice when the tears surprise me. They arrive so suddenly and with such intensity that I can't stop them as they spill down my face, landing on my mat and creating a little puddle of release. I move into child's pose and I can hear my yoga teacher's words in my head, "But surely, tears should be welcomed, dear Em."

He is right; tears on your yoga mat are a good sign. I know this. And I know that the best thing to do is just try to go with it, no need for analysis or stopping what is flowing and releasing. I've cried a number of times on my mat over the years. Sometimes I'm feeling a little out of sorts and I have this niggling feeling that I just need to get on my mat, and I start practising and then all of a sudden, just like now, the tears start flowing and it doesn't feel like they will ever stop.

I'm more welcoming of the tears these days, recognising that they are part of a process, a healing, a letting go of an emotion, or whatever it may be that is stuck, or has been stuck somewhere in my body. The release brings with it an increased sense of lightness and relief that all that holding on, unconsciously or not, has now eased.

I have known students to cry on their mats. Some welcome it and see it for what it is, but others, especially if they are relatively new to yoga, are surprised and consider it a negative thing, a sign of weakness. They believe that yoga has made them feel worse because it has brought up a feeling that they didn't want to feel, or a reaction that they can't control and so they stop practising.

However, it's a cause for celebration when we cry and release. Feeling a sensation in our body during our yoga practice is a gift, an opportunity to focus the mind on the sensation in the body in the present moment and to consciously breathe. The sensation is our body's way of communicating with us – maybe it's time to let go, maybe it's time for change, maybe it's time to just be present to whatever is arising and be OK with that.

Maybe you feel anxious, so rather than trying to distract yourself from the anxiety, you might focus your awareness inside to try and identify where in the body the anxiety is arising. It may well be uncomfortable and you may need some courage to be still and present for it, but you'll notice that the more you 'sit' with it and go right into the sensation, however edgy it might feel, the more it may begin to transform and lose its hold over you.

With practice and patience and a genuine willingness to listen (and to be prepared to hear), you might become (more) aware of the underlying reason, of the manner in which the mind is creating a false impression of reality, or is perhaps even *creating* the anxiety. What is the truth, anyway? Just try and remember that in that moment all is well. You're sitting on your yoga mat, breathing. All is well. Over and over again. Just let the sensations come and go, come and go.

Maybe with practice and compassion, you can begin to move the awareness from the sensation of anxiety into the heart space in the centre of your chest. In so doing, you might be able to transmute the anxiety into love. Or maybe you need to focus on being grounded on the earth, so you make an effort to notice your body in contact with the earth (the ground that you're sitting upon) and you can imagine rooting down, as if you have roots growing out of your sitting bones and/or feet, and experience the support that comes from this grounding and connection to the support and stability of the earth beneath you (allowing yourself to be held by Mother Earth).

Essentially, it's about listening to whatever is trying to get your attention in the body. And it's about being open to hearing whatever needs to be revealed too. So often we don't want to hear our own truth, as this may mean stepping out of our comfort zone and recognising our denial, as well as the manner in which we, yes, *we* can sometimes create our own suffering. Journaling can certainly help, writing whatever comes to mind, and being honest with yourself about how you are feeling – this can be deeply revealing.

Allow the tears to flow. Allow the vulnerability. Allow the healing.

As the tears flow, my headache eases. I close my eyes and rest on my back on my mat with my knees bent and the bright sun warming my tear-stained face. My breathing calms. All of a sudden, I am overcome with this sense that it will be OK. I am sure now that it will all be OK.

However, by the later afternoon my thinking is all over the place again: worries about the trek, worries about my future, worries about my hopes and dreams. It's made worse because I know that worrying is a complete waste of energy.

It was from my Reiki Level One training that I first became aware that energy used for worrying is in essence wasted, as it brings no change to the situation. Up until that point, it simply hadn't crossed my mind. I was a worrier, and worrying had become such an ingrained behaviour pattern that I didn't know I had a choice to be anything other than a worrier! It was a revelation to realise that worrying was not something I necessarily needed to do. That worrying itself was never going to change things, it was simply going to make matters worse.

I've since witnessed myself going into this worried state many times and I almost laugh at myself at the stupidity of it. But there are times when I become so caught up in it that I cannot even recognise that I have entered my worried state in the first place. It is at times like these that I forget that there is a divine purpose to everything and that worrying is not going to change that.

Sometimes it is important to simply trust that things will work out for the best in the end. What is beyond our control cannot be changed and squandering copious amounts of our energy worrying may only serve to diminish our vitality, cloud our perception and create greater limitation. Things will be what they will be; worrying about it will not change this. It's just another opportunity to have faith and trust in the process.

These days most people have heard of Reiki but not many know what it is actually is. They often assume it is a form of religion or massage and they often wonder if it is dangerous. No, is the answer to all these assumptions. It is neither a belief system nor a physically manipulative technique and it is completely safe. Essentially, it is a way of being true to yourself so that you do things consciously, with awareness, sincerity and intention.

The Japanese word Reiki (pronounced *ray-key*) means 'universal energy' and it refers to the free flow of energy in a person. Eastern medicine has always recognised and worked with this energy, which flows through all living things and is vital to well-being. Essentially, Reiki refers to a hands-on healing art developed by Dr Mikao Usui in Japan in the early 1900s based on ancient practices, for personal development and to heal others. Dr Usui believed that by clearing the body energetically it was possible to feel more connected to life, more relaxed, physically healthier and more balanced emotionally.

Reiki is activated by intention and works on every level: physical, mental, emotional, spiritual and energetic. Reiki can be likened to a free-flowing river. The water in this river is like the energy flowing easily down through the body. Occasionally a pebble or a rock may fall into that river making the flow of water a little more difficult. These pebbles can be compared to human emotions such as worry, fear and anger. When these pebbles start to build one on top of the other, they restrict the flow and soon there is only a trickle of water running in that once free-flowing river; at this point, physical pain may be experienced. When you receive Reiki, more energy is offered to the body. This extra energy is like a flood that washes down through our rivers removing and dissolving obstacles in its way.

From my own experience, I know that Reiki offers a great many benefits as it is a holistic relaxation therapy that focuses on the root cause of conditions rather than merely on the symptoms. Thus, not only can Reiki be used to induce a sense of deep physical relaxation, but it can also be used to promote the healing of a wide range of ailments.

These include everything from stress-related complaints such as insomnia to joint aches and pains such as arthritis, headaches, stomach aches, depression, backache, menstrual problems, anxiety, asthma, colds and flu etc.

However, I must admit that when I went for my first Reiki session, shortly after discovering yoga, back in 2003, I had no idea what was really involved. I remember lying on the treatment couch wondering what on earth was going to happen to me. Relaxing music played in the background and candles enhanced the natural light of the room. The Reiki practitioner talked about angels and fairies and when my stomach started to gurgle she told me that this was a sign they were in the room. I couldn't quite relax because at any moment I was expecting to see apparitions and have a strange out-of-body-type experience.

I now know that Reiki treatments tend to last anywhere between 40 minutes to an hour and are carried out with the person being treated lying in a comfortable and peaceful environment. There is no need to remove any clothing and you are often given the opportunity to cover yourself with a blanket to encourage relaxation and make you feel a little more comfortable. The practitioner may gently lay their hands on different parts of the body corresponding with the chakras, working from the head to the toes. You may be asked to turn over so the practitioner can work on the other side of your body too. Back then, I was unaware of any of this.

In my 'out-of-balance, want-to-be-balanced' kind of way, I suspect I was looking for a miracle cure that day – as so many do in this society where we place doctors on pedestals, almost like gods, expecting them to heal us with pharmaceutical drugs, and without us having to make any changes to our lives or take any responsibility for our illness or being out of balance. But, of course, the miracle cure didn't happen. After the session, I still felt like the same old me, a little out of sorts, a little unhappy. The only difference being the fact that I knew a little bit more about angels.

However, regardless of whether I felt the effects of the Reiki during that first session, a seed had been sown. I was clearly drawn to Reiki for a reason and it was only a matter of time before it presented itself to me again – and the second time around, I had not gone searching.

Quite unbeknown to me, I had started attending a meditation class which was led by a Reiki master teacher, Alyssa Burns-Hill. Most of the meditation attendees were Reiki-attuned and there was often much chatter about Reiki and the Reiki courses taught by Alyssa. I would listen to them talking about metaphysical energy, auras, crystals and chakras and wonder what it was all about – it was certainly a different world to the one I lived in at the time.

But times change and only a matter of weeks later I came across an advertisement pinned to the notice board in my office advertising Reiki treatment sessions with – coincidentally (and this is something that becomes more prevalent in the Reiki world (coincidences that is)) – Alyssa who led the meditation classes. I was fascinated as I read the advertisement; it mentioned how Reiki can encourage and support positive personal changes, helping to balance emotions and free you from restrictive mental attitudes and behaviour patterns. It explained how Reiki can help to improve the quality of your relationships, help you to de-stress, reduce your need for alcohol and tobacco, improve your diet and help you to respond more calmly to situations and events in your life.

This resonated with me immediately and while I still knew very little about the 'how', I was at a point in my life where I was willing to give anything a go. After all, I had recently given yoga a go and that had worked out well. This is often the nature of Reiki – you may not be aware of it at the time, but it tends to come into your life when you need it the most; you simply have to be open to receiving it. This is another thing about Reiki: it cannot be forced upon you. You are either willing to receive it and all it may reveal to you, or you aren't, and no amount of pressure from family or friends will change that – all they can do is plant the seed by making you aware that it exists in the first place.

My second Reiki treatment provided a very different experience to the one I had had only a few months earlier. Practising Reiki tends to enhance the intuition of the Reiki practitioner and Alyssa was certainly intuitive – not only that but I felt more of a connection to her and to the Reiki energy. She was able to feel what was going on for me, beyond the ego and the conscious thought patterns, and articulate these feelings to me in such a way that I could not have said better myself. The fact that these feelings were verbalised and given a voice was a liberating and enlightening experience, as I finally started to acknowledge some of those things I had squashed down and tried to push away.

After the session, I felt emotional and Alyssa assured me that this was not unusual. Alyssa explained to me that it is a little like peeling an onion – the more you receive Reiki, the more you remove the layers, and the more you step into authenticity. It is a little like discarding unnecessary baggage, session by session, and therefore a fantastic form of personal development. It is different for everyone though – some people may only want one session to enjoy the many benefits of relaxing, while others will want more sessions to continue peeling away the layers and perhaps making life changes in the process.

Reiki has its own intelligence and the practitioner will be drawn intuitively to those parts of the body where the Reiki needs to go. The body automatically draws in only as much Reiki as is needed, using it in whatever way is most appropriate at that time. The Reiki energy may be felt as a flow of energy, mild tingling, warmth, heat, coolness, other sensations, or nothing at all. It is common to drift off to sleep and you are often encouraged to do so, as it promotes a deeply relaxing experience, calming the mind as much as the body.

Being attuned to the Reiki energy so that you are able to channel this to others doesn't take years of training, nor is it dependent upon intellectual capacity; the ability to channel is simply passed from a teacher to the student through an attunement process. As soon as this happens, you have the ability to channel Reiki for the whole of your life, and it can be learned by anyone. The attunement (which is part of the teaching process) is a powerful spiritual experience and can increase psychic sensitivity. However, like most situations in life, people respond differently and the Reiki attunement is no exception.

There are three levels of study and they are all independent of each other. The first level teaches you how to use Reiki for your own personal self-development, self-healing and also the healing of others. The second deepens your experience of Reiki and teaches you three of the four Reiki symbols, including the distance-healing symbol so that you can heal beyond time and space – (it can take a while to get your head around this!) – and provides you with additional tools to work with Reiki, both on yourself and with others, and enables you to become a registered professional practitioner. Becoming a Reiki Master is the third level and here you learn the fourth symbol. Your experience of Reiki deepens, so you simply 'become Reiki' – there is no separation between Reiki and your life, as it becomes an integral part of it. You can then go one step further and train to become a teacher yourself.

The attunement process starts a cleansing process that can affect you on all levels, as many of the toxins (physical and emotional) that have been stored in the body are released, along with feelings and thought patterns that are no longer required. Each level of attunement tends to increase the strength of the energy, encouraging personal development, self-healing, greater clarity of mind, greater connection to your intuition and a potential increase in levels of consciousness.

Over a period of two years, I undertook all my training and I am now a Reiki Master Teacher offering Reiki treatments and attunement sessions to others. Each level brought with it new insights and it has been an empowering experience, which has not only increased my awareness of the world around me but also changed the way I perceive so many aspects of life. I have a far greater understanding and appreciation of healing, health and well-being, metaphysics, the chakra system and the flow of energy within the body.

Furthermore, Reiki has profoundly helped me on a personal level too – it has literally been life-changing, incredibly empowering and transformative and helped me (and continues to help me) to find the strength, clarity, self-belief and faith to make significant life changes to be more in tune with my true self. In addition, it has helped to support me through many life challenges, not only emotionally, but physically, mentally and spiritually too.

After my yoga practice in Namche Bazaar, to try to distract myself from my constant thinking and fretting, I attempt to read a book a friend has lent to me and I laugh out loud to myself because it's so appropriate, talking about letting go and surrendering to one's reality. I am reminded that the Universe is forever supporting us and trying to help us recognise that we are more often than not the creators of our own suffering! I am also reminded that it's far too easy to get caught up in the seriousness of life on this spiritual path, when actually the spiritual path, with its myriad of practices and lessons, is simply trying to encourage us to lighten up.

This is one of the reasons I love yoga – it encourages me to lighten up! Whether it is a full-on asana class so that I have no time to think because I am too busy moving my body in rhythm with my breath, so that the whole practice becomes a little like a moving meditation, or a gentle class with pranayama and meditation, or a restorative class with Yoga Nidra (deeply relaxing and transforming guided relaxation), they somehow all help, in their own way, to still my mind and brighten my outlook on life.

It may only be temporary, but in that moment of stillness, there is an all-consuming feeling of peace and a profound sense of oneness. There is also a deep knowing that we are all connected, that we are all one and that all is well. It's actually very difficult to put this feeling into words, for there are not enough words to describe it.

But in this moment, right now, there is no stillness, there is none of that feeling of connection, of all being well. My monkey mind is in full swing, from one thought to the next, unsettled, over and over again. The monkey of fear is sounding some alarm too, jumping up and down and highlighting all the things that could go wrong and all the things I need to be wary of, which makes me feel anxious and edgy on the inside again and again.

The Buddha showed his students how to meditate in order to tame the monkeys in their minds. You can't rid yourself of them, for what we resist persists! Instead, the Buddha suggested that we spend some time each day meditating so that we can, over time, tame the monkeys and come to know them better, and recognise when they are starting to get too loud in our heads. The fear monkey in my head is now really loud and I'm delighted when it's time for dinner as it provides a much-needed distraction.

Tonight, the dining room is busy with trekkers of all ages and from all over the world, including a large party of English school children on a field trip. I sit next to Pemba while we wait for our meal to be served. He fascinates me, as it has already become apparent that he is a bit of a charmer with his infectious smile, attracting the Sherpinis from far and wide!

I discover that he is thirty-seven years old and that he was born in a small village near to where we will be staying after the trek. He was sponsored to attend a Sir Edmund Hillary school not far from Namche Bazaar, yet a solid three-day walk away from his home village. He studied hard in primitive conditions, spending most of the year away from his family, always struggling for money and food. However, he feels that the hardships were worth the suffering, because in turn he received a good education and this enabled him to attend university and qualify as a lawyer. He was married at fifteen and became a father a few years later, with the birth of his son. He now has three children, all of whom are studying at a boarding school in Kathmandu.

We talk about education in Nepal. Pemba tells me that after the 1951 revolution, efforts were made to establish a national education system, but children were generally needed to work in the fields and at home, and educating females was viewed as unnecessary.

Pemba says that in this particular part of Nepal, the Khumbu region, many children still forgo an education to help their parents work the fields for subsistence farming, or work as porters in the mountains to guarantee an income for their families. It makes my heart sink to think of the young porters who will spend much of their life trekking up and down these mountains day in and day out, their spines stooping with the weight of their packs so that eventually they will no longer be able to stand up straight – it's a shocking reality.

Pemba tells me that our four porters, who are from Bupsa, will try and find work during the main trekking seasons in autumn and spring, leaving their families behind at home to look after the fields and animals. They return home out of season and will then work in the fields, subsistence living, hand to mouth. Perhaps sometimes they sell their surplus food at markets and they return with goods they have purchased with the money they have earned.

He explains that portering is not an easy job, although I can see this for myself. Others travel to seek porter contracts with people who are sending goods to hill villages. They earn a fixed rate based on the weight of the load and the number of days it will take to reach its destination. This is often the reason that porters carry double loads, or that two porters will carry three loads, so that they can supplement their income. There are some who are professional porters who do nothing else, but the majority only do the work when they do not have their own domestic responsibilities to attend to or work to be done.

I also learn that in 1975 primary education was made free and it became the responsibility of the government to provide school facilities, teachers and educational materials.

Primary schooling was then made compulsory, beginning at age six and lasting for five years.

However, despite the efforts to improve education for all children, Pemba tells me that the caste system still influences access to, and quality of, education. Also, education remains largely city-biased; the majority of schools are found in urban areas. Consequently, if rural families want their children to advance then they need to do what Pemba has done and pay to send them to study in urban areas. Thus education is divided, not just geographically, but also between the elite and everyone else.

Pemba believes that the people living in the villages experience a better quality of life than those who live in Kathmandu. He explains that in the villages they have lots of land and food, somewhere to live, clothes to wear and a simple, family-oriented life, in touch with their spirituality and the land. However, when they move to the city they need to pay for somewhere to rent, buy their food, get a mobile telephone and a vehicle to drive, perhaps. All of a sudden, they need all these things that they didn't need to worry about when they lived in the village – they experience pressures that were unknown previously and life becomes even more challenging.

Pemba tells me that approximately 57% of Nepalis are illiterate and 70% of those are women. I am shocked, as I had no idea. He also tells me that education has been further hampered these last ten years by the violent conflict between the Nepali government and the Maoist rebels, who have been waging a campaign against the constitutional monarchy since 1996.

More than 10,000 people have died during the fighting, with many civilians caught in the crossfire. Education has become a resulting casualty. However, foreign charities have been keen to do what they can to improve educational facilities and standards throughout the country – this is one of the reasons that I find myself here in Nepal, as we too will be helping out at a local village school after this trek.

Our conversation opens my eyes a little to the reality of life lived in Nepal and I realise that I have a lot to learn. For the first time, I'm looking forward to visiting the village school in Bupsa – not only will it be interesting to gain exposure to the rural education system, but I'm keen to experience rural life, as well as gain further exposure to Tibetan Buddhism.

7

And if I only could, I'd make a deal with God,
And I'd get him to swap our places,
be running up that road, be running up that hill,
be running up that building,
If only I could, oh…
"Running Up That Hill", Kate Bush

DAY 4: Namche Bazaar to Tengboche

A barking dog keeps me awake half the night. Even here, we cannot escape their moonlight chorus. It was the same in Kathmandu. I've never known anything like it, not least the number of stray dogs in this country thus far, but also their endless barking throughout the night. Once one starts, another starts, and then they're all howling and barking away. It doesn't happen at home in Guernsey, so I'm not used to hearing it!

In the morning, Lilly's still feeling ill. I wonder whether it may be nerves as she is really very fretful about continuing with the trek. Her concern has rubbed off on me and again, we discuss staying here in Namche while the boys continue with the trek. My headache has eased, but I'm still feeling tired and below par, and I'm also now filled with fear. However, Pemba will absolutely not entertain our concerns and insists we pack our bags and get ready to leave with the boys after breakfast: no further discussion allowed.

Lilly and I mutter and moan to one another.

"But I'm sick," Lilly says. "I'm going to have to keep stopping to go to the toilet all the time, and I can't stomach any food, which means I'm going to be weak too."

"I know," I respond, "it's crazy. You can't be expected to trek in these conditions if you don't feel right. But I have to admit, I really want you to feel OK and keep going, because I can't do it on my own."

"I know, but I'm not sure if I can do it," Lilly says, with pain in her voice, clearly torn between wanting to stay put and yet wanting to make it to Everest Base Camp.

"Well look," I try to reason, "let's see how we get on today. If it's awful, well then we'll just insist that we return here and wait for the boys, however long they may take, maybe six or seven days if all goes well."

There's a part of me that feels that this would be the best option, but there's also another part of me that doesn't like giving up. I'm here to reach Everest Base Camp and I need to make an effort to get there. Furthermore, I've been telling anyone who will listen to me that I'm trekking up the mountain, so I really do need to get on with it. But it's not easy, especially when someone else is potentially trying to find a way to opt out. Namche would be a lovely place to stop too, with all its bookshops and the Gompa to visit.

But the decision has been made. We're joining the rest of the group, and Pemba makes sure that we start out early and get going before we can put up any further resistance, plus we have another long day ahead of us.

The early morning sky is beautifully clear and I take it as a sign that we're meant to keep going! With that, I walk with my head up and am aware of my surroundings and of the number of other people also starting out on their day. "Namaste, Namaste, Namaste," we say to one another, smiling.

There's a pack of donkeys up ahead of us, their tinkling bells echoing throughout the quiet cobbled streets as we navigate our way out of town. The further we climb, the more I am aware of my every breath, yoga in action, as I am encouraged to follow the inhale and the exhale. For me, one of the most enlightening things about beginning yoga was awareness of the breath.

Until that point, like most, I had taken the breath totally for granted; admittedly, the London Marathon made me aware of it, but it was yoga that really hammered the point home. Without the breath we are nothing! It is the one constant in our life, from the moment we are born until the moment we take that final exhalation – we can go weeks without food, days without water, but only minutes without breathing, yet we pay it such little attention unless it is challenged.

When we begin practising yoga, we are often so preoccupied with trying to place our various body parts into the alignment required of any given posture that we are totally unaware of the breath. Certainly, this was my experience, because in those early days my main focus was on my body and trying to figure out my right from my left, let alone identifying with my sitting bones and shoulder blades, or any of the other body parts that a yoga teacher may mention to describe how to get into a pose.

This was, without doubt, one of the first awakenings I received from yoga: the awareness that it brought to the physical body. For many, like me, this may be the first time that they have had to consider their sitting bones and the way they sit, let alone identify with their perineum or tailbone. It was a revelation, and I am always conscious of this when teaching beginners. It is imperative to begin on the gross level – right, left, hand, foot and then become increasingly refined with levels of experience. To this day, I still attend classes where teachers talk about specific muscles and I am sure that the majority of students in the room have no idea what the teacher is talking about!

It's a little like this with the breath. While it is the breath that differentiates yoga from other forms of exercise, initially the breath is something that continues to happen relatively unconsciously until such point as we have a better grip on the body. It is then that we start to pay greater attention to the breath and potentially our whole experience of yoga then shifts.

Over time, we build a refined awareness of it, and capacity for it, and can use it to experience greater space in the body, increased energy levels and a calmer mind. With the breath, we balance giving and receiving, bringing in and nourishing on the inhalation, and letting go and surrendering on the exhalation. We learn whether we are more at ease inhaling or exhaling, and consider how this is reflected in our lives.

Do we hold on or do we let go? Are we givers or takers or a balance of both?

It's a joy to witness the transformation of students' yoga practices, as they shift from one level of awareness to another. There is always someone who will lead with the left when the teacher and the rest of the class are leading with the right and others who will always take a shorter stance than others, because either they struggle to process the instruction or underestimate the length of their limbs and/or distance between their hip bones etc. The image we have of ourselves in our head is often different to our reality. For example, people who view themselves as short take a shorter stance than the norm (proportionally) and long-limbed individuals will often overly-widen their stance and of course there are others who think that wider is best, because they are still caught up in the need to compete, even though yoga is non-competitive in approach.

I was that person once, competing with myself and with others in the studio, wanting to be able to perform the more advanced postures. Little did I realise at that time that there's far more to a yoga practice, and to an asana (posture) practice certainly, than just physical flexibility and strength. There's so much more and yet, sadly, these days most in the West think of yoga as simply being about the postures and often overlook the potential of the breath and the other practices.

Shortly after completing my teacher-training course, and quite by chance, I met a wonderful soul called Emil Wendel who teaches 'beyond the asana'. He is a philosophy and pranayama teacher, and it was the latter that particularly drew me. I ended up travelling to Bali to spend two weeks on one of his 'Beyond the Asana' retreats. It was there that I truly learned and experienced the potential of the breath (and mudra and meditation) to transform how we feel on the deepest of levels. It was mind-blowing, and certainly that trip marked the beginning of my love affair with the Divine, and helped me to recognise the oneness of all life.

Here in Nepal, I long for that connection, although I doubt I will access this through the breath, for it is an effort to breathe. The air is thinner, with less oxygen, and this, combined with the physically demanding nature of the terrain, means that I am virtually sucking for breath. In many respects, you could say that my awareness of the breath is heightened, simply because there is not enough of it to take in. I'm almost gasping for breath at times. This creates a slightly edgy feeling, an inherent fear, primal I assume, that is alerting me to the potential challenge of the simple act of providing my body with the oxygen it needs to exist.

One of the main breathing techniques used during an asana practice, especially during a Hatha vinyasa practice, is the ujjayi breath, commonly translated as 'victorious breath'. This technique means that while you breathe in through the nose, you direct the breath towards the back of the throat and constrict the glottis in the process, creating an audible sound to the breath, a little like the sound of the seashore or, dare I say, Darth Vader from *Star Wars*! This breathing technique offers the potential for calming the mind and soothing the nervous system, and I use it regularly throughout my day-to-day life too.

However, the mere fact I am able to breathe is reassuring now. I've never known air like it. There is no doubt that all of us on this trek have become aware of our breath in a way that we may never have been previously. I'm having to make a real effort to inhale sufficient oxygen to enable me to continue.

Fortunately, we soon stop on the top of a ridge at a chorten, a stone Buddhist monument, adorned with more prayer flags and Buddhist relics. It's incredible and I feel something that I have not felt thus far on the trip: a lightening in my heart and a shiver down my spine. I'm finally touched by the incredible panoramic view of the peaks of Mount Everest, Lhotse, Thamserku and Ama Dablam (or so Tim tells me), rising in the distance, and this stunning landscape.

Pemba tells us that this area was once covered in dense juniper forests, but these have been stripped bare by the locals to be used for firewood to help provide hot food, hot water and warm rooms for we tourists. Removing the trees makes the land more likely to slide during heavy rain and that obviously brings with it a huge risk to the locals. It's the first time that I've started to consider the impact that our being here is having on the environment and its people. On the one hand, we provide a source of income, but on the other hand we place additional strain on the natural ecosystem.

We take photos. I've finally let go of stressing over my broken camera and have accepted that it doesn't work and I won't have my own camera on this trip. Lilly has kindly suggested that we share hers instead. So now I take photos with it as if it were my own and I'm very grateful for this opportunity – it is one less thing to fret about! We're all smiling in the photos because there is something magical about this particular spot. It's funny how you can experience such extreme moods in such a short period of time. Earlier I was nervous and anxious about continuing and now I think the trek is marvellous.

Our every step is bringing us closer to the mountains and the views are stunning. We're all touched in our own ways. I feel it as a vibration of the Himalayas, an energy that lifts my soul and brings joy to my heart. Lilly feels it as well, and I'm pleased, because she's been so fearful of continuing and now she's more positive, which is encouraging. The light seems brighter here too – like we are closer to the Divine (however you determine this).

The trail runs gently downhill to the river – what a delight – and we stop here at one of the guesthouses for lunch, basking in the noonday sun and enjoying views of the river with her cleansing energy. We are all very hungry so we're not very impressed when it takes over an hour for our food to arrive. Still, our patience pays off as I've chosen rice with potatoes and cabbage, which is the tastiest rice, potatoes and cabbage I have ever eaten! The boys eat plate after plate of momos with spicy sauce – momos are stuffed Tibetan-style dumplings, which have been fried – they love them!

After our lunch break, it's a draining two-hour trek up to Tengboche, as we climb through a forest of tall, mature rhododendrons. Lilly wisely bought herself some walking poles in Namche Bazaar, so I now have two walking poles again and it makes a huge difference. I love my walking poles for this very reason – they help to support me up and down hills, encouraging me to dig in on the way up, and creating greater support and stability on the way down. I would certainly recommend that anyone who chooses to trek in Nepal ensures that they have some walking poles with them.

We're following a herd of yaks; their bells pierce the thin air with their tinkling. I doubt I shall ever forget this sound, as it is synonymous with the need to slow down, an indication that there are yaks approaching, or yaks in the way of the path ahead. For us now this means that we have little choice but to reduce our pace, slowly placing one foot in front of the other as we slog endlessly uphill. The trail is busy, not only with trekkers but with porters too.

I'm in awe of the number of porters who pass us wearing only flip-flops on their feet. I can't stop looking at them because I just can't get my head around the fact that they can walk this trail so quickly with such limited support for their feet and ankles, or any form of protection from the increasingly cooler climes. I'm also in awe of the weight and volume that they carry on their backs, not least those carrying three trekking bags in one go, but also those carrying various supplies and others carrying boxes of goods in their wicker *doko* baskets.

We're so spoilt in comparison. We've got clothes available for every eventuality and we are all wearing good quality hiking boots, a necessity, really – well, at least one would imagine that it is a necessity, but the porters are proving me wrong. That's the reason I'm so intrigued – how can they be so hardy? They must be made in a different way to the rest of we 'gentle' Westerners!

I'm so busy staring at one of the passing porters that it takes me a moment to register that there's great excitement ahead. One of the yaks has lost its footing and is starting to slip down the side of the steep earth bank. It happens almost as if in slow motion. Pemba shouts at us all to stand back against the earth bank behind us. He's paranoid about the yaks hurting us. We all leap back as instructed, reacting to the serious tone in his voice, and watch as the yak desperately tries to find its footing.

Two Sherpas who were leading the yaks start shouting at the sliding yak and then shout at each other in Nepali before sliding down the slope themselves to help encourage the yak back up onto the trail. We watch in bewilderment, feeling helpless, as the yak flounders and soil flies all over the place and the Sherpas continue shouting at one another while trying to push the yak back up the slope. I'm just questioning whether the yak will make it when all of a sudden the powerful beast secures its footing and clambers, with the help of the Sherpas, back onto the path again. Phew!

With the excitement over, we wait a few minutes for the yaks to continue along the trail at a safe distance ahead of us, before we follow. Pemba explains to me that these long-haired yaks are greatly valued in Nepal, so Sherpas will do all they can to ensure their safety. As we've seen, they are strong load carriers and are used to help move supplies along the trail. Their wool is woven into blankets and can be used to make ropes too. Furthermore, their dung is burned as fuel and the female yaks offer a butterfat-rich milk, which Sherpas use to make cheese and butter. I can understand now the reason the Sherpas were so keen to save the yak; they have many valuable uses!

The trail soon becomes really dusty and the dust clings to my skin and fills my nostrils. The weather changes too and as we approach Tengboche at the top of the steep and seemingly never-ending hill (3,870m) the fog sets in and it has become so cold that we have to stop to unpack our coats, scarves, gloves and hats from our day packs. I wasn't anticipating this change in climate so soon and wonder how much colder it may get the higher we go.

Finally, after a few tedious hours of trekking uphill, some of it on stone steps that make me very aware of my aching knees, we arrive at Tengboche itself, a village that is scattered across a wide, grassy saddle below a crescent-shaped ridge covered by scrub pines and dwarf rhododendrons. Ordinarily this place offers stunning views of the Himalayas, but we can't see much of anything right now due to the cold fog that clings to the air and makes me shiver to my core.

Tengboche is home to the largest and most active gompa in Khumbu. The first monastery was built in 1916 by Lama Gulu, a monk from Khumjung, but the building was destroyed in the earthquake of 1934, which also killed its founder. A second gompa was built on the site, but this only lasted until 1989, when an electrical fire burned the stone and timber structure to the ground.

With donations from a combination of Buddhist groups, Sherpas, mountaineering and trekking companies and foreign-aid organisations, the monastery was reconstructed and reopened in 1993. It's an incredible building, especially with its history, and it is clearly a testament to the faith and strength of the people who kept rebuilding it. I can't help but marvel at how they got the supplies up the mountain in the first place.

Pemba explains to me that gompas tend to follow a general sacred geometrical mandala design, including a central prayer hall containing a thangka (a Tibetan Buddhist painting like we saw in the little gompa in Namche Bazaar), a number of benches for the monks to sit on when they engage in prayer or meditation and an accommodation area. There are often a number of stupas accompanying a gompa too.

Pemba believes that about 50 burgundy-robed monks currently live at the monastery, which is remarkable really when you consider the austere conditions and the cold temperatures. It's so very cold up here that we walk past big blocks of ice scattered on the ground in the courtyard, and this is in springtime! I can't even begin to imagine the freezing temperatures in the depths of winter without heating and of course the lack of light, without a constant supply of electricity.

At the entranceway to the gompa, we tentatively remove our shoes and place our socked feet on the cold stone floor before being welcomed into the chapel by one of the resident senior monks. I enter the dark and cool room and immediately stand still in awe, for standing there right in front of me is a four-metre-high statue of Shakyamuni Buddha, backed by an ornate wooden frieze of mythical beasts, which Pemba tells me was rescued from the fire.

I walk up to the statue and stand in front of it, hands held together in anjali mudra (prayer position) in respect to the Divine. I bow my head and pray, asking for protection and support on the trail ahead. I also silently give thanks for the opportunity to be here to witness this beautiful gompa and the Everest landscape for myself; I finally feel blessed and full of gratitude.

There's an incredibly light and vibrant energy in the gompa. It's difficult to explain in words, because it's something you feel instead. It's a bit like the feeling you can get when you step into a place of worship like a cathedral, for example, only that this energy is even lighter than that. The boys don't know what to do with themselves. It's an alien environment for them, and yet I know that they can feel something too, as they become silent.

I've become increasingly intrigued by the energy of Tibetan Buddhism and the vibration created by the prayers and chanting of the monks, which positively affects the ambience within the room. The silence is welcome too; the boys are ordinarily relentless in their chatter. All I can hear now is the soft padding of socked feet as we wander around the gompa, following Pemba, and drinking in the sublime energy.

I pause with Pemba at the side of the darkened room to study the beautiful, brightly coloured thangka paintings covering the walls. They are incredibly detailed and must have taken a long time to paint. Pemba informs me that these thangkas serve as important teaching tools, depicting not only the life of Buddha, but also various other influential lamas (the term used for venerated spiritual masters, or heads of monasteries in Tibetan Buddhism), deities (a supernatural being considered divine or sacred) and bodhisattvas (a living being who aspires to enlightenment and carries out altruistic practices). He says that to Buddhists these Tibetan religious paintings offer beauty and are regarded as a manifestation of the Divine.

After we've walked around the room, Pemba and I join the other members of our group, already outside. It's now so cold that my breath hangs in the air as the fog continues to hug the landscape, making it difficult to see very far ahead. It makes me feel disoriented and I'm pleased that Pemba knows the terrain so well.

"Come, come," he says, as he ushers us, "we need to keep moving."

"How much further?" we all want to know. We're cold, tired, hungry and ready for a cup of tea.

"Down this hill," he tells us. "Be careful. It will be slippery, and muddy too. Bistari, bistari."

I sigh inwardly. That's all we need, slipping down the hill!

We gingerly follow Pemba down the slippery slope formed by a combination of muddy soil, full of clay, and cold ice. I'm pleased I've got my walking poles to help support me and keep me on my feet because any minute we're all waiting for someone to slip, and almost wishing it too, not for harm of course but for the potential hilarity of muddy clothes and faces. But it doesn't happen, we're very steady on our feet and mindful of our movement.

It's not long until we arrive at a tiny lodge, our home for the night. We all sigh with relief. It's been another long and hard day and we're all feeling chilled now – like the cold and damp air has seeped through to our bones. We're therefore delighted to find a simple and centrally-placed wood-burning stove at work in the small and dimly lit dining room of the lodge. However, we quickly realise that it isn't yet producing much heat, which is very disappointing, so we huddle as close as we can to gain as much heat as we can, while eagerly drinking cups of hot mint tea, served to us in flasks. The boys devour small packets of sugary biscuits as if they have not eaten for a week, which makes me chuckle because they really are food machines!

We are organised now with the catering and refreshment side to our trip. Pemba keeps a book where he notes down all the group orders for breakfast, morning tea, lunch, afternoon tea and dinner. The innkeeper then tallies up the total billable amount and Pemba pays this before we leave any given eatery. Anything extra that we order, we pay for ourselves. The higher we climb, the higher the prices become, so a cup of milk tea that might cost five rupees at lower elevations, rises steeply in the higher altitudes to fifty rupees. It's the same with the staple bottles of water and the fizzy drinks and chocolate bars that the boys keep consuming.

I contemplate a yoga practice, but I soon realise that there is no space for me to practise on my mat in this lodge, as it is so tiny. I really struggle with this as there's a part of me that has become conditioned to believe that I should practise every day and that if I don't get on my mat then I am an insincere practitioner. It's not only that, but I relish the time out and the opportunity to tune in instead. Anyone who regularly practises yoga will know what I mean. Life can be busy, with lots of external demands and distractions. Even taking just five minutes to lie silently on your mat and notice how your body is feeling and bring awareness to the breath, deepening the inhalation and lengthening the exhalation, can bring some relief, some inner peace.

Often, we can spend so much of our time living in our heads to the extent that we're not even aware of the body and the messages it is trying to give us, with its various aches, pains and sensations. Even those focused on a spiritual path can lose themselves in the ether, floating around in a 'spiritual' bubble unable to manifest on this Earth as they are not grounded and centred within themselves in the body, in this reality on Mother Earth. Practising yoga can help with this, encouraging us to actually embody our experiences – truly live in the body, rather than just living in the head (caught up in our intellect and the whole 'magical thinking' that can take place).

I'm also aware that yoga encourages balance (so too strength, flexibility and stamina, mentally and physically) and that includes a balanced approach to the practice. I am still struggling with this. As a Type-A personality, I'm aware that I have a tendency to do things to extremes and finding the balance is an ongoing work in progress – that whole concept of 'not too tight, not too loose', trying to find the Middle Way, as taught by the Buddha.

During the trek, I have been reading a book about Buddha and about Tibetan Buddhism. I am aware, therefore, that the search for the Middle Way is really a universal pursuit of all Buddhist traditions – the quest for a way of life that would give the greatest value to human existence and help to relieve the world of suffering. It is for this reason that Buddhism itself is sometimes referred to as the 'Middle Way'.

The Buddha's life is an example of the basic interpretation of the Middle Way, as the path between two extremes. Born a prince, and known as Prince Siddhartha, he enjoyed every physical comfort and pleasure. However, dissatisfied with the pursuit of fleeting pleasures, he set out in search of a deeper more enduring truth. He entered a period of extreme ascetic practice, depriving himself of food and sleep and bringing himself to the verge of collapse.

Sensing the futility of this extreme path, he began meditating with the intention of realising the truth of human existence, which had eluded him as much in his life of asceticism as it had in a life of luxury. It was then, in his rejection of both self-mortification and self-indulgence, that Prince Siddhartha awakened to the true nature of life – its eternity, its deep wellspring of unbounded vitality and wisdom.

After his perfect enlightenment, he became known as Shakyamuni Buddha, whose unequalled accomplishment has since guided seekers of wisdom throughout the ages. The Buddha, the Awakened One, then spent the rest of his life teaching others how to be free from suffering and to discover lasting peace and happiness. Rooted in principles of non-violence and loving-kindness, the lessons that the

Buddha taught all those years ago continue to help people to this day.

Tibetan Buddhism contains the teachings of the Buddha as practised and taught in Tibet. Because of Tibet's secluded location, the Buddhist tradition developed there for fourteen centuries in relative isolation, largely unknown or misunderstood by the outside world. A turning point came in the late 1950s, when the Communist Chinese takeover forced Tibetan teachers to migrate to India. Since then Tibetan Buddhist teachers have travelled further abroad and have established teaching centres that now flourish all over the world.

Tibetan Buddhism teaches that we are all potential Buddhas because we are essentially pure and luminous at the most basic level of existence. That purity, called Buddha-nature, is typically clouded over by a dense layer of ignorance and negativity, which can dominate us and lead to suffering. The Tibetan Buddhist path encourages its practitioners to adopt the traits and characteristics of enlightened beings through the use of special meditational techniques, thereby realising their innate Buddha-nature.

Buddhists entrust their spiritual growth and well-being to, firstly, the Buddha as the perfect teacher, secondly, his teaching (the dharma) as the holy path to awakening, and thirdly, the lamas (the Tibetan equivalent of the Sanskrit term guru), tulkus (a person who has been identified as the emanation of a deceased master) and the ordained (nuns or monks ordained in the tradition), who all comprise the sangha. These three objects of refuge (Buddha, Dharma and Sangha) are collectively revered in Buddhism as the 'Three Jewels', and are the basis for Buddhist spiritual commitment.

Tibetan Buddhism is distinguished by its many methods and techniques of spiritual development and for its great acceleration of the spiritual journey. It developed from the Vajrayana tradition of Buddhism and uses advanced yogic techniques in combination with elaborate meditations – it offers, therefore, an esoteric approach to Buddhism. The meditations incorporate visualisations of personified archetypes of enlightenment, frequently referred to as 'meditational deities'. These archetypes are often represented in Tibetan religious art in the form of bronze sculptures, or in painted portable scroll icons such as the thangkas that we have seen in the gompas.

The scriptures containing the esoteric teachings for yogic practices (such as meditative visualisations) are called tantras. These tantras form part of a larger body of Buddhist sacred texts based on the public teachings of the Buddha and are known as sutras. (Vajrayana's use of tantric literature explains why it is sometimes referred to as Tantric Buddhism). Mantras (chanted sacred syllables or phrases), mudras (ritual hand gestures) and mandalas (symbolic representations of enlightened worlds) are all used as part of Tibetan Buddhist meditational practices.

I find it very interesting because I have become increasingly drawn to using these techniques in my own practice. I love to chant different mantras and I have become increasingly fascinated by mudras. I was introduced to mandalas during my Reiki training and I often create mandalas of my own, using the Reiki symbols, and working with the energy of intention and manifestation – I am carrying a little notebook with me on this journey, for example, that is full of very simple mandalas that I have drawn.

I am also fascinated by the fact that in the Tibetan Buddhist tradition the lama is of particular importance. These venerable teachers are often given the honorary title of Rinpoche ('Precious One'). All lamas complete a long course of study that prepares them for their future role as the bestowers of initiations and esoteric teachings.

Lamas introduce students to particular teachings and through 'empowerments' bestow spiritual energy so that specific practices can be successfully undertaken by students. Formal and informal face-to-face oral transmissions of spiritual insight and wisdom typically occur between lama and student. While I appreciate that this relationship is more developed and embedded in the tradition, it reminds me of

Reiki and the relationship that can form between student and Reiki master, and how this can develop over time.

I have become increasingly aware that it's this relationship that is lacking for me in the yoga world, as I don't have one dedicated teacher. I'm lucky though, as I have trained with a number of yoga teachers who inspire me in their teachings, but the trouble is, they mainly live and work on the other side of the world, which is tricky. It's true what they say though, about teachers arriving when the student is ready, and I can certainly relate to this, but I do sometimes yearn for one single teacher who is available to me at all times. For example, there are periods when I'm 'stuck' in my practice, or have a question and would like to have someone on hand to answer it.

But I also have this sense that I'm just not meant to have one single teacher or guru in this lifetime – that essentially, I have my own inner teacher, my heart, and that others come in to guide me to listen to this more clearly, so that I can learn from my own experiences (rather than the experiences of others). So often, people give their power away to others, believing that the other person knows more about them than they know about themselves. Only we know our own truth, but it can be helpful to have others in our life who can guide us from their own experiences.

This is another reason that I love yoga. While you can certainly learn about the theory of yoga in books and from teachers, it is not until you start practising yoga and experiencing it for yourself that you come to 'know' yoga. It is an embodied experience and that for me is crucial when it comes to personal development and authenticity – you cannot learn this from books alone, you need to do the practice, do the work.

A number of people say they practise yoga, when this is merely a notion in their head. They may well have a yoga mat stashed somewhere at home or in their car (just in case) and they may well have the intention to attend class regularly, and perhaps they do attend a class once every six months or so, but really, can they truly say they practise yoga, when they rarely make it onto their mats? And how present are they in the class? (Is it merely a tick-box exercise, "Go to yoga – tick"?) How often do they truly connect with their breath and their body? Or connect their hearts with their inner teachers? This is not to judge, just to recognise the levels of our denial in how we live our lives in our heads and how we actually live our lives in reality; the two often contrast.

Deepening our connection to our hearts so that we can hear our inner teacher is not necessarily an easy process though, nor is living and directing our life from this place. Generally it involves unravelling the layers, undoing the conditioning and journeying deep within so that we come to know our own truth and then have the courage to do what needs to be done to step closer into authenticity (perhaps realising a little more of our potential in the process).

It can be a lonely journey and this is the reason that I sometimes crave a teacher who may help to guide me and prevent me from getting 'lost in the forest' in the first place. Sometimes it can be so difficult to see the wood from the trees, which can be a decidedly edgy and terribly frustrating experience.

However, I have come to appreciate that there is a certain joy that accompanies this process (eventually) and that figuring my way through the forest can be empowering and enlightening, as I am encouraged to truly feel and listen, trust my instincts and continue to put one foot in front of the other in the direction of the light, however far away that seems, or however much that may go against the mainstream.

Something magical happens though when we listen to and act on our heart's yearnings. The Universe is truly marvellous in providing guidance by way of coincidence, synchronicity, illness, books arriving, new people entering our lives, jobs ending and/or the unexpected happening etc. These are all signs sent from above to help us to learn the lesson that we may need to learn, to deepen our connection to the heart, to realign our lives more closely with our truth and true selves, and ground us in the present moment too.

Essentially all of life, for me at least, is a teacher. This trek is certainly a teacher and it is providing me with the opportunity to put my spiritual practice into practice and learn some life lessons in the process. It is also taking me out of my comfort zone and helping me to recognise and face a few of my fears, while providing both the time and space to process this – a true gift that I am very grateful for.

I'm also extremely grateful for the Tibetan Buddhist teachings and for the opportunity to absorb the beautiful Tibetan Buddhist energy. This alone is healing, revealing and heart-opening all at the same time. It is also awakening something deep within – there's a resonance, and I'm keen to continue exploring this as we journey higher into the mountains (I'm always welcoming of anything healing and heart opening).

I'm also hopeful that I shall be helped by the Tibetan Buddhist energy to embody the Middle Way, rather than it remaining solely as a concept in my head. There are times, especially when I was immersed in the Byron Bay yoga scene, that I become far too extreme and essentially unbalanced.

I developed an eating disorder when I was seventeen years old. I starved myself to lose weight because I wanted greater control in my life and because I believed I was not good enough as I was. I was a perfectionist who was not perfect enough, or this is how it seemed to me. My periods stopped and my parents grew increasingly concerned as I spent my days counting calories and finding ways to avoid eating, while also trying to exercise excessively. There were a number of trips to the doctor and an appointment with a psychologist, but the damage had been done.

That same year I went away to university and lost control of starving myself and started a binge-and-starve cycle instead. This went on for many years and was utterly exhausting in its extremes. I was constantly consumed with what I was eating and would exercise as much as I could, and went to ridiculous and dangerous steps to control my weight. It was inevitably a form of self-harm now I think back. I absolutely did not like myself and the media simply served to reinforce this with its emphasis on skinniness-equals-perfection-equals-happiness.

My negative relationship with food went on for far too many depressing years. If I was seemingly in control (ha!) then I was relatively happy (or so I thought), but inevitably I would lapse and then I would be filled with utter self-loathing and absolutely hate myself. It was perhaps no surprise that I ended up with PMS (through the disruption to my hormones with all the up-and-down blood-sugar levels and the loss of connection to my natural cycle and my body's wisdom), cysts on my ovaries (as something ate away at me from that trigger point at age seventeen) and depression (a complete loss of spirit).

It wasn't until my mid-twenties that I knew something had to change. I had found my way, thankfully, out of a destructive relationship, and while those days were particularly dark, they helped to ease me slowly into the light. This is the reason I started running, as it gave me an opportunity to process and to try to run my life forward. This led to the London Marathon, which as I have mentioned led me to yoga.

In my typical way, I got addicted to yoga and couldn't get enough of it. Something about yoga made me feel better and I wanted more of it. It also helped to give me the strength to see a qualified and experienced nutritionist. The nutritionist, Carol Champion, was great. She had a very pragmatic and no-nonsense approach, which was wholly appropriate for me at that time, and she gave me an eating plan, plus some supplements. The combination made a huge difference to how I felt. I couldn't believe it!

Until that point, despite being a competitive sportswoman and being fed well by my mum (when I'd eat!), I had no idea about good nutrition. I ate what I ate depending on what I felt it would do to my weight, as opposed to what I felt it would do for my health. It was incredible, really, to finally appreciate that much of my PMS symptoms were due to my restricted diet, and I came to realise that we are truly what we eat, and with that there was a huge shift in my relationship with food.

However, an eating disorder doesn't just go away overnight and I was still very much in denial that I even had one, or at least the degree to which I had one. It levelled out a lot with the discovery of good nutrition, Reiki and yoga and for the first time in many, many years my weight stabilised – hoorah the Middle Way – and I was eating well and feeling better because of it.

But, of course, there were still trigger points and the yoga world is full of students with eating disorders – the focus on the body in Western yoga inevitably attracts those who have body issues. In Byron especially, I was surrounded by many skinny yoginis, and this was challenging. I wanted to be a proper yoga practitioner which in my perfectionist's head meant that I needed to be light and lean and ever so bendy and stretchy on my mat like those around me. It is a very vicious cycle.

The combination of practising up to six hours of yoga a day in Byron, and eating a predominantly raw and vegan diet (as was the done thing for many there at that time), meant that I lost weight. I loved the feeling of being light and the fact my clothes were hanging off me. It's a control thing and I got a kick out of the control, even though it was counter-productive because the moment I lost control and therefore ate lots of food, I loathed myself both for losing control and for putting myself in a position where I might put on weight. Back home in Guernsey it was challenging to sustain my new lower weight. It was winter for a start and I was back in the office working to save money to go travelling again so I couldn't indulge in six hours of yoga or exercise as I had been doing in Byron with all the walking on the beach, cycling around town and swimming in the sea. It wasn't easy and I began to loathe myself all over again as I redeveloped the whole binge-starve thing.

Sadly, I now associated Byron and practising yoga in Byron with being skinny. It was with some joy therefore that I returned to Byron nine months after initially leaving, in September 2005, for my 240-hour intensive teacher-training course, followed by a few months of training at the Byron Yoga Centre (as it was then).

I began the training course eating my normal diet, as it was incredibly demanding and intense, and I was cycling backwards and forwards to the centre every day up a steep hill both ways. However, it didn't take me long to be influenced by the diets of those around me. One of the ladies involved in the training (who was very skinny) was a raw food expert and she was keen for us to explore this diet properly. (On my first trip to Byron I had been drawn to eat more raw foods than usual, but without any knowledge of this way of eating; I just ate lots of salads.)

So I gave it a go. There are many benefits to a raw food diet in terms of the vibrancy of the food, but I wasn't necessarily following it for that reason. I just wanted an excuse to eat less and lose weight in the process. The perfectionist in me was always looking for new ways of challenging myself to be perfect and here was one – see whether I could exist on raw food alone. It was another trigger, another thing to obsess about. It didn't help that I was living with a vegan couple, so I had that pressure too.

The lady who introduced me to the raw food diet was also very much into juicing, and at the end of the training I joined her on a five-day juice fast. This was a major trigger for me – the challenge of actually not eating. Wow, you can just imagine how great I felt about myself when I achieved this! And, actually, I did feel great. You get this incredible energy if you juice beyond three days, but it wasn't healthy, because it led to months of me not eating properly.

Following the juicing, I decided to give the fruit-only diet a go and existed for a good two months or so just on a few bowls of fruit a day and an awful lot of soya chai. I felt great! Well, I thought I did. Great because I was full-on in the grips of controlling myself, I was the skinniest I'd ever been, I could leap around my mat really easily and I looked the part of the yoga teacher (or how I thought a yoga teacher should look; it's nonsense by the way a yoga teacher should look like they look, there is absolutely no requirement to be skinny!).

The truth was, I couldn't sleep at night and was running on some pretty crazy energy. My adrenals were probably pushed to their limits with all the caffeine and exercise I was doing – the yoga, walking and cycling around town and swimming. Also, my mind was utterly consumed with my weight. It wasn't healthy in the slightest. I was in some denial that I had an issue, I was really in the depths of it. I mean deep down I knew I had a problem, but I was a few years away from really admitting it and doing something about it.

I returned home to Guernsey after five months significantly depleted, totally ungrounded and the skinniest I'd been for an awfully long time. With this weight loss and all the rather yang (strengthening, dynamic and masculine) yoga, my periods stopped again. I blamed the style of yoga I'd been practising rather than the diet. I really didn't want to accept that I was harming myself again, and especially not through yoga. I thought I was just doing what I felt other yoga teachers did – eating a simple (ha, very simple) sattvic (pure) diet to enhance my spirituality and practising a whole ton of yoga. Silly when I reflect back, but that's the nature of the mind. It's tricky!

So, I'm very aware of how the extreme approach to anything, even something supposedly healing and healthy like yoga, can be unhealthy. It really is all about trying to find the balance – the Middle Way.

Furthermore, experiencing the Middle Way is also about being OK with all that arises in any moment. It is about taking responsibility for all parts of ourselves, especially the bits that we don't like. Those aspects that we cast into the shadows will always show up, be that in the manner in which we treat ourselves or through the people we attract into our lives and the unhealthy relationships we have.

If we truly seek a life of truth, integrity, love and compassion, attracting healthy situations and experiencing loving and supportive relationships, then we absolutely need to do the inner work. We need to look at what is not working – at the extremes, at the manner in which we play out the same old self-deprecating stories – and do something to address this. It's not comfortable, but it is essential to our path as truly spiritual and enlightened (becoming lighter) beings.

I know this only too well, but the mind is fickle and my mind still holds on tightly to how it thinks things should be. It has developed a notion of what it might mean to be a sincere yoga practitioner and teacher and a student treading the path of light. This involves consistent yoga practice on my mat, regardless of life circumstances or finding myself way up in the Himalayas with very little room to lay my mat.

If I do not practise, I will feel bad. Because in my head practising yoga makes me feel good. I have this sense of goodness, the need to be good, running through my veins. And when I fall short of my own high standards, I am filled with a sense of self-loathing. It's something I'm working on, and being here in the mountains is providing the perfect opportunity – after all, the Universe creates situations (like this) for us to grow, to let go of how we think things should be, and shift perspective to a new, more resourceful, and essentially compassionate way of being.

The long and short of it is that getting on my mat each day, or not as the case may be, has become yet another opportunity to beat myself up with my (perfection) stick. It would take a few more years of practice to overcome this and lay that stick down once and for all. But right now, I'm not there. The biggest dilemma, and what a privileged life I have that this is the most pressing matter for me, is where to practise some asana!

Well, nowhere really; this is becoming the lesson of this trip – one of accepting my current reality and letting go of how I think things should be. Having zero expectation in the first place maybe. Fortunately, there is another pressing matter at hand that distracts me from all the yoga-practice-thinkings and that's the opportunity to have a hot shower.

Lilly and I are not only feeling cold, but we're also incredibly dusty, and therefore cleaning ourselves is both a priority and a necessity. Thankfully, the Sherpini who runs this tiny lodge is happy to oblige and sets to task boiling a large pan of water on top of the stove. It's a rather laborious process but we are both happy to pay her for this kindness.

The shower is located outside the main door of the lodge in a wooden cubicle, with a door that won't lock properly, so Lilly insists I stand outside in the freezing cold to keep guard, which I do of course, even though the boys all know that she's in there and are being respectful of her need for privacy. We giggle together about the fact we're taking it in turns to stand naked in an outside shower in the arctic weather.

It's a simple shower system and demands a certain attention to timing – you only get the one pot of boiling water each, which is poured into a cylinder above the shower cubicle and runs down a pipe into the shower head itself. The whole process is controlled by a simple tap, which literally goes on and off, or at least that's the concept.

However, there's a fine art to it – turn on tap, quick wet down, turn off tap, apply soap, shampoo, turn tap on and quick wet down, turn tap off and apply conditioner, turn tap back on and wash down until water runs out. Quickly turn tap off, wrap yourself in quick-dry thin trekking towel and hotfoot it back through the sub-zero air into the lodge and up the wooden stairs to your room, hoping no one will make too much of a fuss seeing you run half-naked past them (which the boys do, of course, it's conditioned into their psyches). Then see if you can change very quickly into PJs and numerous layers of clothing in the tiny room, with very little light without getting too cold in the process.

Up in our room, showered and changed, we can't stop giggling.

"It's the funniest thing," I try to say in between my giggles, "our desperation for showers."

"I know," Lilly responds, "it's ridiculous really. I just need a hairdryer now," she says, and with that we burst into hysterics because the concept of a hairdryer up here is crazy, not least because there's not much energy for beautifying oneself in the mountains, but also because there's very little electricity full stop.

Here, the lack of access to electricity makes us all too aware how very fortunate we are in the West to be able to take it for granted. No hairdryers mean that Lilly and I sit beside the wood-burning stove, so that our hair can be dried by the heat it is finally expelling. I can't stop shivering and yet my face glows at the same time with the effort of the day. I feel clean and satisfied after a hard day and now enjoy the opportunity to chill out in front of the roaring fire.

We sit huddled around it, mesmerised by the flickering flames. There's something primitive and healing about sitting around a fire in a circle together and we all feel warmed and calmed by the experience. I'm reminded of the Hatha yoga practice of trataka, which involves gazing at a candle for a period of one to two minutes initially before closing the eyes. It's a fabulous practice which helps to makes the eyes clear and bright while relieving nervous tension, improving the memory and helping to develop good concentration and strong willpower; an excellent preparation for meditation and sleep.

With very little else to do, and time to kill before dinner, I massage Joe's feet (as you do), before reading a few pages of my book. Matt and Ben are avid readers and have their heads in books too. We sip fresh mint tea now, served to us in flasks to keep the water warm, and before too long we've started chattering again. The boys joke with one another, their comments full of sexual innuendos – they can't help themselves! Sometimes it annoys me, but other times I enjoy their juvenile distraction; it serves to remind me how serious I can be in my I'm-so-spiritual way, and I'm pleased that they have helped to make me aware of this (shining lights on shadows).

The boys with their youth and innocence and lack of responsibility, or need to be responsible even, have highlighted to me some of my core values, which keep me trapped and prevent me – at this moment in my life – from experiencing greater inner freedom and peace. The voice in my head, the ego, which tells me what is right and what is wrong is still very strong. Like so many others, I have a deeply ingrained sense of this. Yet, on what is it based? Who is to say that my perception of 'right' is right? Or that my perception of what it means to be 'spiritual' is 'right' either?

And yet, I use my understanding of what's 'right' or 'wrong' or 'spiritual' as a barometer to measure how I'm doing in the world, to beat myself up and give myself a hard time.

I'm becoming increasingly aware of the manner in which my thinking sometimes limits me, simply because (like all of us) I have been conditioned to think a certain way. At some point in my life, I was judged by others and learned to judge myself – therefore I view some of my thoughts as 'good' and some as 'bad'. Furthermore, I consider some of my character to be good and some of my character to be bad. Likewise, some of my tendencies are good and some are bad.

We are constantly evaluating our world, and our experience of the world, based on our limited and judgmental thinking. If we are consumed with fearful thoughts, then we will see fear everywhere. If we are consumed with positive thoughts, then we will see the positivity in life. It's true in that our way of thinking creates our reality. It influences everything from our relationships to the opportunities in our life, and to our health.

There is a fabulous Chinese proverb, which always reminds me of the need to be conscious of our thinking and the thoughts to which we give our energy: "Be careful of your thoughts, for your thoughts become your words. Be careful of your words, for your words become your actions. Be careful of your actions, for your actions become your habits. Be careful of your habits, for your habits become your character. Be careful of your character, for your character becomes your destiny."

I am aware that these boys, who can be so silly at times, offer the potential to teach me how to have more fun, to keep my thinking positive and to go with the flow and allow life to unfold in its own wonderful way. I recognise that in my quest to be 'spiritual', I've lost a little of my sparkle. I've been beating myself up regularly for my shortcomings, based on what exactly? My own limited perception of reality and the beliefs I hold.

For example, I have somehow taken on the belief that being spiritual means being serious. Keeping a tight rein on things. Early bed, early rise, no socialising or partying. Eating clean food. Getting on my mat each day for as long as I can. No intoxicants. No nothing that may challenge this controlled way of living. There's nothing wrong with this per se, but I do recognise that it lacks balance. No Middle Way. At this stage in my life, if I let myself go, then it's likely I'll swing completely the other way and then I'll give myself a really hard time about it. Years later I will come to find the balance, or greater balance, but for now it's very much a work in progress.

I mull over all of this into the evening and am pleased by the arrival of dinner, which is served at 6pm – we've learned now to order as soon as we arrive at the lodge so that we can be certain of a timely dinner. I'm sticking with the dal bhat as it's filling and, let's face it, the Nepalis eat it twice a day every day, so it's got to be OK for you, and it's the only way I can guarantee a vegetable! Dinner finished, there's very little to do apart from go to sleep, so Lilly and I are nestled up in our respective sleeping bags by 7.15pm, which is unheard of at home. How life changes!

8

We are always running for the thrill of it thrill of it
Always pushing up the hill searching for the thrill of it
On and on and on we are calling out and out again
Never looking down I'm just in awe of what's in front of me.
"Walking on a Dream", Empire of the Sun

Day 5: Tengboche to Pheriche

I am woken at 5.30am, when a party of Japanese trekkers, who are also staying at the small lodge, clomp along the wooden corridor and up and down the wooden stairs. I try to ignore their noise, but it's no good, it feels like they're stomping right beside my bed. I reach for my earplugs, but I'm immediately aware that I have yet another headache and I can't be sure if it's due to the altitude, dehydration or the fact my spine hurts from the hard, wooden planks that lie beneath the thin mattress on which I've been sleeping all night.

At breakfast, we discover that both poor Matt and Ben, who do everything together, have been ill during the night. I feel for them; a night spent squatting over the smelly sunken toilet is my worst nightmare. The only positive is the fact that the toilet is inside the lodge, so no traipsing into the freezing cold outdoors. Poor Lilly's still feeling ill too and the rest of us are growing increasingly concerned that we may be next. I'm trying my hardest to keep my thoughts positive as I really don't want to be sick in this environment. Yuck.

All the sickness means that Will, our medical student, is in his element handing out drugs to anyone who will take them. I've come to realise that this boy loves drugs and he is keen to share his love of them with the others. Like me, however, Tim is resistant to pharmaceuticals unless absolutely necessary and the two of us look on in amusement instead.

Will is taking one tablet for one thing and then another to counter the effect of the first tablet. It's a strange concept to me. I've been embracing the more natural approach to healing the last couple of years. All these tablets seem a little counterproductive as Will's now constipated and feeling uncomfortable from this. I don't believe his diet is helping him either. All that fried food is enough to test the most robust digestive system. Matt and Ben have the opposite problem; they can't keep anything in! Illness or no illness, Pemba declares us all fit to trek. Clearly, we would need to be half-dead before Pemba would let us stop!

We begin with a gentle ascent in the cool and fresh air, all of us zoning out from one another and listening to our respective iPods, aware that we're likely to lose power soon, as there was no electricity available at the lodge last night to charge them and we're not sure whether there will be any further up the trail either. It makes us all aware how much modern gadgetry is dependent on electricity. Gone are the days of carrying spare batteries. Even Apple is useless in the Himalayas!

The fog has eased today. Dawn is clear and bright, which helps to lift our spirits. I delight in the landscape as we walk through a forest of dwarf conifers and more rhododendrons with their beautiful pink flowers creating a colourful scene. I really had very little expectation, and no idea what might draw people to this part of the world other than to see Mount Everest. I'm therefore continually blown away by the beauty of the landscape and by the simplicity of the lives of those who live here.

I consider how far removed our lives have become from nature. In the West everything happens so quickly. There's always a sense of rushing. But rushing where and for what purpose? It's perhaps not surprising that so many people suffer from depression and anxiety, as their lives lack the grounding that a steady pace in touch with nature and the elements encourages.

The porters' pace may well be steady, but it's much faster than our own and they dash off ahead of us as we fall into our own rhythm. Sometimes, I zone out from my surroundings as I spend time in my head, thinking and processing. I enjoy the opportunity for contemplation and trying to make sense of things that have been on my mind recently. Chatting with Lilly and the boys helps with this too as we can have some really in-depth conversations in the space of twenty minutes.

For example, Lilly and I will be talking about something quite insignificant, like what kind of tea we'll order at the next lodge, and then we'll suddenly find ourselves talking about our childhoods, and in such an open way that Lilly is getting to know more about me than my best friends. After we've exhausted that conversation, at least for the moment, we're back to discussing menu choices for the evening and bemoaning the lack of fruit and fresh vegetables on the menu! Then our conversation will be interrupted by passing trekkers and the exchange of "Namaste, Namaste, Namaste", and we'll split apart and enter into silence again, admiring the views instead.

Soon the path drops steeply down to a wobbly-looking suspension bridge dangling (or so it seems) over the surging and gurgling white waters of the Imja Khola. That's one powerful river and another opportunity to trust that the bridge will withstand our weight and won't collapse when we're halfway across it! I'd like to say we're getting used to all the bridges, and we are to a point, but I still experience a brief moment of hesitation because each bridge is different in terms of stability, and each bridge takes us further into unknown territory, and I'm never quite sure what that means in terms of demanding terrain!

We stop for an early lunch at one of the lodges in a village called Pangboche, at an altitude of 3,985m. It is located in the Imja Khola Valley about 3kms northeast of Tengboche and is the base camp for climbing nearby Ama Dablam, and trekking. Apparently, it contains a monastery, famed for its purported Yeti scalp and hand, the latter of which was stolen! The village is inhabited mainly by Sherpas, and famed for being the home of Sungdare Sherpa, who held the record in Sherpa climbing history in 1989, for conquering Mount Everest five times.

It's only 10.45am and everyone is feeling the change in altitude with much talk of pounding heads and feeling out of breath. I'm pleased to stop, my blood-sugar levels have felt really low this past hour and I'm experiencing an increasing sense of unease, anger and irritation. My state of mind has changed very quickly, which surprises me.

I'm irritated at feeling out of sorts and at the relentless nature of this journey. It pushes and challenges us again and again and we've still got approximately 1,400m to climb before we reach Everest Base Camp. I'm not sure how I'll cope with the increase in altitude when I'm having such a hard time already. It doesn't help that the weather is changing and a bank of grey cloud has begun to roll in, almost reflecting my mood, which is decidedly grey!

We take refuge in the small, dark dining room of the lodge and settle down on large wooden benches covered with rugs that rest against the perimeter of two of the walls, all sitting one next to each other. I sit on the end of the bench and can't bring myself to speak to anyone. I then make a terrible lunch choice without really realising it. My mood plummets even further when I am presented with a plate of boiled cabbage and deep-fried Tibetan bread.

I'm now furious at myself as much as I am at being here, feeling rubbish, head pounding and blood-sugar levels low. I just want to be back at home! I angrily eat some of the food that has been provided, struggling with the fried nature of it – it's said that you shouldn't eat when you're angry and emotional, but I'm well aware that if I don't eat, I'm only going to feel worse further on the trail. I'm furious though and irrationally irritated, not in the slightest bit grateful for the food, caught up as I am in all-consuming rage and a victim mentality.

Having eaten what I can of the meal, and to cope with my reality, I curl up into a ball and lie on the bench, covering my face with the hood of my coat while wearing my sunglasses. I play the music of Bic Runga on my iPod, which soon brings me to tears. I don't want anyone else to see me and I have a massive block around me, like a force field that says, "DO NOT COME NEAR ME!"

It's a horrible feeling when the rage comes like this, because it consumes me. I'm so angry and have no way of venting. This trekking malarkey is truly hard work. I'm tired of walking and tired of the demanding nature of the terrain and the lack of oxygen in the air. I'm sick to death of the boys and their endless chatter too. I just want some peace and quiet and an opportunity to get on my mat and lie down and rest.

I recall a moment of extreme rage last summer, which was so intense that I eventually ended up laughing (thank goodness). Since discovering yoga, these moments of rage have eased significantly in my life, so I had reached the point where I thought maybe I was done with my anger. So it was a bit of a surprise that summer morning, when the all-consuming feeling arrived just as I was trying to hang out the washing, while my parents and my brother (who was visiting at the time) were sitting on the patio, not far from the washing line.

I got myself into a complete state about something or other and effectively took it out on the washing. In my temper, I ended up pulling the washing that I had pegged onto the line, off the line, and desperately tried to shove it back into the washing basket before throwing this (with the washing in it) across the lawn. It was nonsensical and ridiculous, but I was so caught up in the red mist of rage that all rationality had gone well and truly out of the window.

I'll never forget the moment I realised that I wasn't alone, and glancing over towards my parents and my brother, found them all staring at me in surprise, not sure whether to laugh or be quiet, and curious to see what I was going to do next! This awareness of them watching pulled me out of my mood and brought me back to my senses, the red mist easing.

I then burst into tears as I calmly put the washing back on the line, before returning to the house feeling very remorseful about my actions and sorry for myself that I was still having outbursts of anger (blame the hormones!). It was only then, with all emotion vented and feeling much calmer as a result of it, that I was able to laugh at my sorry state.

Rage is all-consuming and can be hugely effective at allowing one to vent, but it can be ever so damaging if you take it out on someone else, or on yourself, or on your washing! I'm very aware of this as it is a theme that runs through my life, not only the depression, but also anger and frustration (which are often linked with depression). The high standards I have set for myself mean that I often don't live up to my own expectations, which creates the anger.

Anger is a destructive emotion when expressed inappropriately and can cause disharmony in the body. However, anger can also be a powerful motivator for change, provided you are consciously aware of your reactions and take charge of your emotions. This is the tricky bit – becoming conscious of the anger as it arises and acknowledging this, but then responding with love. It's a very fine line and the transition happens very quickly.

One of the five Reiki principles reads, "Just for today, do not anger", so I am aware of the negatives and do try to catch myself before I get into an angry state, but as I've mentioned, sometimes the feeling is so powerful that I react and vent before I've had a moment to come to my senses and try and see the love in any situation.

The key is to let go of expectations – whether those expectations are those of other people or situations, it doesn't matter. We get angry when our expectations are not met, so the best thing we can do is let go of expectation and see the person and situation as it is right now in any given moment.

Clearly, I still have work to do on myself, to catch myself before I allow the rage to take root, before the red mist descends and I can no longer think clearly or indeed rationally. With this awareness, having now become conscious of my changing mood and the need to shift it, I turn to my breath and inhale and exhale deeply. It is only then, with my mind a little calmer, that I recognise the need to let go of expectation – (is boiled cabbage and deep-fried Tibetan food really so bad in the grand scheme of things?) – and to give myself a break in the process.

I manage to pull myself together in time to continue trekking up the hill. I walk on my own though, head down, eyes hidden behind sunglasses, still sulking a little, needing my own space. It's a really hard slog and I'm not enjoying it. What was I thinking – it was going to be easy? Ha, I was kidding myself!

Finally, the landscape pulls me out of my terrible mood as it jogs a memory. As we continue walking uphill through the valley, the weather changes again; thick, low, white and chilling clouds now roll in. It reminds me of walking on Dartmoor, where it's also wild and abandoned, and with the clouds it has a slightly claustrophobic feeling to it, as I've experienced on Dartmoor when the mist comes in. I'm wearing a warm and woolly hat, yet the piercing wind literally whistles through my ears and I shiver with the cold.

I love Dartmoor for its solitude and familiarity. We spent time there as children while my parents oversaw Duke of Edinburgh expeditions for the teenagers that Mum taught (cared for) when she was a teacher. My brother and I would traipse around Dartmoor with my parents seeking out the groups and checking that they were OK and running to schedule. This was my introduction to the wilds of nature and I loved the sense of freedom, of playing in the rivers and of searching for the post boxes hidden among the tors.

The memory brightens me a little, as I consider how one part of our life can link us to another. Why did I get so lost? I ponder. I had been so desperate to go to Exeter University because the city was familiar to me and because it was the gateway to Dartmoor and close to the Devonshire surfing beaches. But I was rejected, the first rejection of my life, and I ended up at Swansea instead, drawn by Gower and the surf, being an avid surfer as I was at the time.

It's funny how we are shaped by things that happen in our lives, the decisions we make, and the consequences. Perhaps if I had chosen different A-levels, I may have ended up at Exeter and perhaps then my life would be very different. But it's not healthy to live on 'perhaps' or to live in the past wondering what might have been.

We are where we are. Sometimes there are periods of darkness and sometimes there are periods of light. Admittedly, we do each have a choice. Every moment of our lives we have a choice. But I've no doubt that something guides us and prompts us and tries to steer us to the path where we may feel more at ease in the world. This path right now, this very path in the Himalayas, reminds me of Dartmoor and this familiarity lifts my spirits.

And yet I recognise the vastness of this land on a scale that was unimaginable until now. It feels like we're all scuttling across the terrain, as if we are beetles in a garden, so small in the vastness (there really is no other word) of this mountainous landscape. We hurry up to a ridge. I'm following Dawa, one of the porters. He's leading the way, while Pemba stays at the back with Lilly and Joe. Will and Tim are at my heels, their heads down, trying to protect themselves from the harsh wind. Matt's to my side and gentle Ben is not far behind him.

Out of the clouds, I notice a party approaching us from the opposite direction. One of them, a man, is wearing very short shorts, which make me shiver. I like his bravado, though, and chuckle because he has lovely legs. I hope Lilly notices because she could probably do with smiling right now too.

Dawa and the boys stop a little way ahead and take refuge, sitting behind some large rocks trying to shelter from the wind. I join them and nestle down on the arid ground beside Dawa, crouching in silence. I don't have the energy to speak to the boys, and the wind makes it difficult to hear one another anyway. I'm not particularly aware of my surroundings. You can't see very far ahead and it's so icily cold and the wind so bitter that I'm huddled in on myself, longing for Pemba, Joe and Lilly to join us soon.

Dawa tells me that we are now above the treeline and on a dry landscape of scattered boulders and alpine meadows. Apparently, we won't see another proper tree now until we drop below the treeline again on our descent from the camp. This makes me feel both excited and uneasy. Excited that we've managed to make it this far despite all my earlier reservations and moaning, but uneasy about what lies ahead in this new terrain.

9

And I say, climbing, forever trying
Find your way out of the wild, wild wood
Said you are gonna find your way out of the wild, wild wood
Wild wild wood.
"Wild Wood", Paul Weller

Day 5: Tengboche to Pheriche continued...

Pemba, Joe and Lilly join us and we stop to drink water. I know I've not been drinking enough water, but as silly as it sounds, it's just such an effort to remove my daysack from my back and lift my bottle out of the side water pocket. It's even an effort to ask someone else to pass it to me. Lilly has cleverly managed to tie her water bottle to the front strap of her daysack so that the bottle hangs between her breasts, easily accessible.

I consider that this may be the reason for my foul moods as I'm not drinking enough water or eating enough calories and I make a mental note to eat more rice and drink more water each time that we stop at a lodge.

We're soon moving again, the wind howling in our ears and the clouds growing increasingly thicker and denser. The terrain is rocky underfoot as we walk up the valley, vast mountains looming all around us, and I have to make an effort to pick my feet up properly.

I experience irrational moments of simply wanting to lie down behind the nearest rock and sleep and I find myself scanning my immediate environment, searching for the most appropriate rock or boulder where nature has bountifully provided shelter from the natural elements.

Soon I begin to hear the small but fast-flowing Khumbu Kola and Pemba assures us that we haven't got far to go now. We follow one another across a small bridge over the river and Pemba tells us that this bridge is washed away every monsoon and has to be rebuilt again. I wonder how on earth anyone can live up here in this hostile and challenging environment.

Arriving at Pheriche (4,240m) we can see houses scattered along the broad valley of the Khumbu Khola, which drains from the Khumbu Glacier at the foot of Mount Everest. Freezing winds scour the valley, drawing away body heat and moisture and making us feel increasingly cold in the process. We long to reach our lodge for the night to be able to warm up by the fire and drink some hot tea.

The main lodging area of Pheriche appears as a labyrinth of stone walls with the main trail cutting through the village leading to the various lodges. We're never quite sure which one we'll be staying in so those of us at the front of the group scour the horizon for our porters, as someone is always waiting for us.

We've all been walking in silence, heads down, trying to protect ourselves from the relentless wind. I didn't appreciate how much the landscape and weather would change over the course of the trek and I suspect we're all trying to come to terms with our current reality, all desperate to reach the warmth of our lodge and rest our weary legs. Lilly is at the back of the group again with Craig, whom I've not really connected with yet on this trek.

It's funny how that happens. You might all be in the same environment, sharing the same experiences, yet your journeys can be so different. Craig and I walk at different paces, which means we rarely walk together so we don't have the opportunity to chat. Furthermore, when we are at the lodges, we tend to sit at different ends of the table and if we do chat, I find Craig defensive and reluctant to engage in any meaningful conversation, so I don't really feel like I know him.

It's with some relief that we soon spot our porters at a lodge up ahead and we virtually fall, one after the other, through the open door and into the warmth of the lodge. We quickly locate the wood-burning stove in the middle of the central dining room and rush to its warmth. You can almost hear a collective sigh as we collapse onto stools, taking the weight off our feet and removing our daypacks from our shoulders. I silently offer a prayer of gratitude that we've made it here. That was a tough day.

Pemba is aware that I've been challenged today – (my miserable face gives it away if nothing else!) – and he gives me a hug. I could cry (again). I'm homesick for my brother and his familiarity. There's been too much time to think and my mind is a jumble of self-deprecating thoughts and concerns. I'm consumed by my thinking, lacking as I am right now in any grounding.

"We rest here now," Pemba reassures me. "Rest day tomorrow. Take it easy, drink lots of water."

I'm pleased we have another rest day to allow us to acclimatise, but I'm already wondering what on earth we'll do for a whole day with very little to entertain us. I voice my concerns to Lilly, who continues to suffer with stomach issues.

"I'll be happy to sleep all day," Lilly says, "and rest my aching legs."

"Yes," I agree, "but Pemba will insist on a walk to help us acclimatise."

Lilly sighs. "I'm still not feeling well so I need to rest." She then voices her concerns about continuing. "I don't know that I can go any higher," she says.

"Let's wait and see," I respond. "Perhaps tomorrow everyone will feel better." I truly hope that this is the case because Pemba will soon be sick of all our moaning!

My mood isn't helped by the fact that Pemba won't let me have a shower. He says it's too late in the afternoon and the staff are now far too busy making hot drinks and preparing dinner for the stream of people arriving to take refuge for the night – thus they don't have the time or the facility to boil hot water for me to shower. I struggle with this as my head is pounding again and I long to stand under the shower and let the water warm and cleanse me. It's also a way of passing the time.

Lilly and I are sharing a room together at the back of the lodge, which we access from the dark corridor that connects the shared bathrooms at one end, with the dining room and kitchen at the other end. Like all the lodges we have stayed in thus far, they are basic and built from a practical perspective to provide protection from the elements and therefore lack much comfort. Still, I'm just grateful that there's sufficient space in our room, between the two simple wooden bed frames, to lay my yoga mat on the floor.

It's 3pm and so ridiculously cold that I have to wear all of my layers to be able to withstand the temperature in the quiet room. There's no heating in the bedrooms and everyone else in the group has wisely taken themselves into the warm dining room, heated by the central stove. However, I'm determined to get on my mat. It's a necessity, really, as I'm craving the time out from the rest of the group, plus my head hurts and I'm hoping that a yoga practice will ease this.

I light some Tibetan incense that I bought in Namche before practising a few rounds of sun salutations to try and warm my body a little, a seemingly impossible task initially, but I'm determined. I then move through an asana practice that I hope will support my digestive system, which has been challenged by all the trekking and the different foods and environments. Like most, I loathe being constipated and I've been trying to do what I can to prevent this while trekking and I'm aware that yoga can help.

I'm also keen to stretch out my hamstrings and thighs and open out my chest to release the tension that has accumulated from carrying my daysack and looking down towards the ground on and off all day. It feels good to move my body like this, easing some of the physical and mental tension as I focus on my breath.

However, it does nothing to alleviate the pounding in my head from the higher altitude; I'm having a hard time adjusting to this. It's funny because, despite expectations, I did have an idea in my head of how life would be lived up here in the Himalayas, but I hadn't factored in the effect that the changing altitude has on the body and mood, nor the cold, nor the simplicity of the lodges in which we are based.

So, while at home the idea of a day and a half to potter without work or anyone expecting anything of me is usually a dream, here it is a challenge because there are none of the comforts of home. It's not like I can check my emails, or Skype someone, or follow a YouTube yoga video. I can barely practise yoga in our room.

I am suddenly aware how much of life, certainly my life, is spent filled with activity, busyness, always doing something – whether that be working, practising yoga, reading a book, chatting to other people, going for walks/swimming, and/or sending emails. There is very little time spent doing nothing in particular, resting or daydreaming and simply being.

Here the busy schedule has been totally removed. There is very little distraction and this is a profound experience as it gives the space to be with whatever is arising. It makes me reflect on the manner in which we divide our lives into sections – working and 'free time' (assuming therefore that life is all about work). Also, how we may set aside certain parts of the day for spiritual practice, whether that be yoga or meditation, for example.

However, I have become increasingly aware that a spiritual practice is not something that is done or achieved, but something that is ever-present, ever-conscious, ever-evolving. It is an opportunity to be fully present to every experience, bringing loving attention to every ordinary moment, not just those few moments that occur within the time we have timetabled for 'being spiritual'.

This trekking experience is certainly providing me with the opportunity to strip apart some of the limitations I have created in my mind about what I've deemed to be 'spiritual'. What does it mean to be spiritual? I keep asking myself this question. However, I'm very aware that by attempting to define it, I'm limited by its vastness and potential for liberation and freedom.

We can engage *all* of life as a spiritual practice – life, by its very nature, will provide many challenges and obstacles that afford us opportunities to put our spiritual practice into practice, moment to moment. It is by being present to the manner in which we respond and react to life's challenges and obstacles that we may begin to recognise the myriad of ways in which we maintain our sense of separation, of allowing our disconnection from the Divine (however you perceive/name this). This separation leads to feelings of loneliness, anxiety, depression, isolation and fragmentation, all so prevalent in society today.

Ultimately, we are all one, connected and supported by Mother Earth, but our fast-paced lives can lack grounding, substance and true meaning (without a sense of purpose, or a sense of faith), and this can lead to our suffering.

This awareness, of how we create our own suffering in the way we respond to life, doesn't make it any easier to bear. I can find many reasons for the fact I feel far from peaceful and happy right now. Clearly, there's still much inner work to do in terms of overcoming the obstacles that *I* have placed in my own way, of the thoughts that I think and the behaviour patterns I have adopted and the tendencies that unconsciously play out, that are all, on some level, preventing me from experiencing the inner peace and contentment that I seek.

This time spent trekking in the Himalayas is providing a much-needed time for processing and examining my life. We don't always have the time or space for this in our busy day-to-day lives, and thus so many of our life experiences can remain unresolved and unprocessed, clogging a part of our body with suppressed emotions, which creates stagnant energy in the energetic body and can lead to dis-ease in the physical and mental bodies.

Furthermore, I'm very cognisant that there is a bigger picture and reason that all of us eight members of our haphazard group find ourselves together in the Himalayas! We act like mirrors for one another and this continually challenges me to examine and rethink how I approach myself and the world. It's not easy. Will, for example, is a challenge for me. There are aspects of his character that irritate me. But then I suspect that he finds me challenging too because we're both strong in our beliefs and our own ideas of what is right or wrong. But really, what does that even mean? One person's perception of right does not necessarily equate to another's.

This awareness makes me feel uncomfortable as it throws into question all that I believe to be 'real' about my life and life in general. It rocks my foundations and I find it unsettling to question my life and the manner in which I'm living it over and over again.

Lilly joins me in the room. We can see our breath in the air, it's that cold, and we wonder how much colder it will get overnight.

"I'm wearing all my layers to keep warm now," I comment to her. "Imagine what it'll be like in the middle of the night!"

"I know," she agrees, "and how much colder it's going to get further up the trail."

"Oh, don't," I say. "My head's pounding enough as it is. I really don't like this feeling and am not sure whether I'll be able to cope with another few days of this."

"Me either," she agrees. "I've definitely got something wrong with my stomach and I don't know that I'll be able to keep going either."

I can't believe that Lilly is still poorly, but sure enough, nothing stays in her tummy for very long, which means she's loathe to eat too much while we're on the move. The primitive toilets are few and far between, although we have grown used to them now. We're just grateful we stocked up on toilet roll and hand wipes as both have been invaluable.

It soon becomes too cold to stay in the room so we join the boys in the warmth of the dining room, where they've kept themselves busy playing cards, while simultaneously quoting from films and cracking jokes. Evening has now descended and it's dark outside, so we sit by candlelight. It's busy in the dining room, with all ten tables packed with groups, chatting and laughing together, the wood-burning stove taking centre stage where the porters now huddle trying to warm their hands and feet.

I've chosen dal bhat again for dinner this evening and I'm longing for it to be served. Food is such an important part of our daily routine, where there is little other distraction. It's a bit like when you fly long haul and even though the food's not usually very nice, you welcome the opportunity it provides to break up the monotony of the flight. Not that it's monotonous up here per se, just that there isn't much else to do besides chat and read our books, plus we're hungry. It's been a long day!

Once the porters have served us our meals, they sit together and silently eat their meal of dal bhat too. They eat with their right hand (the left is strictly for the bathroom) and use their fingers to mould rice together so that they can use this to scoop up some of the vegetable curry before popping it in their mouths. I watch them as they eat like they haven't eaten for weeks, heads down, and fingers spooning one mouthful after another, refuelling after our gruelling day.

The boys are still resisting dal bhat and are instead feasting on an array of deep-fried food including deep-fried noodles, deep-fried Tibetan momos and deep-fried Mars and Snickers bars. It's perhaps not surprising that with the combination of the fried food and the drugs, Will is not feeling his best.

He has the opposite problem to Lilly in that he has been constipated for a number of days now and is in some discomfort. While he can be very challenging in his need to disagree with everything I say, I'm keen to help, and so I massage his hands and channel Reiki on his swollen tummy. The combination of the Reiki and the warmth in the room, causes him to zone out and virtually fall asleep, slouched as he is on the bench. The other boys find it amusing, but are curious about the Reiki.

It's so warm in the dining room that it's quite a shock for us when we walk out into the dark and icy corridor to access our bedrooms. Our head torches are vital in this environment and we'd be lost without them. There's not much time for faffing around in these conditions. A quick clean of our teeth at the rather hideously smelling 'bathroom', using boiled water from our bottles, a quick pee in the grim concrete squatting toilet and then back to our rooms for an even quicker change into PJs, warm socks, a jumper and my woolly hat because it really is that bitter!

I'm finding it nigh on impossible to sleep in this cold and oxygen-deprived environment and I'm still awake at midnight with a chronic headache. I am also very conscious of the effort involved in breathing, as it feels like someone is sitting on my chest. It freaks me out initially as it reminds me of those times in my life when I've experienced bouts of asthma, my body trying to tell me to stop smoking.

I don't have an inhaler and I start panicking that perhaps I need one, and my mind goes into overdrive, wondering what will happen if I have an asthma attack and whether anyone else in the lodge has an inhaler I could borrow. It reminds me how precarious life can be when you don't have immediate access to medical support. It's something we can take for granted so easily at home and yet here the terrain dictates the degree to which one can access medical attention.

With the panic comes the tears and I have to consciously remind myself to let go of the fear as I mentally repeat to myself, "All is well, breathe, in and out." I feel for my torch and reach into my bag to find the emergency aspirin I bought at Heathrow last-minute. I know I need something to dampen the pain in my head, so I swallow the tablet and lie in the foetal position, focusing my awareness on my breath, using ujjayi breathing, creating an audible sound, calming the mind and central nervous system so that I encourage sleep, while channelling Reiki onto the right side of my head and my right shoulder where my hands are placed.

10

Oh the air is thin.
Oh the air is thin.
"The Air is Thin", Jesse Sykes & The Sweet Hereafter

Day 6: Acclimatisation day in Pheriche

My thumping head wakes me before my alarm clock. It's still incredibly frosty in the room and my eyes feel heavy, like they do when my spine is twisted with stress, like a corkscrew, all wound up from hips to neck. Needless to say, I still feel completely out of sorts. Lilly and I moan to one another across the small room. She's still not feeling right and is now worried that she may have a stomach bug that will prevent her from continuing.

Pemba undertakes his usual morning round. We're his responsibility and he is keen to know if we are all OK. There's a resounding "No!" from me and Lilly. We convey our health concerns, but he's not in the least bit concerned – he's his usual jovial self – "Oh, well, see you at breakfast in thirty minutes," he chirps, before leaving the room. We look at each other rolling our eyes and carry on our moaning – there's nothing quite like a good moan with Lilly! Still, we realise that we need to do what Pemba says, so we quickly dress, layering up, before heading to the dining room to join the boys.

Heavy fog was hanging in the air when we arrived at the lodge yesterday so we had no idea of where we were. However, now a very different scene greets us as we walk into the dining room and there ahead of us, through the windows, is a very clear view of snow-capped peaks rising high up into the bright blue and sunny sky.

The scene is incredible and I realise that we are now, quite literally, nestled high up in the bosom of the Himalayas. Tim has already been out taking photos and delights in showing us shots of the scenery. He's almost bouncing up and down with excitement like Tigger from *Winnie-the-Pooh*!

Today is an acclimatisation day to help us try and adjust to the higher altitude. To do this, Pemba insists we walk a further 400m up yet another hill to visit the small Nangkartshang Gompa, overlooking Dengboche, a popular acclimatisation village in this area. While ordinarily I'd be keen to embrace such an opportunity, today I'm not the slightest bit interested in doing any more trekking (nor is Lilly), especially not at this increasing altitude. Lilly is excused because she's still poorly and I'm envious as she gets to stay behind in bed reading her book. It's pointless trying to argue with Pemba though. He insists I'm fit to walk.

Pemba leads the way and the boys and I follow him, the boys chattering and joking together as we approach the first ridge. The air is unbelievably light and clear and the sun shines brightly so that I need to wear my sunglasses to protect my eyes from the glare. It feels a little other-worldly in this environment. There's no one else around and the landscape is exposed and wind-burnt, and carries with it an incredible sense of space and yet a loneliness to it too.

The wind is still relentless, not as cold as it was the previous day, but irritating nonetheless – this valley is renowned for it, there's no escape. I'm pleased when we reach the first ridge and see that our effort of walking was not in vain. The views are spectacular. Below us we can make out the village of Pheriche, where we're staying, with its visible labyrinth of simple stone walls and pastures. We can see about six bright green and blue roofs too, appearing completely insignificant in the expanse of the vast Khumbu valley and yet offering us much-needed protection from the elements.

As well as views of the magnificent mountains that rise in the distance, making me feel totally insignificant, there is also evidence of a glacial-melt river zigzagging its way down one of the mountains and flowing along the valley floor. It's stunning and I forget the pounding in my head as I try to absorb the sublimity of the moment. This is nature at her most powerful, demanding full respect. How can we ever be naïve enough, or so arrogant as to think that we can control nature? Up here, there is no doubt that nature is the one in control.

Furthermore, I have this sense that it shouldn't be seen so much as an us/them, nature/human-type thing. We're all here, all a part of the same world that we all inhabit. We too are made up of minerals, just like rocks and the earth. It's a matter of all trying to get along. Of caring for the natural landscape and Mother Earth as a whole, as we may care for ourselves. The two are often a reflection of each other. The more we care for Mother Earth, the more we may care for ourselves and vice versa.

We continue to the top of the second ridge, home to the small gompa. It's far more exposed up here and the harsh wind whips the dust into our eyes, despite wearing sunglasses. The dust also coats our clothing and I think about how impossible it would be to stay clean living in such a hostile environment. Dawa leads a few of the boys further up the hillside, but I have had enough. It's hard work walking uphill, almost sucking for breath in this light, light air. I find myself a lovely little spot on a drystone wall, where I can lie back and gaze up at the simple and wind-damaged gompa.

The gompa was painted white at one point, but much of the paint has been stripped off by the elements. Prayer flags flutter from it, while the painted watchful eyes of the Buddha gaze out across the valley. A faintly painted question mark takes the place of the nose, a symbol of unity, (it's actually the Nepali sign for one), and there's a painted third eye too, symbolising the Buddha's clairvoyant powers. The base of the gompa represents the four elements – earth, fire, air and water - and the 13 concentric rings on the spire, painted gold, symbolise the 13 degrees of knowledge and the 13 steps that one must take to achieve nirvana or enlightenment.

Life is made of moments, some more memorable than others. This was one of those memorable moments. It stands out because it felt as if time itself stood still and there was only the present moment, the gift of presence and of the peace that arises with this, as I lay on my own, nestled on the wind-damaged wall. It was one of those moments where you know, on some deep level, that we are all one, that everything is connected, and that if only you could get out of your own way, all is fundamentally well; peace reigns.

Of course, such moments pass within the blink of an eye, but that space between worlds, without time, is enough to be etched on your memory for a lifetime. Nothing else really matters. Not the pounding in my head, nor the homesickness rising in my chest, nor the concern about what I'm going to do after this trek, nor even whether I complete the trek in the first place. None of this is really important. All that is important, is that I am here, truly here, in this moment.

I'm held by the landscape, as if nourished by the vibration of the wall, which has many a story to tell, the watchful eye of the Buddha casting magic to all who pass by. I reach for my notebook and for the first time in a long time I write a poem. The energy of this place has touched me and I have a real sense of Grace permeating the Himalayas.

> *Sitting on top of the world, up high*
> *in mountains, white, touching the sky.*
> *Below me gravel and stones,*
> *breathing dust and the air too thin.*
> *The blue eyes of the white stupa*
> *stare down at me.*
> *Should I be here, I*
> *question, again and again.*
> *My head screams in the middle of the night*
> *when I struggle to breathe.*
> *Thumping and thumping, the*
> *mountains suck me from sleep.*
> *But I'm alive and well*
> *And blessed to be here.*
> *There's a beauty in the solitude*
> *That this landscape creates,*
> *a sense of my insignificance,*
> *and a recognition of the Divine in all life.*

Back at the lodge, we have the whole afternoon ahead of us, with no need for further acclimatisation walks, so I make the most of the opportunity to take to my yoga mat again, embracing the familiarity of the practice, in a world that is still decidedly out of kilter.

Once I've finished my practice, I wrap myself in my sleeping bag and sit up on my bed, woolly hat on my head, and meditate. It's tricky to stay present to my breath as too many thoughts keep distracting me, and I grow tired of them. I play with my crystal pendulum to check the state of my seven main chakras. My crown chakra is out of balance, as my headache shows, but I'm puzzled as to the energetics of this.

I'm curious to learn more, and I offer some Reiki to Lilly, who quickly accepts. She's still not feeling well and I can sense an increasing anxiety. So, while she lies on her bed, wrapped in her sleeping bag and covered with a thick blanket, I kneel beside her, woolly hat on my head, and channel Reiki. The Reiki certainly helps both of us to relax and it helps to pass the time too.

I can't be sure that I'm any more sensitive to the Reiki energy here than I would be ordinarily, although I do have a greater sense of what might underlie Lilly's sickness. I tend to work very much on a clairsentient basis, so that I feel things that might be going on for the person, and this experience is heightened when I channel Reiki.

Some people work much more on a clairvoyant basis where they see things, or a clairaudient basis where they hear things, but I always tend to feel things. Sometimes I might be channelling Reiki on to someone's heart chakra and I may all of a sudden feel intense sadness and find that I have tears running down my face. It freaked me out initially because I wondered what was going on. I have now come to recognise that airing these intense feelings is a form of healing and I am merely the instrument for this, as it comes through me from the person I am treating.

I'm still learning how to protect myself from absorbing too much of someone else's negative energy and emotional residue, and establishing safe boundaries. I've a tendency to give too much of myself away, whether that be time or energy, or both. I hadn't realised until I discovered yoga and Reiki, quite how much energy plays such a pivotal role in our lives. We are energy! Everything is energy! I had no idea!

This revelation was like an awakening, because life started to make a little more sense. I could see more clearly the manner in which I had given my power away too easily, giving rise to intense feelings of vulnerability and the resulting anxiety and paranoia. Also, how I had attracted energy vampires into my life who fed off my energy, leaving me feeling depleted and depressed. Further, I became increasingly aware of those people who were in my life simply because they were drawn to the drama (pre-yoga), not because they cared about me per se, but because it made them feel better about themselves.

When you become attuned to Reiki and/or practise yoga regularly then your resonant frequency tends to change and your vibration becomes lighter. This can create a shift in your relationships with others simply because you may no longer resonate energetically with them. It's not unusual for your friendships to change, so that people drop out of your life, especially those who have been draining you or creating drama for you, or who just weren't really meant to be there in the first place.

My friendships have changed significantly since bringing yoga and Reiki into my life. My core best friendships have stayed the same – our energetic connection is extremely strong and while there may have been some shifting, we'll always come back together again in the end. However, many others have dropped away. It wasn't conscious, we just stopped resonating and our lives went in different directions and I lost any inclination to try to resurrect them. My life was brighter without them.

I also stopped attracting the kind of people that I may have attracted previously, because the yoga and Reiki helped me to become stronger and more centred within myself and clearer about who I was and what I wanted from my life – my boundaries became stronger, even if this is still a work in progress (my solar plexus had begun healing). In many respects, I wish I had discovered yoga and Reiki much earlier in my life, as this may have saved me a lot of heartache! But nonetheless I do appreciate that we often need to go through what we go through, to learn the lesson(s) we need to learn (even if we do not learn this/these until many years later) to become a stronger and wiser person.

In 2001, prior to running the London Marathon, I was in a destructive relationship. In many respects, this was a blessing, because without that relationship bringing me to my knees and ripping the life force out of me, I may never have found my way to this more joyful and liberating way of living.

I was a lost soul who recognised this and was attempting to do something about it. I was still studying for my professional exams and working my way up the career ladder, but I was desperate for change. My best friend's sister, Rachel, was also keen for change, and the two of us decided that perhaps we should go travelling together. It was a big decision, as I didn't have the money available to go travelling, and I couldn't quite see how it might work, but something inside me was encouraging me on.

So, we both took second jobs working evenings and weekends in a pub to save the money to travel. Strangely, perhaps, I also moved out of my parents' home for the first time in Guernsey and rented a flat as I just felt that I needed to finally learn to stand on my own two feet. It was a good move in many respects, as I lived with a girl who was also studying and so the two of us became disciplined in our studying, which helped me enormously. I love studying ordinarily, but struggled with the professional exams, as I found the content so dull and boring! Having a study-buddy really helped.

On the one hand, I was trying to take control of my life, as I was sick of life controlling me, and yet at this time, into my life walked a man, who took all my power away from me. He just kind of moved into my life. I like my own space and so I don't know how he managed to move in so easily, but he just had this way of infiltrating other women's lives and is probably still doing it to this day, playing on their weaknesses.

It was a very passionate relationship and was essentially emotionally and mentally violent. It's difficult even now to write about it, simply because I can't believe that I was that person, the victim. But over the course of nine months, my life was turned upside down. Before I knew it, he was living with me, using my phone as his own and driving my car. I was also paying for everything, despite the fact I was supposed to be saving for travelling.

My family and my friends couldn't understand what was happening. They couldn't see what I saw in him and yet they had very little opportunity to share their concerns with me because he was always with me. He dropped me off at work and picked me up at the end of the day. Previously, I swam regularly, but he started to make this difficult for me too. If I did anything he didn't like, he would suddenly come down with a very bad migraine and blame me and therefore I grew scared of doing anything to upset him for fear of making him sick.

It's very difficult to understand the detrimental effect of this type of relationship unless you've been in one yourself and it is also very difficult to break from such a relationship. It is almost impossible to help a person who is in such a relationship. My friends and my family tried when they could, but I wouldn't listen. I was well and truly trapped, believing that my life would be worthless, that I would be worthless, without him in it. The truth of the matter is that my life was worthless with him in it. He sucked me dry. I had no sense of worth left, no power or energy to do anything about it. My solar plexus was extremely weak.

The saving grace throughout all this was the fact that Rachel and I had already booked our flights before this man rocked up in my life, so I had an escape route, even if I didn't realise it at the time. The Universe had my back so to speak, it was just a case of me showing up for the flights and it was this – and my ability to do this – that concerned everybody.

A few weeks before Rachel and I were due to travel, there was an incident that left me feeling shamed, pained, vulnerable and sad. It was a wake-up call of sorts, that would take me many years to process, as I never had the space or support to do so at the time.

My perspective on lots of things shifted after this and I became desperately uncomfortable with the physical side of our relationship. I needed to leave! But it is very difficult to leave a relationship like this – and even though I managed to get on the plane and I managed to make it to New Zealand, via LA and Fiji with Rachel, I had to telephone him every day otherwise I was in trouble.

It's absolutely crazy, totally crazy to look back at it now and think that I was literally the other side of the world and yet I was unable to leave the relationship. But there are energetics to this and the cord he had energetically attached to me was strong and I couldn't seem to get far enough away from him for it to break.

After a few months, he came out to join me in New Zealand and it felt strange. Inevitably I had healed a little from spending time with Rachel and by standing on my own two feet and immersing myself in the natural beauty of New Zealand. I had also started to find a little more of me and my voice again.

However, this didn't stop him from trying to take over my life once more. He ostracised me from Rachel and frequently checked my emails, breaking down my support network, and distancing me from other friends. Fortunately, Ross came out to join us for Christmas and his presence gave me strength, and I have no doubt that he had been sent to me by the angels at just the right time!

When Ross returned home, things went from bad to worse. We were renting a room in a house we shared with two New Zealanders who I was friendly with. I was drinking and smoking a lot at this time – in fact, much of this relationship was based on drinking and smoking and keeping my energy down. We all went along together to a party and strangely I wouldn't leave when my boyfriend wanted to, so he stormed off presuming I would follow him, but I didn't. I stayed at the party all night.

When I made it home the next morning, he shouted and ranted at me and told me we were over, as he had threatened many times previously if I ever did anything to upset him, before storming out the house.

Usually I'd plead with him to change his mind and I'd assure him that I'd be better/more loving/more giving/more of whatever he wanted to just accept me back in his life. It makes me feel a little sick to write about this now. However, this time, when he called me from a café an hour after leaving the house, assuming that I would plead with him to change his mind, I didn't. Instead, I confirmed that we were done and that I wanted to break up, finally.

He returned to the house very quickly after the phone conversation and got very angry with me and shoved me against a wall. But by then my mind was made up, and all of a sudden, just like that, he had no power over me. I was concerned about what he might do though, and relieved when he stormed off out of the house again.

I telephoned my parents in Guernsey who were in the middle of a dinner party. It is one of those moments that they will never forget– hearing the sound of their emotional daughter, the other side of the world, saying that she needs to come home as soon as possible. My parents were understandably concerned and felt helpless to do anything then and there, other than provide support and arrange for Rachel (who thankfully lived up the road) to reconnect. Fortunately, she was forgiving and understanding and helped to comfort me and give me some strength.

The next day, my housemate passed me a magazine to read, which contained an article on destructive relationships. Time stood still. The moment is still etched on my memory to this day. I felt sickened to my core as the truth dawned on me – I had been the victim of a destructive relationship and I hadn't even realised it.

In many respects, it was hard to accept. I always assumed that destructive relationships involved physical violence and beatings and bruising. Yes, there had been the wall-shoving and other stuff, I guess, that I was struggling to accept, but I now realised that destructive relationships can be emotionally and mentally violent too.

I couldn't quite believe that I had been so foolish. Where had it all gone so wrong? Why had I not listened to anyone? This is the nature of destructive relationships, however. We lose ourselves in them and are damaged to the core of our being. It would take me years to heal from this experience.

I returned back home to Guernsey within the week and took up my job again, from which I had taken a sabbatical. I was a mess, depressed and adrift. It was a blessing therefore, a few weeks after returning home, when I discovered that I had passed my professional exams (I'd taken the last exam while in New Zealand) and was now a fully-fledged company secretary (ICSA). As much as I may have loathed the studying, having this qualification changed my life. I received a 30% pay increase overnight and zoomed up the corporate ladder, which gave me a purpose and a grounding.

My solar plexus chakra, which represents our ability to exert power and will in the world, was a mess and my heart chakra, which is all about love, compassion and forgiveness for the self and others, was in pieces. I didn't trust myself and I was full of self-loathing. I didn't know about chakras back then and I didn't even realise that I had given all my power away, I just knew that life was tough and I felt a victim of it. Depression soon set in, and I just concluded that this was how life was going to be. I couldn't see how things could change.

I continued to drink too much wine and smoke too many cigarettes (and joints when I was able), trying to numb my pain. This period of my life was a dark time. "The darkness has come again," I would say to myself. I wondered if I was going mad. Often it felt like I was sinking down a deep, dark hole, a spiralling darkness of decline, which left me clinging on to the edge with my fingernails, looking up at the sky and desperately trying to find a way to pull myself back up to the daylight. The darkness was all encompassing and so powerful that I worried I might never see the light again.

During one particularly low night, and after a few too many glasses of wine, the self-destructive nature of my mind really scared me and my family as I sought the paracetamol from the bathroom cupboard. I felt an overwhelming sense of emptiness and utter despair and I simply wanted to go to sleep and never wake up again.

Thankfully, my inherent anger at the situation and my mum's sixth sense got the better of me. I know my actions were more a cry for help than an attempt to take my own life – it wasn't so much that I wanted to die, more that I wasn't sure I wanted to be alive because being alive was just too painful. It was certainly an awakening experience and probably saved me from myself. Needless to say, things could not carry on in such a manner and as much as it pained me to visit the doctor, I owed it to my parents, and to myself, to address the matter.

Unsurprisingly, the doctor diagnosed depression and prescribed me a course of Prozac. I had been prescribed antidepressants previously but I had stopped taking them after a week or so as they made me feel really 'woolly'. This time around I certainly wasn't prepared to take the tablets because it didn't actually make any sense to me. I realised that it was time to take action and it was then that I started running.

This was now 2002 and, essentially, I was trying to run my life forward, but on another level, it could be argued that running saved me. It got me out into nature and it gave me the opportunity to process what was happening. In addition, the actual physical act of running, released endorphins, which improved my mental state, plus I was able to shift some of the old energy through movement. I was soon running with a friend, Claire, and it was she who suggested we attempt to get places on the London Marathon. We did!

I've no doubt that the angels were flooding my life with support, although I was none the wiser to it at the time. I've since come to recognise that depression, at least for me, then, was simply the result of my soul being suppressed and desperate for recognition and expression in the world. Whenever I get any depression now, I realise that this means I need to re-evaluate my life and make changes to support my spiritual growth.

The running certainly shifted my energy and I started getting much stronger mentally and physically, plus the time spent in nature and talking with Claire was healing. My solar plexus started healing and with that in 2003, a month before running the London Marathon, into my life appeared B. He was my knight in shining armour, as he whisked me into his arms and helped me to heal and start believing in my dreams. With the Marathon run, into my life came yoga, Reiki, healthy eating and crystals, and I haven't looked back since.

So you see, in many respects, I have learned the hard way about energy and about people sucking it from you if you don't protect yourself properly. It's still a work in progress because the solar plexus is tricky, and because I'm the kind of person who likes to give, and because I'm incredibly sensitive to energy. I find that practising yoga helps to keep my energy strong and that spending time in nature helps to ground and protect me from any negative energy (sea swimming helps to cleanse). Being sensitive to others' energy is the reason I find the group more challenging than others might – I'm sensitive to the boys' energies. So it is important for me to take myself away from them when I can, and cleanse my aura with incense in the absence of showering and water.

Fortunately, I am permitted a shower in the afternoon, after lunch and before the late afternoon rush begins. Showering passes the time and feels so good after going so long without washing! I then enjoy lying in my sleeping bag all cosy and reading my book in peace! The boys sit in the dining room alternating between playing cards, drinking Coke, eating chocolate bars and reading their books. Lilly flits in and out between the two of us and I join her from time to time to smoke.

By dinner time we're all restless and pleased that we're continuing with the trek the next day. It's busy in the dining room again and noisy with chatter. Some people are on their way up the mountain and others on the way back down. The porters are huddling once again around the central fire while others rush backwards and forwards serving plates of steaming hot food to those in their group. It's really easy to lose yourself in all the activity and the camaraderie within the room.

After dinner, I channel more Reiki to Will who is still suffering from constipation and feeling particularly sorry for himself. His skin is congested, reflecting his internal state. I feel sorry for him though and hope that he feels better by the morning. We're also hoping that Lilly improves too as she's been poorly for six days now.

11

Suddenly I stop
But I know it's too late
I'm lost in a forest
All alone
The girl was never there
It's always the same
I'm running towards nothing
Again and again and again and again.
"A Forest", The Cure

Day 7: Pheriche to Lobuche

The headache of all headaches hits at 2am. It's freezing cold in the small room and I surmise that perhaps it's the temperature that's making my head hurt so I pull my woolly hat on just in case, hoping that this may ease the pain. I also drink some water, which is freezing cold too, making me shiver inside.

Thump, thump, thump. My head feels like it might explode. I try to focus on my breath, in and out, in and out, conscious breathing, encouraging sleep. The air feels really thin at this early hour of the morning, which Pemba already told me was due to a lowering of blood pressure. It's scary feeling like this and not being able to do anything about it. I finally manage to drift off to sleep.

Will has given Lilly a course of antibiotics to take in the hope that the drugs may settle her tummy. However, this morning she still feels unwell so Pemba decides we should delay our departure time so that she can go and see a Western doctor at the Trekker's Aid Post, a short way from the lodge, which is supported by the Himalayan Rescue Association.

A BBC film crew is filming a documentary about the work undertaken by these Western doctors, but Lilly turns down the opportunity for BBC fame as she doesn't want to be seen talking about her recent bowel movements on British TV. The doctor diagnoses food poisoning, tells her to continue taking the antibiotics and sends her on her way. There's little more that can be done; she's apparently fine to continue.

The porters have already left the lodge by the time we leave and the sun is shining brightly overhead. I'm delighted to have the comfort of my sunglasses, which ease the glare. We're wearing a whole heap more layers now than when we started and I'm pleased about the added protection from the icy winds that scour this valley. It's tough walking at this altitude with the reduced oxygen in the air, let alone with the relentless wind lashing our faces.

The terrain is once again challenging, as we move slowly up the huge, dry valley. The path itself has been kicked into awkward ruts and gullies by a combination of trekkers, porters and yaks, so we have to be mindful of our footing. There are yaks grazing around us, bringing life to the terrain. The trail has quietened considerably since Namche Bazaar and there are very few people up here.

I find it bleak. There's none of the beautiful green landscape that we were used to seeing earlier on the trail. Now it's all brown and angular and there's none of the gentle mountain life of lower altitudes. It's become more austere and serious too, and increasingly hard work. We stop every thirty minutes or so to catch our breath and adjust to the altitude, sitting on large dusty rocks and sipping water.

Tall Matt and gentle Ben soon start to feel unwell. Usually, they're up at the front of the group full of energy and smiles, but before long they're trailing behind us, heads down and quiet. After a while, the rest of us stop to wait for them to catch up and almost laugh out loud, as they both stop walking and simultaneously vomit. It's comical – they do everything together these boys, even if it is unplanned and something as horrible as vomiting in the Himalayas.

After the boys have cleaned themselves up, we continue together, although Pemba now changes our course. Instead of continuing uphill we drop down the side of the valley to a glacial stream and then cross a small wooden bridge, which has no railings, so that we have to be careful of our footing. We then walk up the other side of the valley, arriving at the settlement of Dughla (4,620m) for an early lunch.

We sit quietly in the small dining room, one beside the other on a wooden bench in front of wooden tables that look more like wooden cabinets as you can't put your legs under them. Pemba and Dawa fuss around us, insisting we drink and eat. Will is also now feeling sick and Pemba orders him garlic soup, like he has done for Matt and Ben, as he says it helps with the altitude.

When the soup arrives, it smells utterly revolting. I've lost my appetite, but am told that I must eat, although thankfully not the garlic soup! I've chosen toast, but even this is an effort to eat with the stench of garlic in the room and I also begin to feel sick. Soon we're all feeling nauseous, which doesn't bode well for the journey ahead. Will is insistent he is merely suffering from a stomach upset and he starts moaning about the quality of the food on the trek – I have to try hard to resist reacting with comments about his food choices.

It's a strange hour and I'm very aware of it. I take a few photos of us in our current pitiful state because on some level I must realise that it is a poignant moment. Gentle Ben sits, head in hands, the rest of us attempting to smile, but feeling a little concerned on the inside. I go to the outside toilet located a short walk from the lodge down in the 'garden' and find that it is occupied by an Australian woman who is vomiting. When she's finished, she tells me that everyone in her group is also feeling sick. The thought of her group being sick makes me feel even sicker, especially now there's the stench of vomit in the toilet.

However, Pemba is determined that we all get back on the trail, and we slowly traipse out of the lodge after him, our heads down, feeling a little despondent. There's none of the usual chatter, instead we're forlorn and lacking in enthusiasm. Even Joe is quiet, which makes a noticeable change, as he's usually leaping around trying to share a joke or a film quote.

It doesn't help that the path takes us immediately up a steep hill demanding some effort. Even I'm really having to dig deep now and it's at moments like this that I am especially challenged physically and mentally. Pemba is now leading the group with Will, Matt and Ben up at the front. "Bistari, bistari," he keeps saying. However, and perhaps unsurprisingly, we haven't walked far when all three of them projectile vomit garlic soup. It would've been funny, if it wasn't for the seriousness of it.

Change happens very quickly in these mountains and all of a sudden there's an urgency to the situation. Pemba makes an immediate decision – he believes that Matt and Ben have altitude sickness and must descend immediately. Both boys look very relieved that a decision has been made and within a minute we've said our goodbyes as they're quickly led down the hill by Dawa, the rest of us staying with Pemba.

We are all shocked at the speed of Ben and Matt's sickness, let alone Pemba's decision-making. It's good, we appreciate that we have all been guilty of unnecessary moaning on the trek, but it's reassuring to see that he does take these matters seriously. None of us had quite appreciated just how quickly our health can deteriorate at this altitude and how much it affects how we feel. Ben and Matt are the youngest members of the group and are super-fit too, so it surprises us that they should be the first to go, although Pemba tells us that this is quite usual.

Altitude sickness occurs as the result of failure to adapt to a higher altitude. Acute altitude sickness occurs when fluid begins to leak from blood vessels, most often in the brain or lungs. If fluid collects in the lungs, then you become breathless more easily while walking and eventually more breathless at rest. In its most severe form, a person can drown in a pink frothy sputum fluid if he or she doesn't descend. This is known as high-altitude pulmonary oedema (HAPE).

There's also high-altitude cerebral oedema (HACE), which is another potentially fatal form of altitude sickness, where the brain swells and stops functioning in the normal way. Once initiated, it can take serious hold in a matter of hours, before most people even realise that they are ill. Because of the speed at which this sets in, it is vital that trekkers are aware of the warning signs. These include confusion, changes in behaviour, fatigue, a 'drunken stagger' called ataxia, difficulty speaking, vomiting, hallucinating and then a coma, and death if you don't descend. Both HAPE and HACE can occur on their own or together.

Our bodies have the ability to adjust to higher altitudes if given the necessary time. This is called acclimatisation and this is what we have been attempting to do by spending an extra day in Pheriche, and previously in Namche. If you were flown directly to the summit of Mount Everest from sea level, for example, you would likely only experience a few minutes of consciousness before you would pass out due to lack of oxygen. However, acclimatised climbers have been known to make it to the summit safely without the need for additional oxygen by allowing their bodies to adjust gradually to the increasing height. The British founder of the charity we are supporting here in Nepal has summited Everest a number of times now without needing additional oxygen.

The adjustment happens initially by increasing the rate and depth of breathing. It is understood that those people who adapt well to altitude automatically increase their breathing more than those who get altitude sickness easily. This sensitivity to altitude is supposed to be genetic so some people will be challenged by it more than others. While you may acclimatise at a certain height for a few days, if you climb higher you can still suffer from altitude sickness. The key is to descend if you are unwell.

Descent should be to the last point where you woke up and felt well. This is likely to be the place where you slept two nights previously because cases of acute altitude sickness generally only develop when a person with mild symptoms proceeds upwards. It is recommended that this should be at the least 500m lower in altitude. Once a lower place has been reached, maximum rest is advised, and in theory you should recover relatively quickly.

The rest of us continue along the path as it leads us directly up the terminal moraine (pebbly detritus) of the Khumbu Glacier. It's a hard, seemingly never-ending slog in a bleak, parched, desolate and craggy landscape. Once again, I feel an overwhelming sense of insignificance in the vastness of the valley, surrounded as we are by tall, ominous, snow-capped mountains; it's humbling. We walk among rough boulders, stones and scrub, the dust and sand constantly blowing up into our faces, everything looking grey and brown and wind-burnt.

Soon a large group of yaks approach, which is a relief as it gives us an excuse to stop and sip water and try and catch our breath. All of us are feeling a little on edge now that altitude sickness has become so very real and present in our lives. We sit together huddled among huge rocks beside our porters who position themselves so that their *doko* baskets rest against the rocks themselves. It's bitterly cold and eerily quiet except for the sound of the piercing wind, which blows endlessly through this harsh landscape.

Descending behind, and following the yaks, is a group of South African trekkers who comment to us that they have spent a thoroughly frustrating two hours in this 'yak jam'. This makes me laugh – it sounds silly but it's impossible to overtake yaks on the trail, so once you're stuck behind them then you're stuck. I'd certainly be frustrated following a herd of yaks for two hours too, and am pleased they're travelling downhill, in the opposite direction to us.

I notice that there are two young, blonde-haired children in the South African party, who can't be more than ten years old. I'm in awe that they've managed to trek up here and that their parents have brought them along in the first place! They don't seem in the slightest bit out of place, and despite the 'yak jam', the whole party appear jubilant in their descent. I'm envious!

It starts me thinking about the future and about having children of my own one day, once I meet my soulmate and life partner, and travelling with them to Nepal and introducing them to this environment, so that they grow up with direct experience of different cultures and different ways of living. The trouble is, I have to find 'the one' first, and I have no control over this.

I've lost count of the number of conversations I have had with my friends, all of us desperate to meet our Mr Right and have children with him. It's not that any of us are necessarily ready right now, but we would all love to have the certainty that we will meet him. I think that's the bit that is the most challenging, not knowing whether you will ever meet the right one, and not knowing if you will then be able to have children with him.

In many respects, it's inevitable. I do believe that dreams can come true. But it's the big one for me and a test in trust, faith and patience. Trusting that there is someone out there for me, faith that the Universe will deliver, and patience to wait until the various pieces of the puzzle have slotted into place before he makes an appearance.

Of course, there's the small matter of leaving B to resolve. In moments of weakness, I consider that maybe I'm deluding myself to think that there could be anyone else. But in other moments, I just have this sense that it has to be fully aligned and I know that my relationship with B will not bring me the peace and joy that my heart seeks. I've seen that such a love exists –my parents are soul mates who met at the age of seventeen. On some level therefore, I know it's worth the wait.

At the top of the next incline we turn left into a memorial area known as Chukpilhara. The energy and weather shift so that the sky is now overcast and heavy with huge white and grey clouds, and the wind whistles across the ledge so fiercely that I have to wear my sunglasses simply to protect my eyes from the stinging sandy dust blowing in the air.

It's a very strange place. Ahead of me, I see a row of stone monuments covered in prayer flags in memory of six Sherpas who died in an avalanche during a 1970 Japanese skiing expedition on Everest. There's also a plethora of Mani stones and chortens (shrines). Pemba tells us that this has become a recognised and respected memorial area on the trail and there are now many other monuments to climbers, mostly Sherpas, who have perished since 1970.

I notice that two of the newer and larger chortens memorialise the American climber Scott Fischer who died leading the Mountain Madness Expedition in the May 1996 Everest disaster. This was considered one of the worst disasters in the history of Everest mountaineering. It occurred on 10 and 11 May 1996, when eight people caught in a blizzard died on Mount Everest during attempts to descend from the summit. Over the entire season, 12 people died trying to reach the summit, making it the deadliest day and year on Mount Everest to that date. The disaster raised serious questions about the commercialisation of Everest.

Journalist Jon Krakauer was on an assignment from *Outside* magazine and in a party that lost four climbers on the south side. Afterwards, he published the bestselling book *Into Thin Air* which tells of his experience during that fateful climb. I've seen the book for sale in the bookshops here, together with a huge number of books relaying tales of people's experiences trying to summit Mount Everest, but I can't bring myself to read any of them. Matt has been reading *Into Thin Air*, however, and says that it is fascinating, but I know it has a sad ending and that puts me off reading it!

It's obviously an incredible achievement to summit Mount Everest but one fraught with enormous risk – you're certainly increasing your chances of an early death. And here, at this memorial site, the reality of death and dying in these mountains hangs in the air. I imagine that if you're on your way up to Base Camp with the intention of summiting Mount Everest that you might take a reflective moment here.

What also touches me is discovering the number of Sherpas who indirectly summit Mount Everest in their effort to establish the trail and ensure that the ladders are securely held in place for the Westerners paying big money to have a shot at summiting. There's a memorial, for example, to Lopsang Jangbu Sherpa, a Sherpa mountain guide who was killed in an avalanche on Everest in September 1996 while on an expedition to climb Everest for the fifth time. The fifth time? Incredible.

There's a shrine to the late Babu Chiri Sherpa here too, and I attempt to write notes, removing my glove in the process, and my hand is quickly frozen numb in the cold air. He was born on 22 June 1965 and started his career as a climber at thirteen years old. By the age of thirty-six he had summited Everest ten times (twice in two weeks!) and spent an unprecedented 21 hours on the summit without the aid of any oxygen – unbelievable and insane! He also became the fastest climber of the world's highest peak, climbing it in 16 hours and 56 minutes, creating a further world record. On 29 April 2001, while on the summit for the eleventh time, he fell into a 200-foot-deep crevasse and died.

Reading this makes me feel sad and reflective, but the rest of the group have started moving again and Pemba urges me to join them. There's definitely a strange energy here, as if it's a ledge of restless ghosts. I have complete respect for those who have perished doing what they do best, following their hearts and passion for summiting Everest, but it makes my own heart feel heavy.

12

Come on now
I hear you're feeling down.
Well, I can ease your pain
And get you on your feet again.
"Comfortably Numb", Pink Floyd

Day 7 continued: On the way to Lobuche

The clouds continue to draw in and it feels progressively colder and windier as we continue along the glacial terrain on the western side of the valley beside the frozen river. We're surrounded by imposing mountainsides and we have to walk around massive boulders, which are iron-oxidised – the colour reminds me of the pebbles pebbles on beaches back home.

My head is now pounding ceaselessly and we're walking very slowly and even this requires incredible effort. I've never known cold like it, and the wind is beyond testing as it whistles fiercely through this bleak valley and pierces my hat and into my ears. My head's down and my only thoughts are of making it to the lodge. Nothing else seems very important to me right now: "Must get to the lodge, must get to the lodge" has become a mantra, as I put one foot in front of the other.

It feels like an endless afternoon of ascending this desolate valley with the air becoming increasingly thinner. I'm frustrated and desperate to get to the next lodge to lie down, so I make a decision to pick up my pace and get there as quickly as I can. That's all I care about now, to go to sleep and experience some relief from the constant throbbing in my head and seek refuge from the penetrating wind.

We're all silent, all battling with our own demons. It feels as if we're stumbling over the loose moraine, ghosts now ourselves, bodies here but minds elsewhere, dreaming of escaping from the freezing temperatures and the constant pounding in our heads. There's no sense of joy whatsoever.

I'm too tired to be angry. It's just about survival now, trying to take in enough oxygen from the thin air.

Finally, in the distance, I make out a small cluster of lodges built to the left side of the valley. It's like seeing an oasis in a desert. I sigh with relief. It's beginning to snow and we can hear thunder in the distance. "Must get to the lodge… Must get to the lodge" goes over and over in my mind.

One of our porters joins us and walks beside us to make sure that we make it safely to the lodges. They tell us that there may be avalanches with the thunder. This spurs me on to make it to the lodge even quicker: "Must get to the lodge. Must get to the lodge." Breathe. I'm on a mission, I've just got to get there.

Originally a summer village for herders, Lobuche (4,940m) now exists solely to service the trekking industry. It's not a particularly attractive stopping point, but to be honest all I care about is getting to a lodge and lying down. I've been rushing ahead so that no one had the chance to tell me to go slow, to ease my pace, to allow for the changing altitude. Nope, I just kept going, thinking how much I need to lie down, get it over with, and rest.

So now I'm totally disoriented. I'm on my own and I don't know which lodge to go in. It's bitter, with snow filling the air and wind slicing through my hat. My head is pounding, pounding, pounding and I just want to lie down; please can I lie down? I stand still and try to focus my eyes to look for the familiar faces of our porters, confusion etched all over my face. Where are they? Where shall I go? I feel very alone.

And then, all of a sudden from nowhere (or so it feels), Pemba is at my side. I'm dazed and confused, numb almost, as he takes hold of my arm and helps to lead me through the door of the lodge. I lean heavily on him with my arm as I stumble over the ledge; I can barely put one foot in front of the other. It's almost too much of a contrast for my eyes, as I step into a bright, hot room and focus in on the familiar and smiling faces of the porters ahead of me.

I'm shivering uncontrollably and my head is really hurting. I stumble forward among the porters, who stand in front of the dung-fuelled central stove. Pemba leaves me with them to go and attend to the rest of our group and they start to fuss around me, clearly concerned.

"Namaste, Namaste, Namaste," I can barely whisper the words as they each try to help me walk, leading me through another door into the cold and dark corridor and on to the small basic room that Lilly and I will be sharing for the night – the others are following, moments behind me. I'm physically and mentally exhausted.

I collapse onto the edge of the small, hard, wooden bed and hold my head in my hands trying to ease the pounding. I'm wishing it away. "Please make it go away" is now my mantra and my prayer. Soon I begin to cry; the pressure in my head is unbearable. I've never known this before and I'm scared. I want the pounding to stop. It feels like my brain may explode in my skull.

Pemba comes into the room and asks me if I am OK, but I can't respond. It hurts too much. He can see that I'm crying and he tells me to lie down on the bed, but I can't move. I just want the pain in my head to stop and go away. Pemba insists I lie down and he helps me to move my hands away from my head so that I can lay down onto my side, before he goes off to check on the rest of the group who have now arrived at the lodge.

Lilly comes into the room and asks me if I am OK. I mumble to her that my head hurts and she asks me if I need anything. "No, no, no, thank you," I respond. I just need to be on my own, alone, in the quiet. I can't cope with any noise.

I'm aware that it's freezing in the room and I'm lying on my bed fully clothed, wrapped in the thick blanket that was on the bed. I reach out and grab the hard, yellow-stained pillow to my side and stuff it into the corner of the wall. I then jam my head against it, right into the very corner, hoping that this will relieve the pain. I will do anything, absolutely anything, to release the pressure in my head right now.

I lie motionless, waiting and waiting, silently praying, please, please stop it feeling like my brain is about to burst in my skull.

I stop crying and remember my breath – inhale, exhale, inhale, exhale, inhale, exhale – rhythmic, calming, and on and on, breathe in, breathe out, breathe in and breathe out. I want to feel normal again.

After some time, the pounding eases a little. However, I don't want to move and I keep my awareness on my breath, as it seems to be calming me. I've lost all sense of time now, in that liminal space, where time is unimportant anyway, breathing in and breathing out, over and over again, deep breaths, trying to breathe in as much oxygen as I can to my head.

Finally, I reach a point where I need to move. I'm still hurting, but I've been soothed by my breath and my brain no longer feels like it may explode in my head. I'm less anxious now and less panicky too. I have a sense that I will be OK.

I move slowly up to a seated position, though it's the only speed I can move at this altitude. It's the strangest feeling, like I'm here but not here at the same time.

Life is precarious in these mountains, I can feel it. We've almost doubled our altitude in a day and I've trekked far too fast. I should've slowed my pace like Lilly, who was the slowest trekker in our group, and feels fine.

Fortunately, I still have an appetite, which means I can't be that bad, although it's my need for tea that encourages me up off the bed, out of the room, and into the warm and bright dining room. It's such a contrast in here from the bedroom and it takes me a while to adjust to the light and activity, let alone the din of people talking. I sit on one of the empty wooden benches along the side of the room, resting the back of my head against the thin wooden wall.

Lilly and Will are sitting to my left, nestled beside one another on a wooden bench in front of one of the simple wooden window frames. Outside, darkness is slowly descending and I can see that the snow is falling thickly now. Joe is hunched over, knees drawn to his chest, resting against the opposite corner of this small yet cosy dining room. Craig and Tim are nowhere to be seen.

Pemba is pleased to see me. He orders a flask of hot, sweet, milky tea and I sit, staring into space, drinking cup after cup of the warming, comforting tea. The combination of sugar and caffeine is just what I need right now.

I'm aware that there are a number of other trekkers in the room and that the majority are sitting around in silence, looking dazed and staring into space. It seems that the high altitude is challenging everyone as it take us some time to adjust to the lack of oxygen.

Joe, our usual happy-go-lucky jester of the group, tells me he is feeling rough too; it's unusual to see him so quiet and withdrawn, and he looks like he might cry. I gesture for him to come and sit beside me so he's not on his own. He shuffles his way over to me and tells me that his head hurts too. He looks pained and vulnerable, no longer the teenager-wants-to-be-a-film-gangster, more like the little-boy-who-needs-a-cuddle-from-his-mum.

I encourage him to lie down beside me so that I can channel Reiki onto his forehead with one of my cold hands. I know that his head is thumping as much as mine, so we sit like that for a while, the Reiki calming us both. It's incredible how much comfort it provides in my life, even now in these extreme circumstances.

Joe soon decides that he needs to go to sleep, so I walk with him to his room to check that he's OK. Pemba is in the room talking to Craig, who I see is sitting on the edge of the bed, with his head in his hands. Pemba is crouching in front of him, trying to work out whether he is OK or not. It's all very strange and I know I need some heat and some distraction from the focus on my head, so I leave them to it and head back into the main dining room.

Lilly and Will are now sitting up on the bench, perched together drinking flasks of tea. They both feel fine, which annoys me slightly because I don't understand how we can all feel so different. I consider myself fit and healthy and yet here I am suffering from the altitude. How come they feel OK?

"Have you taken anything to ease the pain?" Will asks.

"No," I respond.

"No?" Will retorts, "Take some paracetamol. It will make you much better."

"But I don't like to take anything," I tell him, and I really don't. I loathe tablets, the drug companies and everything they represent. I appreciate that there are many instances when they help and some people require medication their whole lives to manage a condition, but I am also very well aware that the human body can heal itself given the right condition – helped by yoga and Reiki of course!

Needless to say, yoga is not really an option for me right now. Not only is there nowhere to practise it, but honestly, I don't think I could even if there was. I'm just feeling so rotten that it's just not even in mind as an option. It's interesting how a change in circumstance can create a whole new perspective on things. Right now, my yoga practice is about getting through the day. It is about breathing and being present and OK with all that is happening.

I'm beginning to recognise that yoga absolutely does not need to look a certain way. Not the clothes, not the postures, not the space. It's a constant surrendering to life as it unfolds and trusting in the process. Plus, having patience.

I'm reminded of this now. I've been holding on so tightly to my idea of how life should be, and here I am suffering. Lilly passes me some paracetamol. "Take them," she urges. I'm really torn. Part of me is so determined to hold off, given my disdain for taking these things, but the other half of me is questioning my stubbornness and is very aware of the continuous pounding in my head. Plus I am aware that I took some aspirin a few nights ago in desperation.

I know I need to surrender to the moment. In the grand scheme of things this is such a small thing, but for me it is also a huge moment. I surrender. There's nothing more for it, the pounding in my head is slowly driving me mad and someone is offering me the option of doing something about it. It's time to loosen the grip on how I think things should be and take what is being offered to me. The Divine has many guises; the key is to see beyond the limitations of the mind.

So, I take two of the tablets, washing them down with tea. It doesn't take long for their effect to kick in and the pain in my head eases, and with that I feel an utter sense of relief. It is an amazing feeling and I only wish now that I had not been so resistant to taking them earlier. I cannot fully explain the joy of not being so completely consumed by the thumping and pounding sensation in my skull.

I shall never forget that moment. I feel as if I am truly coming back to life again. And with that, I suddenly grow aware of the activity in the dining room; the porters sitting by the fire warming themselves and the other people collecting in groups, as if the world has become visible again.

Together with Lilly and Will, we chat with a group of other trekkers who settle themselves down beside us on the long, wooden benches. They are English and jubilant, as they are on their descent, having trekked to Everest Base Camp earlier that morning. They tell us that the air will become even thinner tomorrow as we continue with our ascent and that we will need to trek very slowly to acclimatise to this. I'm learning the lesson – slowly is best. "Bistari, bistari," as Pemba keeps saying!

It's now dark and snowing heavily as Lilly and I wrap up in our layers and venture outside for a smoke. There's a party of Koreans laughing and smoking together and we all hop from one foot to the other, trying to keep warm. I wonder how on earth people can stay warm enough camping in this environment. They must be mad! Unsurprisingly, smoking makes me feel dreadful because I'm having a hard enough time breathing as it is, and I question the stupidity of the nicotine addiction.

Back inside the dining room it's busy now with about 40 of us squeezed along the wooden benches or huddled around the central wood-burning stove. The room is filled with activity, as the porters serve supper and the trekkers talk loudly through their meals. Craig, Joe and Tim join us from their room just in time for dinner. Everyone is relieved to be feeling a little better and we laugh, joke and smile with one another again – what a turnaround in a matter of hours, as our bodies adjust to the altitude.

With Dawa further down the mountain looking after Matt and Ben, the responsibility for serving us our dinner falls to the younger porters and they fuss around us, making sure that we're OK. I'm really hungry and am grateful for the warming and tasty dal bhat. Needless to say, the boys are eating their usual fried food, despite Pemba trying again to insist that everyone should eat dal bhat to help fill them up.

I chat to two of our younger porters, one twenty-five years old and the other twenty-six years old and both very shy. I learn that they are both married and have left young sons at home with their wives. They show me photos and I can see that one is a toddler and the other a younger baby. They tell me that they miss their families very much while they are working as porters in the mountains, but that this type of work is a financial necessity.

It makes me feel ashamed that here I am making such a fuss about how awful I feel, when I made the decision to trek and paid for the trip. No one has forced me to be here. It's not that the porters have been forced either, only that there is such little choice for them in how they make money living in this rural area of Nepal, so in many respects, the decision is made for them. The contrast in how easy it is for me to earn money sitting in an office back home, in comparison to these men in the mountains, makes me feel uncomfortable. Our lives are so incredibly different and yet we are somehow drawn together in the same environment, in the same moment, all people.

This is the same the world over and it is very easy to be ignorant of the manner in which other people live, especially coming from an affluent place like Guernsey, where so many earn a very good wage from working in the offshore finance industry. Yet I am well aware that there is more to happiness and contentment than money alone and that the pursuit of material wealth can take us further away from happiness.

Because, despite the simplicity and austerity and the apparent hardships of the porters' lives (in comparison to my own), they are always smiling, gentle in manner and go out of their way to be helpful and kind too. It is clear to me that they have good hearts and you cannot put a price on this.

But more than anything, I am humbled by their ability to accept their reality, to provide for their families in the best way they can, and get on with living, taking each day as it comes. It makes me aware that sometimes we can become so caught up with the idea of being 'spiritual' (and feeling therefore that we need to live a certain way to be considered a spiritual person), that we forget the essence of life (think Maslow's hierarchy of needs) and the need to work hard, root down, and do what we can to provide food and shelter for ourselves and our children. Ultimately, it's about being responsible and taking responsibility as these men are doing, without needing to label their efforts or approach to life 'spiritual'.

I've witnessed many times over the last couple of years the manner in which spiritual seekers forget to live in the real world in their pursuit of what they feel it means to live a 'spiritual life'. They may try to be 'spiritual' and wise, floating around on their spiritual cloud, and yet they're not able to manifest in the world and struggle to support themselves and their families financially and/or emotionally. Often, they lack any grounding, living their lives in the ether, out of their bodies, and yet kidding themselves that they're living a life in alignment with their heart and soul; "But I'm so spiritual," they say.

Many of them are sometimes so caught up in their spiritual ego and their idea of what it means to be spiritual that they don't even realise that they're limiting themselves and their potential experience of the world in their quest 'to be spiritual'. They're so busy 'doing' the practice, spending the time on the mat, sitting in meditation, doing the self-care, the journaling, the attending courses and workshops, that they totally separate the spiritual from the rest of their lives and forget about the 'being' and the 'living' and the potential that may come from this.

There are also a huge number who are 'spiritual bypassing'. This is a term that was coined by psychologist and Buddhist teacher, John Weldwood, in the early 1980s and refers to the use of spiritual practices and beliefs to avoid dealing with uncomfortable feelings, unresolved wounds and unfinished developmental tasks.

For example, while some people may appear to do the work, and appear 'spiritual' and want everyone to know about it, in actuality what they are really doing is just using their 'spirituality' like any other avoidance or defence measure, such as alcohol or drugs, to distract themselves from their feelings and emotionally numb out and repress them. "It's all about transcendence," they might say, as they check out, rather than check in.

In reality, 'being spiritual' means being present to everything, not just the perceived positive aspects of self. A true spiritual practice involves trying to make friends with *all* aspects of ourselves, including the shadow, (every positive has a shadow), which includes those parts of ourselves that we often try to ignore or deny such as the anger, loneliness and/ or self-loathing, the dark sides of our being.

A spiritual practice will help support us as we bring the shadows to light and as we go through the often painful process of learning to befriend and love all aspects of self. It means being in this world, and in the body, and being in the present moment, whatever it happens to look like in that moment. It's not easy, but having a genuine spiritual practice can help.

The fact is – and this is what I am learning by being in the mountains and being in Nepal – that each moment provides an opportunity for spiritual growth. All of life can be a spiritual practice, a 'sadhana'. We just need to be honest with ourselves and do the work that is required to bring the shadows to light and step into an increasingly authentic version of ourselves in the process. I too have been caught in the spiritual ego at times, taking myself out of the world rather than living in it, and I have spiritually bypassed too, trying to deny my feelings, ignoring the shadow side, and forgetting that we are having an embodied experience here on Mother Earth.

These kind and gentle porters here live authentically. They're not trying to be anything other than what they are. They haven't had to go on a mindfulness course or a yoga retreat to recognise this. They've just gotten on with their lives, accepting their fate, their dharma (sacred duty) and have made a go of it, taking responsibility for their own lives and for that of their families. There is much that I can learn from them and their lives rooted in a combination of Tibetan Buddhism, a sense of belonging in the mountains and their family life. It raises the question of who really is richer and the role that money plays (or doesn't play) in this.

This brings us to a whole other question though, about recognising our sacred duty in this world. It's difficult sometimes to accept this. For example, I didn't consciously choose to become a professional company secretary. It wasn't something I sought or dreamt about; it was something that just happened. It has been very helpful in enabling me to earn the money I have needed to be able to travel and do the training I've wanted to do the last few years, and it enables me to be in Nepal now. But it is not something that is very exciting, or that makes me feel as enlivened and uplifted as I do when I have been teaching yoga. But it is something that just won't go away. Like a boomerang, every time I try to throw it away, it comes back to me again. On some level it is my dharma and the sooner I accept that, the better for everyone!

We studied the Bhagavad Gita during our yoga teacher-training course. This is an epic poem between a distraught warrior named Arjuna and the Hindu deity, Krishna. Lord Krishna counsels Arjuna at a time of despair, and though Krishna is speaking to this warrior, he is really speaking to all of us.

There are many things we can learn from this text, but essentially it teaches us about the concept of dharma and sacred duty. So it goes that each and every one of us is born with this 'sacred duty' that we must fulfil during this lifetime. For Arjuna, his sacred duty was being a warrior at the time of war. For many of us it may be the duty of being a daughter, or a friend, or a company secretary, for example! In theory, we can use this idea to help us cope with our responsibilities in life and see them not as burdens, but as our sacred duties.

When we see our responsibilities in this way, it can inspire us to fulfil them with honour. We are encouraged not to question the responsibility, but to accept it as a necessary sacrifice. If we are able to see it in this way, then we can transform the way we think and see life – and our role within it – in a more meaningful way. We may come to recognise the cosmic order to all life and our role within this.

In the poem, Arjuna the warrior stops in the middle of a battlefield, thereby forfeiting his sacred duty. Lord Krishna then comes along and demands that he takes action. We can probably all relate to Arjuna in this scene – in difficult times we stop, paralysed by fear and doubt. The lesson here is to never stop what has already been set in motion because when we do, we bring our growth to a standstill and potentially waste our lives. Lord Krishna tells us that it is only through disciplined action that we can grow. It is a reminder that we must remain grounded and disciplined in our daily lives.

It's the same with our yoga practice – I'm increasingly recognising that yoga is not about the aesthetics. It's not about whether we're wearing the right clothes or lighting incense (although I do like to light incense as long as it's herbal and not synthetic), it's about being disciplined in everything we set out to do (whatever that looks like to us, it doesn't have to look a certain way). As Lord Krishna says, "The disciplined man attains perfect peace; the undisciplined man is in bondage."

The Bhagavad Gita also says that there is one thing in our lives that is unchanging and that is the self, our true essence. This is why the answers that we seek can never lie in the external world, but within us. Lord Krishna tells us that we must part the clouds of ignorance with self-knowledge. We must get to know ourselves better. Our knowledge is obscured by our desires; we think that material things and the titles that we are given can sustain us, but the truth is, they are only fleeting. Lord Krishna asks Arjuna to look inside himself and to fight this war because it is his duty, regardless of the consequences (and having no attachment to them). Lord Krishna says, "So sever the ignorant doubt in your heart with the sword of self-knowledge, Arjuna! Observe your discipline arise!"

It seems to me that these wonderful porters recognise their sacred duty in this lifetime and have honourably taken on the responsibility to provide for their families (often the extended family) in whatever way they can, accepting their reality and just getting on with the task at hand. I am both fascinated and humbled to see this in action.

After dinner, despite all my earlier resistance and reservation, I take as much paracetamol as I am allowed before we all crash for the night. I still manage to make it into my PJs although I also wear my fleece and my trekking socks. There's not a shower in sight, but I've moved beyond that now too, wrapped in my sleeping bag with a huge blanket on top of this. Even then I'm only just about feeling warm enough to sleep.

13

If God will send his angels
And if God will send a sign
And if God will send his angels
Would everything be alright.
"If God Will Send His Angels", U2

Day 8: Lobuche to Gorak Shep

I wake at 2am with a thumping head again. It has become a routine now and I'm no longer scared. I move as quickly as I can to grab my woolly hat on the floor beside me and shove it on my head, before swallowing yet more paracetamol washed down with icy water from my water bottle, and curling up into the foetal position.

The trouble is I still can't sleep because rather annoyingly I need the toilet and this is a mission in itself. I scrabble around to find my head torch and begrudgingly extricate myself from my warm sleeping bag and put my cumbersome trekking boots on my feet. Then, as quietly as possible, toilet roll in hand, I slide my way out the barely open squeaky door and walk as lightly as I can down to the rancid squat toilet at the bottom of the corridor.

The toilet stinks. There is no smell quite like it and absolutely no getting used to it. I try not to breathe too much as the stench is truly overpowering. It's really not ideal using these toilets at the best of times but certainly not in the middle of the night when it's dark, freezing cold and I'm trying not to wake anyone. It's a balancing act too, trying to make sure that no part of my clothing or body touches any part of the fetid room.

Relieved, not least to have peed, but also to be able to leave the revolting toilet, I tread my way quietly back to the bedroom, the wooden floorboards occasionally squeaking, causing me to suspend myself in the silence that follows.

I pass our porters. I can see them lying side by side on wooden platforms nestled in the space between two rooms and I try and move quickly without waking them. I'm jubilant to make it back to the room and into the warmth of my sleeping bag, mission accomplished, now keen to get some sleep.

Lilly and I wake at 6am, and the lodge is already a hive of activity as people clomp past our room, making it impossible to sleep. It's Easter Sunday back at home and I momentarily think of my parents on holiday in Portugal and my friends back at home eating Easter eggs. The warmth of Portugal and the ease of chocolate-egg-eating seem a world away to me right now!

Lilly asks me how I'm feeling and I tell her that I'm OK. It is a relative term – as long as I take paracetamol then I seem to have some control over the pounding in my head. Lilly is feeling much better now and I can't help thinking that it has helped her psychologically to know that Ben and Matt have already had to drop out of the trek, as I think a part of her was worried that she would be the first one to have to stop.

We congregate in the dining room for breakfast. It's porridge this morning and while I don't like to appear ungrateful, it tastes revolting; a combination of keroscne and some kind of bleach. Yuck! I am just pleased for the sweet milk-powdered tea – while I know that also sounds fairly horrible too, and I would never dream of drinking it at home, it works well up here, warming and energising at the same time.

Craig is not feeling well this morning and sits quietly, slumped in a chair, his head held in his hands; he's certainly not his usual chirpy self. Will is feeling unwell too and tells us how he has been vomiting in the rancid toilets on and off all night. The thought of this is enough to turn my stomach. Urghhh, poor thing, that can't have been a pleasant experience. He sits quietly, trying to compose himself, as he is determined to keep going and still figures the sickness is a result of food poisoning rather than the altitude.

Joe is looking pale and tired, but he tells me he feels much better than he did when he went to bed and he manages a thumbs-up when we take a photo, all of us sitting together in the dining room, trying to be brave in our own ways and reflective about the day ahead. Lilly is now probably feeling the best out of all of us. A memorable moment indeed.

It's a beautiful morning in this frozen world as we head out from the lodge. The bright sun once again demands sunglasses to prevent the glare from blinding us – how do the porters get by without wearing these? Fortunately, the wind has died down overnight and everything looks pristine and white. Furthermore, there is a resounding silence, which merely adds to the purity of the landscape. It's sublime and I recognise again that this is a special part of the world, that the Divine is certainly present.

We trek slowly this morning, making the first footprints in the fresh snow – another one of those memorable moments because we're all very aware that we're the only ones to have stepped on this particular part of the Himalayas today! We're also excited because we've not got long to go now to reach our destination – just one more night in a lodge further up the trail and then tomorrow we'll be able to trek to Base Camp before descending to a kinder altitude.

Already, I'm looking forward to the coming back down again! I know it sounds silly as we've not made it to the top yet, but I'm very aware that the next twenty-four hours are likely to be the most challenging of the whole trek. We'll have to adjust to an even higher altitude and I can't imagine what this might do to my head, especially in the middle of the night. Plus, I'm concerned about the decreasing temperature and how I am going to stay warm in this hostile and freezing environment.

Needless to say, it's extremely hard work as we trek along the western side of the broad Khumbu valley. The air feels as if it is becoming thinner with each step, so that we really feel the effort involved in both breathing and moving simultaneously. The snow and ice melt a little as the sun rises higher into the sky and while we can feel the heat of the sun on our faces, it does little to warm our skin (not that much of our skin is on show as we are now wrapped up in layers of clothes with hats and scarves, hoods and coats).

Will stops to vomit halfway up a particularly steep section of the trail, before rinsing his mouth with water and blowing his nose. He then simply carries on, as if it is the most normal thing in the world, to take a vomit stop. I have to give him credit for his determination to complete this trek, but I question whether it's safe to keep going, when he can't keep anything in his stomach.

We're all quiet this morning, the air is far too thin for chatter, and we trek slowly, with our walking poles steadying us, eyes focused on the ground and ensuring the safe placing of our feet. It feels as if we are moving in slow motion and I wonder how long it will take us, but I don't like to ask Pemba because it is always longer than I want it to be, so perhaps it's best not to ask in the first place.

Initially the trail follows a narrow gap between the glacial moraine and the mountain wall, and to the right of us the Khumbu Glacier gurgles and sighs under a covering of a mish-mash of ground rocks and gravel. Tim has told me that global warming means that the glacier is shrinking away from the moraine wall at an alarming rate. This means that the route regularly changes as the edge of the moraine tumbles into the glacier.

The trail is littered with stone cairns left as markers by those moving before us. We've passed a number of these stone cairns along the trail and I've become very fond of them because they demonstrate to me the spirit of this trek, people trying to help others make it to Everest Base Camp (and beyond) safely by marking the route.

We continue along the western side of the Khumbu Valley, which ascends gently (relative to other parts of the trail) beside the glacial moraine. Inevitably, the ascent becomes steeper and rougher as it crosses several side moraines.

Despite the challenging altitude, I'm in awe of the beauty in everything around me today – the majestic snow-capped mountains with their frozen rivers of ice, the grey-tinged, jade-coloured waters flowing through gaps in the ice (forming ice caves) and between the large boulders of this amazing moraine terrain. We are so far removed from civilisation; from anything I have ever previously known.

The six of us endure three long and hard hours. We're constantly passing a stream of people walking in the opposite direction, joyous in their descent as we acknowledge one another: "Namaste, Namaste, Namaste." Not to say it's easy going for them either. They may be descending, but the path goes up and down, so they have to walk uphill at points, as the path winds its way along the side of the valley. The trail can get a little uncomfortable too at times, elevated as it is on a ledge so that you have to squeeze in to allow others to pass.

After a while, it becomes apparent that Craig is struggling. Following a particularly steep ascent, we stop to rest to the side of the trail on some rocks, the bright sun glaring overhead, and he slumps down with his head in his hands. We ask him if he's OK and he mutters that he's fine and lifts his head to be able to eat a Snickers bar. We don't stop for very long, just enough time for snacks, water and catching our breath.

Progressing along the path, we soon round a bend in the trail and I recognise the trekkers descending towards us. They are the teenagers from England who were staying in the same hotel as us in Namche Bazaar. I'm amazed at how quickly they've managed to ascend and descend ahead of us. This spurs me on, as I know that we don't have long to go and I am really looking forward to our descent, as they look so jubilant!

Finally, after what feels like a very long morning, we make it to the end of the path and up onto a ledge beside the valley, so now we only have a short descent onto the flat and sandy bowl of Gorak Shep (5,160m). This was the base camp for the 1952 Swiss Everest Expedition, but subsequent expeditions established an advanced base camp just below the Khumbu Icefall. Like Lobuche, where we started this morning, Gorak Shep is ramshackle lodges, which provide food and space to sleep, but nothing more than that. This is the last place on the trail with lodges, as people stay in tents further up at Base Camp. In 1953, the British Everest Expedition called this 'lake camp' as it has a small lake that is usually either dry or frozen.

You cannot actually see Mount Everest from Gorak Shep as the peak is hidden by the shoulder of Nuptse, but you can get some good views over the Khumbu glacier. Dotted around the ridge above Gorak Shep are several more monuments to climbers who have died during various Everest expeditions. Since 1921, more than 200 climbers, Sherpas and porters have perished here, either on the peak or in helicopter crashes at Base Camp. Two expedition members, Rob Hill and Andy Harris, who perished in the 1996 Everest disaster, are commemorated here.

It's lunchtime and bitingly cold when we arrive at the lodge where we are due to stay for the night. I didn't know that air could be this thin and I try to imagine how people cope with the decreasing temperatures and lack of oxygen even further up the trail to Base Camp and beyond.

There's a strange energy at Gorak Shep; a combination of the sandy nature of the terrain, and the snow-capped mountains looming over us, gives the impression of being on another planet. It's both an expansive and yet edgy and slightly claustrophobic energy for me. I can't quite put words to it, perhaps a seriousness that I have not yet properly perceived earlier along the trail.

Tim and I are the first to arrive and we head straight to the large dining room, slumping onto a wooden bench at the far end of the plain and utilitarian room. The two of us have been walking at a similar pace the last few days and are both at ease in each other's company, despite the age gap. Tim is a really good guy, kind-hearted and sensible, and I know that he'll follow his heart in all he does. Perhaps this is the reason that we get on, as we understand this perspective to life.

It is following our hearts that finds us here together on this trek. I'm still not sure yet of the bigger picture, of how this trek fits in with what lays ahead for me, but I am aware that it is giving me the space to process all that has been and to essentially let go of this. Furthermore, the very fact of being here, and of seeing and experiencing life from a different perspective, is also helping to shift my awareness and resonant frequency, and further open my heart in the process – especially with the Tibetan Buddhism energy permeating the air.

Tim and I comment on the thinness of the air. This a common conversation. You'd think we'd tire of it, but we are constantly challenged by the lack of oxygen and the effect this has on how we feel. However, all of a sudden, our chatter is interrupted by the others joining us, as Craig collapses onto a basic plastic chair, his eyes half closed and dazed. I can see that he's clearly not in a good way. His lips are blue and he's complaining of feeling dizzy. Pemba is soon beside him, crouching down to be at eye height. "I'll order you some soup," he tells Craig, "chicken soup. It will make you feel better." Then he disappears from the room to place the order.

We all move closer in towards Craig while Will kneels down beside him, reaching for Craig's arm and trying to find his pulse. Will's concentrated face then starts to show concern as he struggles to find Craig's pulse. He tries to engage with Craig, but Craig is having trouble speaking and can't answer Will's questions and mumbles incoherently, his head lolling from side to side, his eyeballs now sinking into his head. If I didn't know better I'd say he was very drunk, but of course he isn't very drunk, it's simply that we are 5,160m above sea level and his body cannot cope with the altitude.

Will, being a medic, is rightly concerned and says that we have to get Craig back down the mountain quickly, as he's really not in a good way. No one moves as we try to process what's happening, all of us staring at Craig, trying to figure out what's happening to him. "He needs to descend NOW", Will shouts at us in a panicky and serious way.

Things then happen very quickly.

Pemba still hasn't returned from the kitchen, so Will virtually drags Craig out the door. We follow, trying to help where we can. It's blindingly bright outside in the midday sunshine and we all squint trying to adjust to the light while simultaneously establishing our bearings. Will's urgently looking around trying to figure out which way to go, while the rest of us are trying to see if we can spot Pemba and our porters.

It feels very surreal, as if we're in the scene of a film and the action shots are happening around us, but have no idea of the role we're meant to be playing or the outcome. While all this runs through my mind, someone finds Pemba and the porters, and they work quickly together, Pemba shouting at them in Nepali, as they untie Craig's rucksack from the other two bags that the porter has been carrying up the trail this morning.

Joe, Tim and I stand together outside the door to the lodge and watch helplessly as Will and Dawa (who has now rejoined us after settling Matt and Ben into a lodge further down the trail) carry Craig between them, one arm and one leg each, halfway up the hill we have recently descended on our arrival into Gorak Shep. The path will ultimately descend down to Lobuche, where we stayed last night, but the path ascends initially out of Gorak Shep. From there the men will make their way to safer and lower altitudes.

Both Dawa and Will seem to have found extra energy, as they ascend incredibly quickly, despite the altitude. We watch helplessly, noticing that Craig's head is noticeably flopping from side to side.

Lilly joins us and starts crying. She's known Craig much longer than the rest of us and she can't believe that this is happening to him. None of us can really take it in. It's very scary how quickly things can change in the mountains.

Pemba soon joins us too. "Why haven't you called a helicopter to take him off the mountain?" demands Joe. The last few days especially, I think we've all been considering the merits of being helicoptered off the mountain, Joe particularly.

"We don't have time," Pemba tells him. "He needs to descend right now and organising a helicopter would take too long." Tim joins in, "But why has no one thought to use a Gamow bag?" A Gamow bag is a portable pressure chamber.

Tim's been talking about them regularly on this trek. I'd never come across the term previously. "There just isn't the time," Pemba tells him. "He needs to descend the mountain as soon as possible, to a lower altitude. It's the only way."

None of us can quite believe what is happening; we've all been aware that Craig has not been feeling well, but he's been insistent that he should continue the trek. However, this is often the trouble with altitude sickness – people do not always like to admit that they have it, and when you come this far and are so close to achieving your goal, well, you just want to keep going. But it's incredibly dangerous and, as we have witnessed with Craig, your condition can deteriorate very quickly and then there isn't any time to do anything other than descend.

It can only have been a few minutes, when all of a sudden Will appears in the distance. He's running back down the hill that he's just run up with Dawa and Craig and he is in a visible state of panic, his walking poles in hand and yet flaying around him. He shouts out to Pemba in his broad Scottish accident, "He's not going to make it. He can't walk, his brain is swollen, he's in a really bad way! I think he has high-altitude cerebral oedema. We need a yak or something to take him down the hill, otherwise he's going to die."

Die? I hadn't realised the severity of this situation. How precarious that space between life and that last breath.

Will is pleading with Pemba to take some action, to do something, desperation etched all over his face, which is also now bright red with the exertion of running in this high altitude.

"It will take too much time to sort a yak," Pemba tells him, before he shouts out in Nepali to the remaining porters, authority in his voice, his hand gesturing down the mountain. The porters look as helpless as I feel, but all of a sudden, on Pemba's command, they run off together in the direction of Craig and Dawa and up the incline to the path that will lead them down the mountain again.

There is nothing we can do apart from watch, as the porters and Pemba disappear over the top of the hill that

Will's just run back down. We stand in silence for a moment, trying to take it all in, before turning towards Will and checking that he is OK. He's visibly shocked, and keeps saying, "He needs to get down. They need to carry him down. He shouldn't have been up here. He needs to get down. They need to carry him down." We try to reassure Will that Craig will be OK, but none of us can be truly certain of this.

We walk slowly and quietly back to the lodge, all of us with our heads down, trying to process what's just happened and make sense of it.

While there have been other moments to remind us of the risk in these mountains, it is only now that we all truly appreciate the danger of the altitude, the thin line between life and death and the speed with which things can shift. You can't afford to be arrogant or foolish in the mountains because they are much more powerful than us, and will remind us of this if necessary.

14

It's just the sun rising
It's just the sun rising
It's shining.
"The Sun Rising", The Beloved

Day 8 continued: Gorak Shep

Dawa's familiar face is soon smiling at us from the doorway to the dining room. He's quickly followed by Pemba, who assures us that Craig is fine, that the porters are literally carrying him down the mountain, all the way to the lodge where Matt and Ben are staying in Dingboche, a little higher than Pheriche where we stayed two nights ago. It's crazy to think that they will trek so far in such a short time, but Pemba reminds us that it is much quicker to descend than ascend, and I look forward to experiencing this for myself soon.

The porters are incredibly strong men. Not only have they trekked all the way up here with us today, carrying a couple of our bags each in the process, but now they are carrying Craig back down the mountain, before having to turn around and trek back up again to join us tomorrow. It makes me feel exhausted just thinking about it and especially as these men don't have the luxury of extra cash to buy themselves chocolate bars like the boys have been doing to help fuel them.

Pemba tells us that he will soon leave Gorak Shep to join the boys in Dingboche and that Dawa will take responsibility for us instead. This new plan means that we will rise early the following morning and head up to Everest Base Camp, which is about a six-hour round trip from the lodge.

We'll then spend the night in this lodge, and rise early the following morning for a four-hour round trip from the lodge, to trek up Kala Pattar, from where we will be able to see Mount Everest (you can't actually see Mount Everest from Base Camp), before continuing our descent down the mountain to join Pemba and the boys in Dingboche.

My heart drops. Right now, the thought of spending two nights up here, in this altitude, with a massive headache, and feeling completely out of sorts, is enough to fill me with sheer dread. A few days ago my main concern was whether I could have a shower and whether I might be able to get hold of some fresh fruit and vegetables, while now, I'm just concerned how I might make it through the night at this altitude and what on earth I might do with myself during the rest time at the lodge.

It's only 1.15pm and the whole afternoon stretches ahead of us. Dawa orders our lunch, settling into his new role as primary carer. You can tell things are bad, because I order fried noodles like everyone else. They arrive covered in pungent yak's cheese, and I eat this with a large dollop of tomato ketchup on the side. I can scarcely believe it myself and I almost chuckle as I think how surprised my mum would be, seeing me eating this now.

Lunch over with, we still have what feels like an endless afternoon ahead of us. It is absolutely freezing and definitely basic up here at this altitude and I feel decidedly challenged. There is no way that I could manage a yoga practice on my mat, as I'm struggling to breathe simply sitting still in the dining room. Furthermore, there is absolutely no room in our tiny bedroom to lay a mat, and even if there was, it would be far too cold for a yoga practice to be enjoyable or of any benefit.

The thing is, I'm feeling so out of sorts, that it doesn't even cross my mind to go and practise yoga. It's very difficult to explain in words quite how debilitating it feels to spend time at this altitude. Perhaps it's worse because I'm an island girl and I'm used to living at sea level, or perhaps it's simply that being at this height is not for me. Either way, my practice right now (hoorah!) is absolutely all about surrendering to the moment and being able to exist, mentally, physically and emotionally in this environment.

I love to read and there is definitely no shortage of books on this trek – the lodges often have a collection of books that you can take in exchange for leaving a book of your own. Lilly, Joe, Matt and Ben are all avid readers too, so between us we have quite a collection. But it is impossible for me to read at this altitude either. The thumping in my head makes it difficult to concentrate and I can only manage a few pages at a time.

I'm at a loss to know what to do with myself. Even sleeping holds no interest for me, as I'm concerned that I will not be able to sleep later in the evening, or overnight, and then what would I do with myself? Thus, I am keen to join Tim when he goes outside to take some photos of the sandy crater at the base of Kala Pattar.

The summit of this dark mound of mountain rubble is rumoured to provide perhaps the best views of Mount Everest in the Himalayas. However, I regret my decision almost the moment I step outside the lodge. Not only is it exceptionally cold, but I find it a struggle to walk and breathe at the same time. I just can't be bothered with the effort involved and after only a few minutes I return to the lodge, fighting back the tears of frustration and self-pity.

Back in the dining room, I slouch against one of the wooden benches and am pleased when I'm soon joined by Tim, who is feeling much the same as me. I'm heartened by this, because I've started to get a bit down on myself, questioning my physical and mental ability to withstand being so out of my comfort zone. This really is a test on so many levels, and I have renewed respect for all those who make it their mission to summit mountain peaks.

Tim and I order a large flask of Nepali tea, and soon Lilly joins us, and we share a tube of Pringles. I'm ravenous, especially for junk food; it's the oddest thing. I can't remember the last time I ate a Pringle, and I'm certainly not proud of it now, but it feels like a necessity. Perhaps it's the salt that my body craves, who knows? But it is certainly an indication that there has been a letting go and surrendering to the need of the moment, even if this wasn't quite how I imagined it; I'm not sure there's a spiritual element to Pringle-eating, but I like the spiritual spin on it!

As always, time passes, and soon Joe and Will join us for afternoon tea and biscuits. By then I really need the toilet, but it takes me a further twenty minutes to get the energy together to go there. The thought of having to unpeel my layers doesn't help, because it really is very cold, and everything is such an effort.

I notice a group of Russians sitting at a table to one side of us chatting away and becoming very animated at times, so that you cannot help but look over at them. There's also a group of Italians sitting on the other side of us, playing card games over and over again. I can hear an American guy across the room, sitting on one of the wooden benches, typing messages using a satellite phone. I'm so used to not having my phone with me, that the thought of communicating with the outside world from up here is an alien concept.

A group of English climbers sit beside the American guy, directly across the room from us. We learn that three of the men and one of the women are due to summit Mount Everest during the window of opportunity at the end of May, a few weeks away. They tell us that they've had to stay here for fifty days to acclimatise to the altitude. Fifty days? My gosh, the boredom would kill me before the altitude! It certainly shows a depth of character, albeit that I think they must be mad, or very passionate!

What's even more crazy to my mind, is the fact that at some point they will need to camp as they move further up the mountain. In many respects, the opportunity to acclimatise in this lodge must feel like a blessing when one considers what lies ahead. However, for us, a single night is challenging and we confess to one another that we have no interest in staying up here for two nights. We're keen to descend as soon as we can and after some discussion, conclude that we should skip Base Camp and focus our efforts on Kala Pattar instead.

It was a difficult decision to make, as we were sold the trek on the basis that we would visit Everest Base Camp. But this is a six-hour round trip, so if we do go there, we will need to spend an additional night at the lodge. However, if we just go to Kala Pattar, we can achieve the four-hour round-trip that this demands, and then continue down the mountain so that we will only need to stay the one night in the lodge.

Furthermore, we have been told that there's very little to see at Base Camp (5,340m) aside from a semi-permanent village of brightly coloured dome tents and prayer flags, wedged between rocks at the bottom of the Khumbu Icefall. Apparently, you can't even see Mount Everest as the mountain is behind the icefall and the clouds often roll down from the peaks. So, going to Kala Pattar makes more sense, as we are told that it affords views of Mount Everest.

In many respects, it's a shame not to make it to Base Camp. I'm intrigued by the mountaineers who are intending to summit Mount Everest and would've liked to have had more of an insight into their lives up here in these conditions. Because of the altitude, Everest cannot be climbed as a continuous ascent, so expeditions have to zigzag up and down the mountain range in order to acclimatise, which leads to a lot of waiting around at Base Camp. I'm told that a lot of gambling, card-playing, eating, reading and guitar-strumming takes place up there!

With the decision made, and little else to do, we're in bed by 8pm. The air temperature is definitely below zero and I've got such little energy that I don't even bother to change out of my clothes. Instead, I simply crawl into my sleeping bag, channelling Reiki onto my shoulder, and wish the night away. I'm sick of this trek and the morning can't come soon enough so that we can just get on with it. Lilly feels the same as I, and we moan ourselves to sleep.

However, I'm not asleep for long. The plywood 'wall' is so thin that the man snoring in the room next to me sounds as if he is lying in bed beside me. I feel dirty and tired and there is absolutely nothing I can do about it, apart from taking some more paracetamol. This is the only thing keeping me sane and easing the endless pounding in my head. I tell myself 'never again' and try to focus on my breath, but even this is challenging when the air is so thin.

15

Life has a funny way of sneaking up on you.
Life has a funny, funny way of helping you out
Helping you out.
"Ironic", Alanis Morissette

Day 9: Gorak Shep up to Kala Pattar and down to Dingboche

I awake early feeling terrible again; not only do I have an awful headache, but I'm also feeling nauseous. Furthermore, there's something disconcerting about waking up wearing the same sweaty clothes I've been wearing the last few days and which I will have to continue wearing the rest of this day too.

It doesn't take Lilly and me long to pack our bags, as we didn't really unpack anything when we arrived. Thus, we soon join the boys in the dining room just a little before 6am as planned. Breakfast is waiting for us, although I struggle to eat my muesli or drink my milk tea, which is strange for me, especially as I don't have much energy.

We're keen to get going as soon as we can with Dawa now guiding us, the porters waiting back for us at the lodge, as they aren't needed to carry our bags just yet. However, stepping outside into the dawn light, we're immediately struck by how difficult it is to walk and breathe simultaneously in this environment, especially with it being so early. I keep saying it, but it feels like I'm having to suck for air, which is unnerving. I also can't shake the nausea.

I'm aware of my every step, as I slowly place one foot in front of the other, like I'm walking on the moon, or at least that's how I imagine it might be.

We trek in silence, dealing with our own discomfort and inner demons. The sun hasn't yet properly risen from behind the mountains and my glove-covered hands are feeling the cold. However, I cannot bring myself to stop and remove my thicker mittens from my bag because I figure that if I stop, I may never start again.

The crater of sand at the base of Kala Pattar is our first challenge. Walking on sand is not easy at the best of times, and certainly not at this altitude. Before long, however, we begin to zigzag our way up the slippery, steep hill of Kala Pattar. Within minutes my fingers are numb, but I still cannot bring myself to stop. It sounds ridiculous, I know, but I just need to keep walking, numb fingers or not.

Sadly, the numbness in my fingers just adds to the overall level of discomfort I'm now feeling. The nausea grips me and I'm also feeling light-headed and physically exhausted, so I'm forced to slow my pace. I try and enter into a rhythm, to force myself up this steep hill, one slow and heavy step after another.

Soon Joe, Will and Lilly overtake me. Lilly's surprised. "Are you OK?" she asks me, but I can only nod at her in response. I don't even have the energy to speak.

I begin to question whether I should continue. Does it matter if I don't make it to the top? A part of me wants to keep going, I've come this far after all, but I'm feeling really sick now and my body is struggling to keep going. The nausea is all-consuming and while a part of me is reticent to vomit, another part of me longs to vomit simply to ease the feeling.

My mind keeps swinging back and forth: Should I keep going? Should I stop? Should I keep going? Should I stop? I'm loathe to admit defeat, to give up, to have to accept that the mountains have gotten the better of me, and yet I'm no longer sure that I can keep going.

This is a new experience for me. If I've made a decision to complete a task – in this instance to make it up to the top of Kala Pattar – then I complete it. I don't do giving up. I ran the London Marathon and, while it wasn't always very comfortable, not once did I question giving up. I committed to a 240-hour intensive yoga teacher-training course and, while it challenged me on every level, not once did I consider giving up. I studied for my professional qualifications and, while I found this very hard work, not once did I consider giving up.

However, my body is currently telling me that it needs to stop, that I have to let go of my resistance to giving up, and that I need to quickly come to terms with this. I'm very aware that sometimes things just don't go to plan, at least not our plan, sometimes the Divine has other ideas… and one has to learn when to surrender to this.

But I'm not ready to surrender. I don't want to be the only one in this final group not to make it to the top of Kala Pattar, just like I don't want to be the first one in the group to give up. My mind is overwhelmed with the indecision and all the while my body struggles to continue the zigzagging ascent.

I feel wretched. My head is thumping relentlessly now and my stomach aches with the nausea. Furthermore, my fingers are numb and I'm desperate to make them warm again. Shall I keep going? Shall I stop?

It's like a higher power takes over, because all of a sudden, I stop walking, just like that. I stop walking and surrender to the moment. I could cry with the relief.

We can battle our whole life against this, but when we finally surrender, when we finally let go of trying to hold it all together, of trying to make life look a certain way, well it allows Grace to enter instead. It's a little bit like saying, "Even though things don't look exactly the way I'd like them to look, life isn't exactly turning out the way I'd like it to turn out, I'll accept my reality, I'll be okay with what's happening, I'll allow its expression." I've heard it said that surrender and serenity are synonymous, that you can't experience one without the other, and this is certainly my experience.

Tim is following behind me and I move off to the side of the thin path to let him pass.

"Keep going," I tell him as quickly as I can, "I need to sit here and rest. I'm not feeling great. I'll meet you all back in the lodge later."

Tim is concerned, "Are you sure you'll be OK on your own?"

"I'll be fine," I try and reassure him, even though I don't know whether this is true. "Just go on and join the others." I wave my hand in the direction of the others further up the hill and try and encourage him on his way.

"Are you sure you're OK?" he asks again.

"I'll be fine," I repeat. "I just need to be on my own. I need to descend and warm my hands and lie down for a little while. I'll meet you in the lodge in a few hours' time," I tell him.

Still concerned, but needing to keep going, Tim continues his ascent as I half-collapse down onto the dusty hill, just off to the side of the path, and remove my daysack from my back. My priority is warming my hands, but they're so cold that I struggle to open my bag. I catch my breath. I am sucking for air, feeling sick, head pounding, thoughts all jumbled. I don't want to be here. I want to lie down and just go to sleep.

Tim notices me sitting on the ground and walks back down to me. He is concerned and asks again if I am OK. I reassure him as best I can that I really am OK; I just need to warm my hands and catch my breath before I descend back to the lodge. I just need a moment to compose myself and accept my reality.

I am keen for Tim to continue, and try to give him a smile, again ushering him on his way before focusing on finally removing my warmer gloves from my bag and pulling them over my freezing cold hands. I then take my water bottle out of my bag and sit back, looking towards the mountains that literally soar up into the sky in front of me. This is the first time I've been properly on my own in these mountains and I relish the opportunity. There's something about solitude that I find deeply healing and comforting; it's the silence and space it creates.

Furthermore, with my hands now adequately gloved and water sipped, I have a moment to collect myself and take in the views around me.

These mountains are truly enormous, sublime, majestic, real and yet so incredible and perfect, that they almost seem unreal. Am I really here? I almost have to pinch myself. "I'm in the Himalayas," I want to shout out.

It's then that the Divine enters my life, the Grace of the surrender.

I have no concept of time, of how long I'm sitting here – perhaps it's only a few minutes, I don't know – but suddenly I become aware that the sun is beginning to rise behind the mountains, the sky lightening with the glow of its bright reflecting rays.

I sit mesmerised, consciously breathing the cool, early morning air.

And then all of a sudden, quite unexpectedly, the first rays of light appear, reflecting and bouncing off the snow-capped summit of the mountain, glistening in the thin, pure air, like a star, transforming the air into a glow of sparkling lights, like the glinting of a crystal in the sunlight.

I forget about everything else – the cold, my hands, the nauseating feeling in my stomach and my pounding head.

I sit and I watch.

The.

Sun.

Rising.

Over.

Mount Everest.

I am on top of the world.

I witness the unfolding beauty of nature, the simplicity of life on Mother Earth, as the sun does what it does every day. No drama. No big deal. It has a role to fulfil, and it does it without complaint, without impatience or frustration, without rushing or being rushed. It just does its thing.

It rises from the horizon high into the sky, peeking above Mount Everest in the most magnificent, awe-inspiring and majestic way, shining light over the world.

This is beauty. This is poetry. This is joy. This is love.

This is everything that Hafiz and Rumi tried to convey in their poetry.

Tripping Over With Joy

What is the difference
Between your experience of Existence
And that of a saint?

The saint knows
That the spiritual path
Is a sublime chess game with God

And that the Beloved
Has just made such a Fantastic Move

That the saint is now continually
Tripping over Joy
And bursting out in Laughter
And saying, "I Surrender!"

Whereas, my dear,
I am afraid you still think
You have a thousand serious moves.

Hafiz, *I Heard God Laughing: Poems of Hope and Joy*

The funny thing is that I don't have a camera to capture this image. A few days ago, this would have been the worst thing imaginable, but now I'm delighted, because it means I'm not distracted from this gift, this opportunity to watch the most amazing natural show on Mother Earth: sunrise over Mount Everest.

I could never capture this moment on film anyway, and I'm delighted at the manner in which life unfolds, reminding me that everything happens for a reason, that we need to get out of our own way and stop trying to control life instead of allowing it to flow.

My soul had been touched and I shall be forever grateful for the sickness that caused me to stop, for the loss of my camera that caused me to watch, and the Grace of God, for bestowing the gift of light upon us all, and which is heightened (trust me) in the Himalayas, deepening my faith in the natural order of all life.

16

You can turn this world around,
and bring back all of those happy days
Put your troubles down.
It's time to celebrate.
Let love shine,
and we will find
a way to come together
and make things better.
We need a holiday.
"Holiday", Madonna

Day 9 continued: Kala Pattar and down to Dingboche

After the sun has risen, I descend the hill as quickly as I can. I'm almost running with the urgency to return to the lodge to lie down, feeling a little vulnerable on my own.

The dining room is busy with trekkers and Everest summiteers preparing for their day and I quickly scan the room for a spare bench. I see one to my side and take it over as mine, laying my head down on my daysack as I curl up into the foetal position, hanging my booted feet off the bench and to the side.

My head is still thumping, and the nausea has now become all-consuming. I'm desperate to sleep to distract me from my discomfort. It's easier said than done, as there's a real din in the dining room with the morning chatter, but I zone in and out, channelling Reiki onto my tummy and trying to breathe deeply.

An hour or so later (although I have very little concept of time) Joe joins me, shortly followed by Tim. Both boys tell me that they started to feel ill too and decided to descend rather than taking any chances. By now the dining room has quietened with most of the people having left. Joe lies down on another bench and Tim sits in one of the plastic chairs. All of us zone out, trying to manage the effects of the altitude in our own way.

Before too long, the jubilant faces of Will and Lilly appear in the dining room. They're high on their experience of making it all the way to the top of Kala Pattar and beaming from ear to ear. It just goes to show that you can never be sure how you'll fare in this environment. Lilly may have been the slowest walker and fretted more about the trek than the rest of us, but perhaps she's been the wisest for she paced herself well.

Tim, Joe and I are keen to leave immediately, but Will and Lilly are both exhausted and need some time to compose themselves. We grow restless waiting for them. Joe starts sulking, Tim starts pacing, and I pray that we can soon get moving! It seems to take ages for everyone to get their stuff together before we can finally leave the lodge and begin our descent.

Tim keeps asking us if we're OK, but no one is really OK, in fact, I'd say that we are a little miserable, certainly not what one would expect on a descent! The trouble is, we have to ascend to descend, and it's hard work as our legs feel so heavy from the morning's exertion.

Lilly suddenly bursts into tears. Not only is she tired from the trek up to Kala Pattar, but she's overwhelmed by the enormity of her morning and the fact we're rushing her down the mountain when she hasn't had a chance to process her experience. She's understandably proud of herself, but hasn't yet been able to celebrate.

I try to be compassionate, but it's difficult as I feel so wretched myself. Will encourages her to eat a Snickers bar to fuel her as we continue along the trail. We're all desperate to drop to a lower altitude as soon as we can. Easier said than done though, as we're not the only ones on the trail and we follow behind others on their way down to Lobuche too.

I'm not very aware of anything other than the horrible sulphuric taste in my mouth and the tightness in my stomach. I'm desperate for the sensation to ease, but I have a horrible feeling that I need to be sick first. Joe and I traipse along together, both looking pale and miserable and yet determined to descend as quickly as we can. We have a mission ahead of us today.

Fortunately, the descent to Lobuche is much easier than the ascent from there to Gorak Shep and we make it to the lodge where we stayed a night ago, in time for lunch. Unfortunately, the lodge brings back bad memories of headaches and food poisoning and I'm not keen to stop for too long. I'm not even that hungry, but I know that I need to eat and order myself some toast. Tim is feeling so sick that he can't even bring himself to stop for lunch and carries on ahead of us with one of our porters, who are now accompanying us.

I force myself to eat some toast, but it sits heavily in my mouth and no amount of chewing makes it any easier to swallow. A familiar Dutchman sits opposite us. He was staying in this lodge at the same time as us and he comments to Lilly that we all look unwell. Lilly relays the activity of the last few days. "You've all got a touch of altitude sickness," he tells us. "You've ascended too quickly and now you need to get down the mountain."

He's probably right, we should have taken our time, spent longer acclimatising. But the trouble is we've all been a bit gung-ho and naïve and just wanted to get on with making it to Base Camp, without having any awareness of what that actually meant in terms of altitude and its effect on our bodies – we're certainly learning the hard way.

I'm desperate to get going, but again it takes a while for Lilly and Will to get their things together and prepare to leave. It's snowing by the time we make it back outside and I'm now feeling very sick. We've not been walking far when I suddenly become very hot and start sweating profusely.

I know what's coming next and, sure enough, I find myself vomiting among the rocks of the moraine terrain. Gross. Will is quickly by my side and hands me a toilet roll and water, while Joe comes over and tries to make me smile, "I know that there is nothing I can do to make this situation any better," he says to me, "but… girl power", and with that he gives me a thumbs-up. I smile inside.

On we go, and I know that I'm going to be sick again. I can taste it in my mouth. Sure enough, fifteen minutes or so later the same thing happens. I become really hot and sweaty before I vomit all over the rocks to my side. Will hands me more toilet paper and water. "Done?" he asks. "Not sure," I say. But I am, thank goodness. The nausea has finally abated and the pounding in my head has eased.

As the next hour passes, I begin to feel more like my normal self and with each step down the mountain, I become more energised and my mood lifts. The increased energy is almost a little overwhelming and, at one point, I have so much energy that I am virtually running down the hill to Duglha where we stopped for lunch a few days ago when Matt and Ben were both really unwell. Running, free, descending, high off the extra oxygen in the air, I cannot believe the difference it makes to my sense of wellbeing and energy levels.

After Duglha we drop down to a bridge situated over a gushing stream that flows out of a glacier, and here the weather suddenly changes; the air cools and the wind picks up. I'm feeling tired now and the boys overtake Lilly and me, leaving us to walk with Dawa for what feels like an eternity. We're following an endless ridge where the yaks are sent out to pasture and I'm reminded of Dartmoor again as we continue through windswept and damp long grass. Soon the clouds close in around us limiting our visibility and it feels very bleak, reflecting my mood.

Lilly gets really angry. She's exhausted and longs to make it to the lodge and here we are, endlessly walking with the mist all around us; it's hard work. Dawa makes the mistake of telling us that it would only take a further 40 minutes to reach the lodge where we will be staying for the night, but after 30 minutes he tells us we still have another 30 minutes to go. Light snow starts to fall again and the light is decreasing. I begin to wonder what would happen if we got lost in these mountains.

Lilly moans to me about Dawa underestimating the distance, "How much longer? How much longer?" she asks him over and over again, as if pleading with him to tell her we don't have long. But he's learned not to give us a timeframe, and responds with, "Soon, soon, come, come", as he ushers us along with him.

The wind soon whistles along the ridge and we have to hug in on ourselves to escape the penetrating cold. I can feel Lilly's anger. She's beside herself with agitation and I let her vent her frustration. "I'm sick of this trek. I just want to get there," she almost shouts at me.

"I know," I tell her, "me too, but try and focus on something positive, like the fact we'll soon be able to have a shower."

This is what is keeping me going. It's been days now and with being sick I'm keen to change out of my dirty clothes and wash my body clean. I long to brush my teeth, too, and drink some tea. I'm also looking forward to having a rest day tomorrow to recover from the trek thus far and to have the opportunity to get back on my mat and drop into my space; I feel adrift when I don't have this opportunity.

Eventually, I see the stupa where I sat and wrote poetry a few days ago, and I know that it can't be far. We just need to drop down the ridge. I try to tell Lilly this to lift her mood, but she won't believe me. She's now seething with anger. Nothing I say will appease her, but I know we'll be there soon. She just needs to hang on a little while longer.

We dip down the other side of the ridge and I'm overcome with relief as it's sheltered and we're gifted a break from the wind. Furthermore, in the distance and walking towards us out of the clouds and the dusk, appears Pemba, with a big smile on his face. We're delighted, and Lilly smiles for the first time since returning from Kala Pattar earlier in the morning.

I can't see too much of Dingboche, as the clouds and mist are hiding it, but I'm told it's a beautiful village of scattered houses, with views of the snow-capped summits of Island Peak and Lhotse. It's often used as a place to stay on the descent from Base Camp, being 130 metres higher than Pheriche, so trekkers generally stay at the lower elevation of Pheriche on the ascent and walk here on rest day to help with acclimatising. (We made it halfway here when we trekked to the Stupa on our rest day.)

The high pastures in this region are sometimes referred to as summer villages and Sherpas with homes lower in the valley often own the small stone huts in this higher region and occupy them in summer while their herds of yak graze in the surrounding pastures. It's interesting to me how the landscape and terrain can change so quickly – there's life again down here.

Pemba leads us into the small and cosy dining room of the lodge where all the boys are sitting together drinking tea. It's lovely to see Matt, Ben and Craig looking so well. They tell us that they've been waited on hand and foot, lying in bed reading books and eating biscuits. Bless them, everyone is the happiest they've been all week! Craig says that he can't remember anything about being in Gorak Shep yesterday. I think he is a little embarrassed about the whole incident.

Lilly and I share a lovely spacious and light room with large windows and I look forward to rolling my mat out for a yoga practice on our rest day. Right now, though, my focus is on having a shower, and I cannot tell you how excited I am about this.

The shower cubicle is located in the backyard, a little out of sight of the dining room. It takes twenty minutes for the water to boil. However, it's worth every minute of that wait and every rupee I pay for the privilege. It's also worth every moment that I'm cold, as I remove my clothes in the mountain air and stand barefoot on the cool slate, which forms the base for the shower.

When the warm water washes over my body I smile, for it feels so lovely. I've been dreaming of this moment all day. It's not the longest shower I've ever taken. There's just the one bucket of water so I have to use the water wisely, but I manage to wash my body and my hair, which makes me feel like a new person!

I catch a glimpse of myself in the small mirror perched on a wooden beam within the cubicle. I haven't seen my reflection since we started the trek and it's strange to see my face, let alone my body, which is certainly thinner than it was when we began in Lukla.

I cover myself with as much of my small travel towel as it will allow, before running back into the lodge and up the stairs to our room. Combing my tangled hair is a challenge, but I manage this eventually. The real delight, however, comes in putting on my comfy pyjamas, my big woolly Tibetan socks I bought from a Tibetan trader in Namche Bazaar, my shawl, some earrings and a bright pink scarf – it's the best I can do to try to look pretty!

I join the others in the central dining room where the energy is high as everyone is relieved to be on the descent. Pemba is insistent I eat, even though my stomach still feels a little delicate after my earlier vomiting. Dinner is served and I feel like a princess sitting cross-legged on a heap of pillows placed on the bench and positioned at the head of the table, in front of the window. I'm on top of the world compared to how I felt earlier in the day.

The boys are hyper, Joe particularly, and they chatter and joke incessantly. Everyone is happy with the extra oxygen nourishing their brains. Not one of us truly understood what life would be like on the way to Everest Base Camp, and it's amazing that we survived as well as we did. Trekking in the Himalayas is certainly not for the faint-hearted and demands a certain level of respect.

After dinner, Pemba tells us that we will be celebrating with the porters tonight – he's worried that we've all had an awful time on this journey and he is eager for us to have some fun. Given the events of the day, I just want to go to bed and read my book, but there is no getting out of it as Pemba is very determined that we will celebrate together as a group.

So it begins, celebrating the Nepali way – or the Pemba way at least. He pours everyone a shot of whisky with Coke – Craig and I decline. Neither of us likes to drink alcohol these days and Pemba respects our choice. Then the chairs are cleared to the side of the room and the proprietor of the lodge rigs up an old stereo and Nepali music soon fills the air. Within minutes the porters are up off their chairs and dancing around the room, the whisky warming their blood and the music touching their hearts and souls.

We sit and watch with a look of utter disbelief on our faces – we've never seen anything like it. The men dance with such femininity, moving their hips and twirling their arms. They dance towards one another, like lovers, acting out a story, around and around each other, joy illuminating their faces, gesturing with their hands, their arms, their eyes and their bodies. What a dance. It is utterly incredible and totally mesmerising.

Pemba encourages us all up onto the dancefloor. I resist as long as I can, not simply because my stomach hurts and my pyjama bottoms threaten to fall down but because I enjoy watching everyone else and taking photos of their antics. Joe makes me laugh. He is dancing like he is at a rave, while Matt is all arms and legs and Ben is very shy and doesn't know how to move his body.

It's such a funny scene, everyone trying to dance to this unfamiliar Nepali music. The two Polish men and two South African women who are also staying in the lodge for the night join in and the older porters are particularly animated. They look so happy as they drink their whisky and gyrate their hips. They clearly love to dance and let their hair down.

Pemba tells me that the joy of dancing, and watching others dance, is a predominant Nepali pastime. It's a very poor country, but that doesn't stop the locals from wanting to have fun, and for many dancing is the surest, if not the only, form of entertainment available to them. As I'm discovering now for myself, peer pressure is integral to Nepali dance – it seems to me that this involves playing some loud music, goading everyone up off their chairs and then dancing around them clapping and gyrating your hips.

It's a lot of fun, spirits are high and the room is filled with the sound of laughter. Lilly and Will buy everyone more whisky and Coke and the dining room is now really warm from a combination of the heat from the stove, all the dancing and the red whisky-touched faces. We've bonded over dance in the Himalayas, it's hilarious.

However, we're also exhausted and in bed by 9.30pm, late by our standards. I couldn't be happier though, snug in my sleeping bag, with no headache, safe in the knowledge that I've gone as far as I could on the trail and that earlier that morning I saw the sun rising over Everest! I wonder what delights still await us and mentally make a note to try and enjoy every last bit of the trek.

17

Look at me standing
here on my own again.
Up straight in the sunshine.
No need to run and hide.
It's a wonderful wonderful life.
No need to laugh and cry.
It's a wonderful, wonderful life.
"Wonderful Life", Black

Day 10: Dingboche (4,410m), rest day.

It's a miracle; I awake at 7am without a headache. What a relief! Lilly and I rejoice at feeling normal for the first time in days.

"Oh, my gosh, this is amazing," I say to Lilly.

"What?" she asks

"Lying here in my bed feeling cosy and knowing that we don't need to go anywhere today. It's such a relief."

"Yay, we just get to chill out today," Lilly agrees. "What are we going to do?"

"Well I don't know about you," I tell her, "but I'm going to do a really lovely long yoga practice because I haven't practised for three whole days, which is the longest I've ever gone without practising."

"You're going to have to teach me," Lilly says.

"Oh, don't worry," I respond. "When we get to the rural village I shall make it my mission."

And I mean it. Joe is interested too and I've told them that I'll teach them when we have more space available to us and it's not so cold, so we can practise outside. Today, I have the space in the room and I cannot wait. It's going to be a real treat.

Before then, Lilly and I make the most of the opportunity to sit outside on a stone ledge beside the lodge with the early morning sun shining on our faces as we leisurely drink our fresh mint tea and smoke. It's a little warmer down here than it's been the last few days. We no longer need scarves and gloves – it helps that we're sheltered from the wind too.

We watch a couple of young local children with snotty noses wandering around to our side, holding small bowls of porridge in their hands, eating on the go, their faces and clothes covered in dirt.

"It's got to be tough," I comment, "trying to keep clean out here."

"Definitely," Lilly agrees. "I guess you just get used to it, and anyway it's more challenging than at home."

She's right, life is different in Nepal, especially in this mountainous environment. There are no washing machines, or purpose-built bathrooms like we enjoy back home. You're much more vulnerable to the elements and to this unforgiving landscape where you have to walk everywhere. Washing your clothes and your body becomes less pressing than it might for us back home, where we have hot clean water available to us at the turn of a tap. It's so easy to take it for granted and coming here has been a good lesson in gratitude.

There is a saying that gratitude turns what you have into enough and more. Yet it's all too easy to overlook what you have in the quest for what you don't have. Seeing how happy people appear along the trail, when they have so little, makes me think. So, too, considering all the mod cons we have at home, let alone economic, political and environmental stability. It's far too easy to take this all for granted, to forget how lucky we are, and to feel gratitude. I'm pleased of the reminder and increased awareness.

Soon the boys are also awake, feeling happier than they have done the last few days.

"The changing altitude made us all depressed," Will comments over breakfast.

"Hmm, interesting," I respond. "You're right, we were all a bit down. I just hadn't associated it with the lack of oxygen."

And it is interesting because there is probably some truth in Will's observations. I believe we were all challenged in our own ways by illness and by feeling well and truly out of our comfort zones. Certainly, the lack of oxygen didn't help with all that and I'm grateful for the insight that this experience has provided too. This is probably the reason yoga, with its emphasis on breathing, can help so much in relieving depression. Having more oxygen in our blood, nourishing our cells, let alone the extra prana running through our energy channels, can only ever be a good thing!

We're also feeling positive not only because we're on a rest day and there's more oxygen in the air, but also because we're descending the mountain and will soon be closer to civilization (as we know it) and the opportunity to contact our families and friends back home. I've never been out of touch from my family as long as I have been these last few days. It's a strange feeling not being able to telephone home at a whim or send an email or check for messages on my phone. In many respects, it's refreshing.

We're in no hurry to do anything, so I rejoice in the opportunity to return to bed after breakfast and read my book. It feels so decadent and yet so guilt-free because we're meant to be doing nothing and resting, and that's the joy of life in these mountains, as a trekker at least. No one is demanding anything of me and there's no deadline(s) to meet. I can't get the Internet and my phone doesn't work in Nepal. It's bliss!

I join the rest of the group for lunch and discover that they've been playing card games together all morning, while drinking steaming cups of black Nescafé coffee and consuming large quantities of chocolate. They've eaten all the Snicker bars and have now moved on to Mars bars.

After lunch, it starts lightly snowing again, so I wrap myself in my sleeping bag and lie on my bed, gazing out through the large window. To the side of our lodge, and visible from the window, are some small fields separated from one another by neat drystone walls. From what I can tell, the locals use the fields to grow crops. To plough the land, oxen are still used, as there are no tractors.

Unfortunately, the farmers are having a hard time getting the oxen to plough in a straight line, and the furrows are all haphazard. I watch as the farmers whack the oxen on their hindquarters to try and encourage them back in line. At the edge of the field, I can see our porters and a few local men standing around together all wearing jogging bottoms and T-shirts, with plastic sandals on their feet (it's snowing!), watching the scene like it's reality TV.

To be honest it's the closest thing to TV or indeed live entertainment around here at the moment and that's not a criticism, just a reality! In the field adjacent to the oxen, a Nepali woman and a young girl are turning the hard soil by hand to plant potatoes, the staple food in the mountains. It looks like such hard work, especially in this cold weather, and the disparity between our lives makes me feel a little uncomfortable. Here I am loafing about, while they are working hard just to be able to feed themselves.

I ask Pemba about the agricultural situation in Nepal and he tells me that it is based on subsistence farming, particularly in the hilly regions, where the locals live off these fragmented plots of land cultivated in difficult conditions. Some manage to make a meagre income from selling any additional supplies. Pemba believes that as much as 80% of the population is involved in agriculture and the most widely grown crops are rice, wheat, maize, sugarcane, oilseed and potatoes. There is livestock too, mainly cattle, goats and poultry.

Once the oxen get back into their stride again and start ploughing straighter lines, I drag myself out of bed and enjoy a long overdue yoga practice on my mat. It's blissful to be able to lie down and breathe consciously while stretching my aching limbs after the days of trekking and the nights of sleeping on the relatively uncomfortable wooden bedframes with the thinnest of mattresses upon them.

There's a certain feeling of coming home to myself the moment I get on my yoga mat, particularly after a few days away from it. That's not to say I haven't been aware of how

I've been feeling; far from it, the mountains have demanded total awareness of all aspects of my being. In particular, I've been aware of the strain that the trekking has placed on my body and I've also been aware of my monkey mind with all its thinking, and the manner in which I've been emotionally challenged, and spiritually uplifted.

However, there is a certain comfort that comes from lying down and having the time and the space to truly check in and see what is going on, to ask the question, "How am I feeling?" and to check through each of the energy centres in turn, while also gaining an awareness of where I'm feeling tension in the body and whether anything is playing on my mind and what's going on emotionally and how my energy levels are doing (where is the energy stuck?). Also to see how I'm feeling in spirit – connected or lonesome.

I feel lighter. Not least in body, having lost weight trekking, but energetically too. I feel like I've let go of some of the emotional stuff I've been carrying, what with the tearful outbursts and the releases that have accompanied them. Also, there's been a shift in my mental state, as I've been encouraged to let go of stuff that I've been holding on to, whether that be trekking to the top of Kala Pattar, or not being able to use my broken camera, plus of course the letting go that accompanies being out of the comfort zone. I have a greater sense of the energy within my body, as if the mountains somehow enhance this connection, and I feel increasingly energised as we now descend.

Spiritually I feel nourished by the exposure to Tibetan Buddhism and my interactions with the porters. I'm also inspired by the Buddhist teachings with their emphasis on the Middle Way. I'm also touched by the notion of living with compassion for all beings, which is at the heart of the Buddhist teachings. Often the greatest challenge is having compassion for ourselves, and this trek has helped me to notice some of my self-deprecating tendencies. I have also become increasingly aware of the manner in which we can judge ourselves and others (and be judged!).

There is something transformative about being in the mountains, and with the boys, the combination challenging me on every level. It's a joy to have space and solitude away from the rest of the group for the first time properly in days. I've missed this. I can truly drop in. There's nothing that I'd rather be doing right now than breathing consciously on my mat in peace!

18

People they come together
People they fall apart
No one can stop us now
'Cos we are all made of stars
People they come together
And people they fall apart
No one can stop us now
'Cos we are all made of stars
"We Are All Made of Stars", Moby

Day 11: Dingboche to Tengboche

By the time Lilly and I make it to breakfast, Craig, Ben and Matt have already left the lodge with Dawa to climb Island Peak (Imja Tse), a 6,189m peak a bit further east. It's something that they organised prior to arriving in Nepal – it was an additional option on our gap-year programme that I hadn't realised. We just hope that they can all cope with the terrain and the altitude, and laugh about the fact it was the three of them who got altitude sickness in the first place.

We also laugh because Pemba is hungover today. He tries to deny it, but we can smell it on his breath and see it in his eyes, plus he is extraordinarily quiet – he hadn't returned home by the time we went to bed, so we've no idea where he got to, but surmise he must have been having some fun. He really is a charmer with the Sherpinis that one!

Today we're trekking to Tengboche, so we need to drop down (down!) the valley to Orsho, and follow the west bank of the fast-flowing Imja Khola to Shomare and on to Pangboche. From Pangboche we'll retrace our footsteps down to the Imja Khola again and up through the forest, past to Debuche Nunnery and into Tengboche. I suspect that it will be much easier and more enjoyable than our ascent!

It helps that today has dawned beautifully bright and sunny, quite a contrast to yesterday, and Lilly and I are both jubilant as we walk and talk – this morning's topic is about what we are going to do when we finish the trek. We've been told that we'll be staying in a rural village called Bupsa, a day's trek away from Lukla, where we'll be helping out at the local village school, building a new classroom.

I haven't really given it too much thought, but now we're here, and gaining a sense of life in the mountains, I'm both excited and apprehensive. We've also been told that we'll be staying in a house on our own and we'll have access to fresh and locally grown vegetables. This certainly makes me feel happy. If there's one thing I'm beginning to miss, it's fresh vegetables. I'm also missing fresh fruit. The most we've managed is the odd bit of cut apple in our porridge, quite in contrast to both the amount and volume of fruit I eat back home – there's been no 'five a day' this last week!

I really love the passing landscape today. I'm much more aware of it than I was on the ascent, simply because it's much easier going downhill than it was going up! We pass terraced fields marked by drystone walls and walk through small hamlets containing stone-built houses with brightly painted door frames and roofs (lots of blues and greens, albeit faded by the sunshine). The spring energy is in the air again, and I feel as if the spring has returned to my step.

The three boys walk on ahead of us, Tim the sensible one, while Joe and Will stop every so often to play-fight with their walking poles, pretending they're starring in a *Star Wars* film. It's very entertaining, especially when we pass other trekkers who think the boys are crazy! That's the great thing now, we're the ones descending and full of smiles, while those ascending are much more serious in comparison, "Namaste, Namaste, Namaste".

The trail is busy today, especially late morning, after our tea stop. I'm still absolutely in awe of the amount of stuff the porters carry on their backs and I can't stop commenting on it to Lilly.

"But look at them, it's amazing," I say. "They're so strong to be able to carry such loads on their backs."

"Yes," she agrees. "There's no way people back home would be able to carry those loads, at least not without complaining."

"And the incredible thing," I add, "is the fact that they do it with a smile on their faces."

"I know," she agrees. "I'm just thankful I haven't had to carry my bag while out here."

"Tell me about it, and it's incredible that they've been carrying two or three bags at a time, when we couldn't even carry one! It's the furniture I'm most blown away by," I add, recalling to mind the porters I saw carrying six-foot wooden doors up the mountain the other day, let alone those carrying stacks of plastic chairs somehow attached to their backs.

We pass Sherpini porters too, short Nepali Sherpa women who grimace with the weight of their loads, wearing skirts, old t-shirts, head scarves and simple trainers. I feel irrationally guilty again for the stark contrast in our lives and the inequality in this world – here I am walking beside these struggling Sherpini women, a Western woman, able to afford to pay someone to carry her bag and to wear proper shoes on her feet, just because I was born in one of the more affluent parts of the world.

At lunch, Will and I are at loggerheads. I know I need to let it go, but we have this tedious conversation about what to eat in the mountains. He has this thing about the menus up here offering Western food – it's not exactly Western food as we imagine it, or indeed know it to be, and he cannot understand why the restaurants don't simply stick to Nepali dishes.

I appreciate his sentiments, and agree that perhaps there really is no need to pamper to the Westerner but he contradicts himself repeatedly by choosing the Western dishes and then being bitterly disappointed with what he is served. Needless to say, this lunchtime is no different as he,

Joe and Lilly order cheeseburgers while Tim and I stick to the more 'local' option of sweet and sour vegetables and rice.

Admittedly Lilly and Joe do nothing to assist this situation as they reminisce about the large and succulent cheeseburgers served in one of the pubs back home in Guernsey. All three of them grow increasingly excited therefore about the prospect of the cheeseburgers they've ordered.

But we are in the Nepali Himalayas.

Supplies are limited.

Life is simple.

There is no electricity and no running water in most of the lodges.

There are no ovens, grills or microwaves, no fridges and freezers.

Food is cooked on a wood-burning or kerosene stove.

There are no supermarkets or grocery stores.

Supplies must be carried here, on foot, by porters.

Needless to say, when the cheeseburgers are served they do not quite live up to expectations.

"This is not a cheeseburger," Will laments, as he picks up the crumbly, semi-toasted and long-life piece of white 'bread', which smells of preservative and promptly falls apart in his hand, to reveal a cheeseburger – quite literally – a concoction of something resembling cheese shaped into a burger. "Can they get nothing right?" he laments in a frustrated tone. "They just have no idea, these people. Why do they bother to put Western food on the menu when they don't know how to make Western food?" He gestures to the mess on his plate. "This is not a cheeseburger," he repeats, exasperated.

I can't resist. "They're trying to please people like you," I tentatively start. "You order Western food, so they continue to serve Western food and therefore you're simply fueling this situation."

"But it is not Western food," he retorts. "It's what they think is Western food, but I bet none of these people have ever been to the West, and anyway," he looks at me, "you've been moaning about the food too." This is true, but I have also accepted that it is not going to be haute cuisine up here. I'm more concerned about the lack of fresh fruit and vegetables and the effect this is going to have on my state of health, rather than my taste buds.

I sigh. It's a hopeless conversation. Thankfully, Lilly and Joe find the whole situation hilarious and we all laugh as Lilly attempts to pick up her cheeseburger and eat it only to find that it literally disintegrates in her hands too.

It's a beautiful afternoon with bright, sunny skies as Lilly and I trek with Pemba through the woods, so that we're soon surrounded by tall trees in spring leaf, both grounding and slightly ethereal – there's something about woods that always finds me looking for nymphs and fairies! I love hearing the birds singing and chattering to one another and smelling that woody and earthy smell that accompanies wooded landscapes. What a joy to be alive! I'm really beginning to love this country, and especially now, in springtime.

At Tenboche, our porters greet us at the lodge where we're due to stay. We've been told that it's one of the best lodges in the region, but there's disappointing news for us. The lodge is very busy and they don't have enough rooms for us so we'll all need to sleep together in the attic. We take a look. It's a large room accessible by a ladder, with plastic sheeting covering the windows and five mattresses laid out next to each other on the floor – it seems fine to us, warm at least.

I'm pleased to have the opportunity to roll out my yoga mat in such a spacious environment and, while the others play cards downstairs in the dining room, I practice asana, stretching my still-aching limbs while focusing on my breath. I feel so much more energised than I have done for days and much more centred and balanced. I listen to sacred chanting playing on my iPod, oblivious to the noise downstairs, enjoying the time on my own and the solitude that this provides.

There is more joy ahead – a gas-heated shower in a proper bathroom. How novel, indeed! We each take a turn, and when it's mine, I make the most of the opportunity to stand under the shower head and allow the hot water to wash over me. I could stand here for hours, it's the most amazing feeling to have a proper shower again, but I'm also acutely aware that someone has had to carry the heavy gas canisters all the way up the mountain, and I don't want to add to their burden unnecessarily.

It's taken a week or so, but I'm beginning to appreciate the impact I'm having on this environment and the fact that my every action has a consequence. It's all very well all this yoga and trying in some small way to help myself be a happier and more peaceful person, but it can't just stop there, it has to move beyond the mat and help to impact positively on the outer world, in the decisions I make and the manner in which I live. As Gandhi said, "If we could change ourselves, the tendencies in the world would also change. As a man changes his own nature, so does the attitude of the world change towards him…We need not wait to see what others do". (Often quoted as 'Be the change you wish to see in the world.')

That's one of the reasons I've become frustrated with Will's attitude the last few days. He very much sees the Nepali people as separate to him, as if he's better than they are. It's ridiculous, as we're all the same, we're all people, and the Nepalis are doing their best to earn an honest living, just like we do back home in the West. But sadly Will can't see this and maybe he never will, which is a shame because the world needs more people coming together and respecting different cultures and ways of living.

Dinner is an exciting affair for us tonight; roast chicken for the carnivores and a vegetable curry with potato, carrots and cauliflower for me – heaven indeed. The boys are beside themselves with excitement about the chicken, although find complaint even here – it's too bony apparently! Bony chicken aside, we're not surprised that this is such a popular lodge, as it's luxurious in comparison to the other lodges we've stayed along the trail.

After dinner, we sit around playing cards together while drinking fresh mint tea. It's a sociable thing this trekking malarkey. The lack of TV and Internet encourages us to find other ways to spend our time, and playing cards is good fun. We're soon joined by a group of five Australian men who are ascending, and we tell them to take it slowly, learn from our mistake. I want everyone to learn from our mistake. If you find yourself undertaking a trek up high, then take it slowly please, "Bistari, bistari!"

Bedtime adds a challenge to the day. We're all lying in our sleeping bags in the darkness. I'm at one end of the line and Tim is at the other end, with Will, Joe and Lilly in between us. I'm just falling asleep when all of a sudden Will and Joe launch a surprise pillow attack on Tim. Poor Tim deals with it all in good humour, much better than I would do, and I grow tired of Will and Joe chuckling. Still, sleep comes easily in the mountains and I drift off without a pillow being thrown at me!

19

Every breath you take,
every move you make,
every vow you break,
every step you take,
I'll be watching you.
"Every Breath You Take", The Police

Day 12: Tengboche to Namche Bazaar

The dining room is a hive of activity this morning; we discover that twenty people are staying here as part of a BBC Horizon documentary about the effects of altitude on the body. They have to keep testing each other's vital signs throughout the day to check for subtle changes and it is intended that their findings will be shown on television in the following autumn.

The early morning sun rises behind the trees and the grass glistens with dew, while a sense of peace and new beginnings permeates the air. Will and Joe run around each other, pretending to be Luke Skywalker again, play-fighting with their walking poles. I have to laugh. How did I find myself trekking in Nepal with these boys?

We walk up the hill to Tengboche Monastery where we stopped almost a week ago now. Today the scene is very different to the foggy and icy one we experienced previously. Instead, the sun shines brightly and there's not a cloud in the sky. It's like visiting a totally different place – I can now see the scrub pines and dwarf rhododendrons, which grow on the crescent-shaped ridge that the village is scattered within.

I am surprised to find horses trotting in the meadow across from the monastery and near the Sacred Land Eco Centre. We're blown away by the manner in which the weather has shown a whole new side to the village – it's very pretty and strangely reflects my changing mood – foggy and distracted the other day and now clear and present!

Pemba leads us up to the top of the hill, where we are provided with awe-inspiring views over the mountains. *Wow!* Looking north, and over the saddle of the town, we can see the distinctive peak of Ama Dablam, standing proud of the massif containing Mount Everest, Nuptse and Lhotse. Looking south you can glimpse Kantega, Thamserku and Kongde Ri. I'll admit that if it wasn't for Tim, I wouldn't have a clue which mountain is which, aside from Mount Everest!

Tenzing Norgay, the first man to reach the summit of Mount Everest with Sir Edmund Hillary, was born in this area and was once sent to Tengboche Monastery to be a monk. I imagine that with views of those stunning peaks staring at you every day, you'd definitely be keen to get closer to them.

We continue along the trail. It's challenging for my knees as we make a steep descent down the very dusty steps of the narrow path to the river valley below. I'm pleased I've got walking poles to support me; in many respects, it's as demanding as going up in the first place, just in a different way. The dust continues to cling to our faces and congeal in our noses, causing Lilly to sneeze frequently and me to blow my nose constantly. It's an irritant and I'm grateful for my sunglasses, which are essential to protect my eyes.

We stop briefly for morning tea at the base of the valley. Pemba is keen for us to keep moving as much as we can today, as we're headed for Namche Bazaar and we've got a good distance to cover. We're keen to get there as soon as we can too. The prospect of technology and the opportunity to send emails and telephone family back home is creating some excitement within our little group.

But it's turning out to be another day of hard trekking, as we have to climb up the valley and around to the next ridge. The boys rush off on their own and Lilly and I try to distract each other from the uphill hike by chattering again about our lives and what on earth we're going to do after our time in Nepal.

"I just don't know that I want to return to Guernsey," I tell Lilly. "I'm definitely going to get my Indian visa like you and just go to India and see what happens."

"Yes, let's definitely go to India," she agrees. "Tim and Joe have got their visas too, so we could all go together."

"Maybe," I say, "although I'd like to go and see the yoga places and I'm not sure the boys will want to do that."

"Well, I'll come with you," Lilly says," although I've only got a month before I have to return to Guernsey for work."

"You're lucky that you can take time out from your job like this," I tell her, knowing that her employer has given her a three-month sabbatical on top of the other sabbaticals she's had over her years of travel.

"I know," she agrees. "They're really decent to me."

"You never know what might happen over the next two months in Nepal," I tell her. "Maybe we'll meet our soulmates and never leave," I joke.

"Well you never know," she jokes back at me, "although I can't imagine living in Nepal."

"Oh, I don't know," I say, "there's something about this country that I love already, but we've still got so much to see. I just wish my life would move forward after this trip. I've either got to commit to B or move on from him, but it's so difficult to get clarity on this," I tell her honestly.

"It's difficult, isn't it, but do you really think B's the one for you?" she asks.

"Oh, I don't know," I tell her, desperation in my voice, knowing deep down that he's not, but not yet ready to admit it to myself.

I've been so consumed by surviving the trek that I've not given too much thought to the future. Instead, I've either been processing (or attempting to process) the past, or coming to terms with the present. Now that we're descending and I'm not experiencing any of the negative effects of the altitude, and as we move closer to completing the journey, and with that, the first stage of my trip to Nepal, my attention has shifted again to the future.

B and I are accustomed to this separation now, as I have been travelling on and off the last few years. We're also accustomed to the fact that our relationship is stuck. It's easier for us both to overlook this rather than deal with it head-on. I have a feeling that B is hoping that I will get travelling 'out of my system', but being away and experiencing different cultures, countries and ways of living, only serves to fuel my passion for travel, not dampen it.

Our relationship is a conundrum that will no doubt continue to play around and around on my mind while I'm in Nepal. Ultimately, I need to step into the fear of being on my own, but I'm not ready to do that yet. There's still some processing and inner work that needs to be done first.

We stop for tea at the top of the long climb to Kyangjuma, where there are various lodges and vendors' souvenir stalls. Nepal has always been a nation of traders, with most of the trails having evolved from the trade routes – generations of porters have carried goods back and forth from India and Tibet, as people have little choice but to trade by foot.

It's getting warmer the closer we get to Namche and I lean against a stone wall enjoying the morning sun, while watching Pemba and our porters studying the trainers for sale. Pemba comes over to tell us that the trainers are much cheaper here than they would be in Kathmandu. They're also considerably cheaper than they would be for us to buy back at home in the UK.

The boys chatter about trainers and I lose interest, focusing my attention instead on four young girls sitting on a handmade wooden bench outside the door of a simple stone house that looks little more than one big room. It's clearly hair-washing day, as all four girls have wet hair and the eldest moves from one to the next brushing each sister's long dark hair. One of the younger girls cries. She clearly doesn't like her hair being brushed any more than little girls back at home.

I imagine what it might be like living here and conclude that life would be very different. There would be a simplicity that is lacking to my life in Guernsey, even 'time' seems to have slowed down. There's much greater awareness of the changing seasons, as life is dependent on a good harvest to provide food for the family. Then there's the whole water issue, as the villagers use a central tap, and the water is cold – no hot showers or long and lazy baths! You've also no guarantee that the water won't cause tummy upsets.

The houses tend to be split between two levels and are built of stone. The lower level is used to house livestock, fodder, food and firewood, while the upper storey houses the living quarters. The floor of this room is wooden and covered with carpets and rugs. There's often very limited furniture; platforms and benches are used for sitting and sleeping, with the whole family (when children are younger) sleeping together. A small area of the house is set aside for the altar, where incense may be burned – I like this idea. At home, the best I can manage is the corner of a room!

In terms of health, if you're sick, it's not a case of simply driving to your local doctor's surgery or to the hospital. Furthermore, education is not necessarily on the doorstep either. Fortunately, though, the Sherpas have benefitted in both respects from the Himalayan Trust, which is a non-profit humanitarian organisation first established in the 1960s by Sir Edmund Hillary, who led the Trust until his death in 2008.

Sir Edmund was passionate about the country and the welfare of the Sherpas, having been the first mountaineer to reach the summit of Mount Everest on 29 May 1953 (with Nepali Sherpa mountaineer Tenzing Norgay, referred to earlier). It is said that he never anticipated the acclaim that followed the historic ascent. He was knighted in 1953 shortly after the expedition returned to London. From 1985 to 1988 he served as New Zealand's High Commissioner to India, Nepal and Bangladesh.

The Himalayan Trust aims to improve the health, education, and general well-being of people living in Solumkhumbu (the Everest region of Nepal), and is a registered charity, with its headquarters in New Zealand. The first major project of the Himalayan Trust took place in 1961 with the building of the first school in this region of Nepal. The Trust ended up building 26 schools in total over a period of 30 years.

These schools were initially staffed and funded through the Trust until 1972 when the Nepali Government took over the administration of all schools and education in the area. However, the Trust has a formal agreement with the Nepali Government to continue to provide teaching resources and support to schools within this region, including teacher training, adult literacy classes and scholarships.

In 1964, Sir Edmund Hillary recognised that the transportation of building materials needed to be easier, so the Himalayan Trust built an airstrip in Lukla (the one we flew into). This is now the second busiest airstrip in Nepal and is fundamental to the trekking industry in this part of the country, which provides a much-needed income to the Sherpas. That same year, the other Trust projects included the construction of a school in Namche and a bridge over the rough waters of the Dudh Kosi.

In 1966 the Himalayan Trust built a small hospital at Khunde to improve healthcare in the region. The building of Phaplu Hospital followed in 1975, helping to improve access to medical facilities. Both hospitals were initially staffed by volunteer doctors from New Zealand and Canada working for periods of two years. Eventually, both hospitals were handed over to local doctors. However, the Trust continues to provide funding, training and medical supplies to the hospitals and also to 13 village clinics.

Pemba tells me that there has been a positive shift in community health since these clinics were set up, including the eradication of TB for example, and also the elimination of goitre (an abnormal enlargement of the thyroid gland) through something as simple as iodine injections. There have also been major improvements in maternal care, meaning that not as many mothers and children die in childbirth and early childhood.

Furthermore, (as if what they have done isn't already amazing!), the Trust has planted over a million trees and built micro-hydro plants. The Trust also helped to restore Tengboche Monastery (which we have recently visited) and Thame, the community's central sacred sites. It is hardly surprising, perhaps, that Sir Edmund Hillary was made an honorary citizen of Nepal in 2003!

We soon continue along the trail towards the settlement of Sanga, passing a huge Mani stone in the process. This stops us in our tracks and has us reaching for our cameras – it's a surprise, and yet I should know now to expect the unexpected while in these mountains! When we reach Sanga, which is primarily inhabited by Tibetans, we stop at one of the many teashops and sit inside to escape the burning heat of the sun's midday rays. (Hoorah for the sun and its much-welcomed warmth, even though it is burning strongly.) However, the smoke from the wood-fueled stove becomes so overpowering (a good insight into the living conditions of the local people) that we decide to go outside and risk the sunburn instead.

Pemba rushes around helping the elderly Tibetan lady cook our lunch. He insists we all eat the same dish of vegetable fried rice, with an optional fried egg and yak's cheese. We can tell that this is important to him and for once we don't complain. We're just grateful for the food and I'm pleased that we can somehow help this elderly lady make a small income.

There's a souvenir stall selling Tibetan wares to the side of the trail, and I go over to take a look. The smiling Tibetan lady is selling an assortment of trinkets, jewellery and spiritual knick-knacks, the kind of stuff I love to buy. After a little deliberation, I decide on a Tibetan turquoise necklace. I then have to barter with the lady and while she offers me a price of 350 rupees, I bravely knock down to 300 rupees. I'm delighted when she accepts my offer, which is a little over £3, but a sufficient amount in Nepal. I've no idea whether I've got a good price, but what does it matter? It's Tibetan turquoise and here I am surrounded by Tibetans in the Himalayas. It's worth every rupee!

The afternoon is a chore – there is no other way to describe it, as we seemingly trek solely uphill, one dusty step after another. We're following the trail to Pemba's old school at Khumjung (3,780m) and we're making his life a misery as we endlessly moan at him. Joe, in particular, just cannot help himself and he reminds me of Kevin, of the teenagers in the film *Kevin & Perry Go Large*, who goes on a trip to Ibiza with his parents and sulks an awful lot. Joe's sulking exactly like Kevin, hiding behind the hood of his bright red hoodie, head down, twiddling endlessly with his hair and whinging and moaning on and on – even the rest of us are sick of him!

He doesn't help himself because at one point we're walking up yet another set of steps, when he announces that he has accidentally left one of his poles at the bottom of it. How did he not notice? Needless to say, he's now too tired and too sulky to be bothered to walk back down to retrieve it. Lilly and I volunteer, but he won't hear of it. We can only laugh at him, revelling in his sulkiness and frustration. Poor Joe!

I'm amazed when we finally arrive at Khumjung, as it is far larger than I had anticipated, and much grander too. Pemba tells me that it's the largest village in the Khumbu region and many locals own tracts of land further north along the valley. It's clearly a wealthy place as the neat and tidy stone houses are large and ostentatious, built as they are into the crook of the sacred peak of Khumbila (5,761m) above.

It's clearly a well-cared for place too, as the majority of the houses are painted cream or white, with blue and white painted window frames and green painted roofs. I'm tickled because not only does the village house the 'Highest Bakery in Nepal' (or so the sign claims), but excitingly (and perhaps an indication that this is an affluent area) it contains one central electric 'street' light, which Pemba tells us is paid for by the local community.

We all stand and stare at this light as if we've never seen one before. We take photos of it too, to prove that it's here. It's such a novel sight, as it is completely out of place up in this mountain environment where some houses don't even have access to electricity. Yet here, in this posh village, they have one outdoor electric light as if to prove their wealth! It's just a shame that we won't be staying after dark to see it in all its night-time glory! I laugh – I feel like I'm having one of those days where it's best to expect the unexpected!

In the middle of Khumjung is the original Hillary school, established in 1961 (just eight years after the conquest of Mount Everest). Pemba received a scholarship to study at this school for six years. Now that I'm here, I have a much greater awareness of how brave he and his fellow students must have been in their quest for an education. It would take Pemba three whole days of walking in this challenging terrain to reach home – it would take me less time to fly halfway around the world to visit my brother in Australia.

Today it provides primary and secondary education for more than 350 children from surrounding villages, making it easier for those children to access free education. Many children in Nepal are not so lucky, and those in remote villages often don't have access to education past the primary level. Furthermore, many students leave primary schools after they learn to read and write, but without additional education these skills may be forgotten.

State education may be free (in 2000 the Government committed to providing free universal education from grades 1 to 10; children start around six years old and finish when they are fifteen or sixteen years old if they manage to stay to the end to take their School Leaving Certificate (SLC)), but the standards are said to be low due to a lack of skilled teachers and by the Ministry of Education's neglect of textbook reform. (The 2015 earthquake caused havoc to the education system as many schools were destroyed.)

If parents can afford it, and can access it, then they will try to send their children to private schools where the quality of teaching is said to be far superior than in the government schools. Lessons are usually conducted in English in the private schools (Nepali in the public schools), and this in itself is a privilege, as English is a commodity in Nepal – the ability to speak and write in English potentially opens up a whole new world of opportunity (that and knowing how to use a computer).

I struggle a little with the idea of formal education, as it tends to focus on developing the left and logical side of the brain to the detriment of the right and creative/intuitive side of the brain. However, I can say that having been fortunate to experience a high standard of free education from the age of four to eighteen and quality university education (albeit at substantial cost coming from Guernsey) from eighteen to twenty-one years, it is easy to take for granted the opportunities that my education has created for me and the ease with which I can earn money, and find myself in Nepal, for example.

I feel humbled by this visit to Pemba's old school. I recognise how lucky I have been to be born in Guernsey. Life may still have had some challenges, and it hasn't always been easy at times, but, nonetheless, I have never had to worry about my education (beyond whether I've made the right A-level choices and which university I should choose!) and have been blessed with good healthcare and stability too.

One must remember that Nepal has recently experienced a civil war. In 1996 the Communist Party of Nepal (Maoist) began a war against the government. Approximately 13,000 people died in the ensuing conflict. By early 2006 (remembering that we are trekking now in spring 2007), the government's control of the countryside was weak to non-existent, while political turmoil in Kathmandu aided the Maoist rebels. In May 2006, a new government in Kathmandu offered to negotiate with the rebels and the Maoists agreed to begin talks. The Nepalese Civil War ended with a Comprehensive Peace Accord, signed on 21 November 2006, six months ago at the time of writing. Ultimately this replaced the centuries-old feudal monarchy with a secular, federal and democratic republic.

During the civil war, the Nepali people suffered severe threats to their state of political, social, economic, psychological and physical well-being. There were a large number of deaths, disappearances, dislocations, displacements, violence, damage to property and infrastructure and an economic downturn. Needless to say, the conflict adversely affected education within the country, although it is said that it also encouraged more girls to seek education and helped support the women's empowerment movement.

I can't even imagine what it must have been like to have lived through a civil war, and I notice that Pemba is reluctant to talk about it. This alone makes me aware how fortunate I am to have grown up in a safe and secure environment in Guernsey and to have been blessed with a British passport upon birth. This has enabled me to fairly much travel wherever I choose throughout the world and is the envy of many a Nepali who is unlikely to travel beyond India, unless they are granted visas to work abroad.

Working abroad is a reality for many Nepali men in particular. It's said that every village in Nepal has someone who is working or has worked abroad. One third of the country's GDP comes from overseas workers. Mostly the men work in Malaysia, Qatar and Saudi Arabia within the construction or clothing industry, or as security guards. They may be away for two years at a time, their monthly salary being sent home to support their families and enable them to save to build a house.

This is the reality for many people and just serves to make me even more aware of how lucky we are in the West. It's perhaps not surprising that a number of Western trekkers who come to Nepal and learn more about the country and its people's hardships throughout their trip, perhaps forming a friendship with their trekking guide or porters, end up sponsoring the guide and/or porter's children.

This means that the child can access better quality education than would have been permitted if they were not receiving a sponsorship, increasing their chances of gainful employment in the future, without having to become a foreign worker. This is what has happened for Pemba and for the other Nepali families involved with the charity, whose children are all receiving private education.

Pemba leads us along the dusty 'playing field' where he used to play volleyball and cricket, and onto a statue of Sir Edmund Hillary where we stop to take photos. We then follow him along a dusty walkway lined by drystone walls – Pemba tells us that people walk backwards and forwards along this walkway as part of their daily exercise – before continuing our journey past more Mani stones, and up yet more seemingly endless and spacious steps.

Tim bounds off ahead and while Will has been complaining of feeling nauseous these last few hours, he still manages to find the energy to race off after him. Lilly, Joe and I walk with Pemba and moan relentlessly again. Perhaps it's a Guernsey thing, I don't know, but we're tired and Pemba refuses to give us a clear indication of how much further we have to trek; it's infuriating!

In reality, we're acting like spoilt children, annoyed at Pemba for leading us the long way to Namche. In our sulking moods, we totally overlook the fact that he was keen to show us his old school and give us an inkling of what life was like for him, helping us to recognise how lucky we are in comparison. We're all too self-absorbed to see this clearly.

Finally, we make it to the top and sit down together on a stone wall to catch our breath. The views are stunning and I'm overcome with the enormity of this place, of the vastness of the landscape with its space and the lightness. I have this 'thing' about the need for space. Sometimes in Guernsey, I can feel suffocated by the lack of space and at times like that, I need to take myself out to the coast and onto the cliffs to gain a view of the endless sea stretching to the horizon and beyond – space!

The light here is amazing and I'm surprised I wasn't touched by this more often on the trek. However, I was often consumed by my physical, mental and emotional 'suffering', which meant there was little energy or interest in the potential for romanticising the landscape and witnessing the joy of it – until I saw the sun rising above Mount Everest! There is something about changing light that I find enchanting. The light of sunrise and of sunset, the light of the full moon and the light of cloudy days. It can truly change a place, bring up something in me, the need for creative and soulful expression.

I consider how the light in the mountains must change season to season and I reflect on the Sherpas living so closely connected with the land, aware of the seasonal shifts and the manner in which this affects them. When I was working in an office, before I discovered yoga, I had little awareness of the signs of the changing seasons. I knew it was summer because it was lighter and warmer and I knew it was winter because it was darker and colder. But I never really noticed the transitions between seasons and I never had much fondness for autumn (which usually signified returning to school/ university) or spring (I always found this a frustrating time when winter was almost done but it wasn't yet warm enough for outdoor summer fun.)

The London Marathon started to shift things for me because I was outside running so much of my week! I noticed the changing light as autumn gave way to winter and winter gave way to spring and I was aware of the changing hedgerows as the autumnal blackberries died back and then nothing seemed to happen until the daffodils appeared, brightening the landscape. The primroses and the violets soon arrived and the cliffs were awash with purples and yellows. On it went, as the spring colour made the whole world feel alive and awake again.

Surfing throughout my teenage years, and while I was at university, meant I was frequently at the beach and I still have a strong sense of belonging in the sea. Through surfing, I learned about the moons and the tides and became very aware of the weather patterns and moon cycle. When I stopped surfing and started working in an office, I became disconnected from all of this. Perhaps it's hardly surprising that I became depressed as I lost my connection to nature and the Earth.

I may well have played competitive netball outdoors throughout the winter, but I was playing on tarmac and rarely made it to the beach or onto the cliffs. Living with my brother in town, I missed the west-coast light and the sunsets that I had grown up on, living just minutes from the main west-coast surfing beach. I rarely knew whether it was high or low tide and I had to make a conscious trip to see the sea.

It's easy to overlook the effect of our detachment from nature; so many of us are oblivious. Our busy lives creep up on us, so our disconnection happens subtly. We don't realise the impact this has on how we feel, challenging our sense of belonging and rootedness to Mother Earth. Through my healing work, I have noticed that those who are deeply ungrounded have a tendency towards depression and anxiety, as if their roots have been cut, and as a result they feel a separation from Mother Earth.

I wonder what happens to people when they move from this environment in the Himalayan mountains to the urban sprawl of the Kathmandu Valley. Their souls must shrivel under the weight of the pollution and the urban environment, so far removed from the lightness of this landscape, the colours of the Earth and the bright sky. I wonder how long we will continue to view 'progress' as moving away from the land and into cities with all the bright artificial lights (when there is electricity!), technology and promise of material gain.

When will we recognise that our soul yearns for freedom and for greater meaning, for connection to the Earth that sustains and nourishes us and gives us a greater sense of belonging? It was yoga that helped me to reconnect with the Earth. The more that I continue to step into greater authenticity and recognise my own true nature, the more my love of nature and need to be within it has increased; there is less separation (both within myself and with my connection to Mother Earth). Furthermore, I have become increasingly aware of my own cyclical nature and the cyclical nature of the moon and the passing seasons.

We follow Pemba as he leads us down a slippery grass hill across an incredibly small landing strip (it seems so out of place) and then along to the ridge overlooking Namche, which still seems so far away. Needless to say, more moaning and sighing ensue as we all try to figure out how much farther we have to go!

"I'm so sick of trekking today," Lilly complains.

"Me too," I agree. "I can't wait to just get there now. It's been such a long day and I'm tired of this wind blowing in my face."

"I know, it's so frustrating," Lilly agrees.

"I'm never trekking up here again," says Joe. "Silly hills, silly country."

"It's not a silly country," I defend Nepal.

"Its hills are silly and its food isn't very good," Joe adds.

"Definitely bad food," Will adds, "and the people can be so stupid."

"They're not stupid!," I exclaim. "They're actually incredibly strong, kind and courageous and the food is tasty, if only you'd try some Nepali dishes."

"I don't want to eat lentils!" retorts Will, with disgust in his voice.

"But you've not even tried them," I say. "You might find that you actually like them!" I am beyond frustrated by the conversation, as Will mutters under his breath and walks off ahead of me. I pick up my pace too and soon Joe is beside me, keen to make progress, while Tim dashes off ahead.

"Slow down," Lilly shouts out at all of us. Her knees are hurting and the hill is slippery. We dig our walking poles deep into the slope, the boys not sharing our concern, and rush off ahead, desperate to get to Namche and the Internet.

Eventually, we pass the brightly painted gompa we visited when we were resting in Namche on our ascent. We're delighted, especially when moments later we're back within the familiar territory of the main street of the town.

Lilly and I are jubilant and hug each other. "We've made it," we both shout gleefully. "We're back in Namche!"

I'm keen to let my family know about the trek. This is the longest that I've been out of contact from them, and this feels strange. But equally, I'm not sure how I can convey to them the enormity of what we've just experienced, not least seeing Mount Everest and being up closer to the top of the world as we know it, but also educating them about altitude sickness and the conditions along the trail.

20

When lonely days turn to lonely nights
you take a trip to the city lights
And take the long way home
Take the long way home.
"Take the Long Way Home", Supertramp

Day 12: Namche Bazaar

Lilly and I shriek with joy to find that we're staying in a modern room in the main accommodation block of the hotel where we stayed on our ascent. We have a proper bed each with a proper springy mattress and there's carpet on the floor. I can't tell you the delight – it's the simple pleasures in life, and I'm appreciating these much more than I've ever done previously.

We both enjoy hot showers and sort our clothes for the hotel wash. It's a joy to feel so clean and to wear lighter-weight clothes. We delight too in lying on our incredibly comfortable beds and chatting about what we might do next – there's a choice, that's the amazing thing!

After tea – you can't do anything out here without some tea – it's time for shopping. The altitude no longer affects us like it did when we were here previously and I feel like my normal self again despite being 3,440m above sea level!

We head straight to the overpriced Internet café, both of us excited about using one of their international telephones to call our parents back at home in Guernsey. However, my parents don't answer the phone and then I remember that they're on holiday; typical! It crosses my mind that I could telephone B (for the first time since I've been in Nepal), but something stops me; I'm happy in my own space and don't yet have clarity on what is next.

Back at the hotel, Will's still not feeling well and he spends the afternoon sleeping in bed. I practice yoga in our room, while Lilly lies on the bed reading her book and intermittently checks on Will. I enjoy lying on my mat in Savasana (corpse pose) with the comfort of the carpeted floor beneath me. It's an incredibly different experience to my previous yoga practice in this hotel, on our ascent. Back then I was feeling decidedly out of sorts. My head was hurting and I couldn't stop crying. I recognise now that I was well and truly out of my comfort zone and full of fear. I knew that there would be challenges on the trek: climbing a mountain is never going to be easy, as it provides the opportunity for journeying in so many ways, but I don't think I truly appreciated the depth of the inner journey and the challenge this alone has been.

I hadn't expected to process (my thoughts/past events etc.) as I have done, nor to be so touched by the Nepali people or the Himalayan landscape, which is permeated by the energy of Tibetan Buddhism. The trip has been extremely hard work on every level, but I feel a sense of coming home to myself in a way that I haven't felt previously. It's as if I have been able to let go of some of my self-imposed limitations.

I have become increasingly aware of my attachment to my mat based practice, regardless of the environment in which I find myself. I am also aware that the practice has been incredibly supportive in allowing me the time and space to drop in and try to centre myself in those moments when I have felt so out of balance.

I don't believe that there is any right or wrong way to practise. Instead, I feel that we must practise in a way that supports us, depending on what is going on in our lives (and the stage of our menstrual cycle, for example). Some days I have felt the need to practise actively because the restless nature of my mind needs distracting with the intensity of active movement. Other days, like today, I feel the need to move slowly and enjoy lying in Savasana, resting my weary body and allowing its weight to be held by the comfort and support of the carpeted earth beneath me. Perhaps tomorrow I will need to move actively again.

There have been times, certainly, when I have felt that I needed to move my body in a certain way, or practise certain postures, or continuously develop my asana practice as I strove towards the more advanced (or those deemed advanced) postures, and pushed myself to achieve these. But to what end? Did this make me a more advanced yogi? And even if that were so, what would that actually mean?

I don't believe that we can fast-track enlightenment, or accelerate our spiritual growth. And I'm not sure I would want to do that anyway. Yes, I am motivated towards a more peaceful, loving and harmonious state of being, but I am beginning to recognise that this comes with adopting a more balanced Middle Way approach to life. This, and living with a deep reverence for Mother Earth and having a sense of purpose.

Something was awoken in me in Bali when I (re) connected with the Divine and I have a sense that spirit, the Universe, or maybe just coincidence (not that I believe in this, of course) has led me here to Nepal where I can deepen my experience of yoga off the mat, so that yoga becomes a way of life rather than something that is limited to time on my mat, wherever that might be.

What was once solely a physical practice has become so much more than that. It has become a sadhana, a spiritual practice, with asana forming only a part of that. There are other ways that I nourish myself spiritually, and I can feel this deepening and shifting as a result of my experiences on this trek, and the manner in which I have been exposed to Tibetan Buddhism with its focus on compassion and wisdom.

The Buddha taught that to realise enlightenment a person must develop two qualities: wisdom and compassion. In *Essence of the Heart Sutra*, His Holiness the Dalai Lama wrote, "According to Buddhism, compassion is an aspiration, a state of mind, wanting others to be free from suffering. It's not passive – it's not empathy alone – but rather an empathetic altruism that actively strives to free others from suffering. Genuine compassion must have both wisdom and loving kindness. That is to say, one must understand the nature of the suffering from which we wish to free others (this is wisdom), and one must experience deep intimacy and empathy with other sentient beings (this is loving kindness)."

My time in Nepal has made me begin to question the nature of suffering and the manner in which we can create this for ourselves. It's also made me ponder the nature of compassion, recognising that to have compassion for others we need to have compassion for ourselves. This has made me increasingly conscious of the way in which I give myself a hard time and the manner in which I am anything but compassionate to myself, with my high standards. It has also made me realise that every moment offers the opportunity for sadhana, not just on my mat.

When I first arrived in Nepal, I sensed this but was yet to embody it or even put it into words. I knew that there was something about the stereotypical Western approach to yoga, with its emphasis on advanced yoga postures and skinny yogini/yogi bodies, that wasn't resonating with me – you just have to look in any one of the many adverts in any yoga magazine to know what I mean about the perception of the modern-day yogini.

I now recognise that my dissatisfaction with the Western approach is due to the fact that it often lacks freedom and heart, the very two things that yoga promotes. This is freedom to honour our own intuitive guidance and wisdom, and heart to meet ourselves just as we are, regardless of how we look, or how we practise, with compassion.

Essentially I am beginning to recognise that underlying all of this is love. Interesting, therefore, that Nepal is said to stand for 'Never-Ending Peace And Love'. I've only been in this beautiful country with its warm-hearted people for a couple of weeks, but I am feeling the love and peace more than I have done previously – it permeates the air!

The people we have met in these mountains may have so little in terms of material possessions, yet they have so much in terms of heart. You cannot put a price on this. You cannot buy love, just like you cannot buy peace. It must come from within.

This shift in awareness has been helpful. I have felt the pressure to conform to the Western notion of what it means to be a sincere and dedicated yoga practitioner for too long now and I have experienced the detrimental effect of this as I've tried to be someone that I am not. I can only be me and slowly learn to love myself just as I am in any moment – this is a life-long journey.

The trek, being in the Himalayas, processing, watching the porters, learning more about Tibetan Buddhism and being positively affected (and heart-opened) by its energy, has helped me enormously. I am finally recognising that the teachers come in many guises and that these don't need to look a certain way either. It's been both refreshing and enlightening.

By dinner time Will's feeling better and we're all in good spirits as we sit in the dining room with our porters. Will buys them beers while Joe and Tim flitter back and forth from the Internet café spending vast sums of money (relatively) updating their Facebook profiles with pictures of the trek. I'm happy reading my book and sitting back in a comfortable chair, knowing we only have one more day to go before we begin the next part of our journey.

21

Look at the stars
Look how they shine for you
And all the things that you do.
"Yellow", Coldplay

Day 13: Namche Bazaar (rest day)

We're meant to be leaving today, but Will's still feeling ill. He's been on and off the toilet all night and he tells Pemba there's no way he can walk today. All of us silently cheer, none of us fancy trekking anywhere today either, and Pemba agrees that we will have another rest day.

We're treated to another beautiful day, not least because the weather is warmer and sunnier than it's been this whole trip, but because we have no agenda. Lilly and I spend the morning sitting in the sun and alternating between reading our books and chatting to the boys, who come and go – Tim and Joe go to the Internet café where they're *still* updating their Facebook status, and Will to his room.

We drink our way through a couple of flasks of hot mint tea in the process, which goes down rather well with a roll-up – a delight of Namche Bazaar is the opportunity to buy Golden Virginia tobacco and skins! And, get this, we're able to enjoy a salad for lunch, as the lettuce and raw vegetables have been washed in iodine to make sure that they don't make us sick. Salad never tasted so good (well sort of!).

In the afternoon, Joe and I spend a few hours wandering around the shops looking for books. We've all been getting very excited about James Frey's books, *A Million Little Pieces* and *My Friend Leonard*. Now that they've been read, we're trying to fill the void. Lilly and I also delight in pottering around the many Tibetan jewellery stalls lining the crooked narrow and steep steps of the town. I'm a sucker for this sort of thing and while I've still not got the hang of bartering, I have fun nonetheless. We also stock up on supplies at the overpriced supermarket, indulging in real Swiss chocolate, another delight!

It's a truly joyful day, enjoying the energy of the town and not having to answer to anyone else. I feel very blessed to be able to take my time practising yoga in our room with carpet underfoot. This for me is the joy of travelling, not having to rush, just being able to go with the flow of what life presents day by day. I doubt I shall ever grow tired of travelling, or of experiencing life in different countries around the world.

There is something about Nepal particularly that really resonates with me and I'm looking forward to seeing more of the country after I finish. I'm still not entirely sure the reason that I'm here, but I suspect it will all become clearer over the next couple of months. I'm keen to explore the yoga community in Nepal and see what it has to offer and how this may further influence my life.

22

"If I live to see the seven wonders
I'll make a path to the rainbow's end
I'll never live to match the beauty again
The rainbow's end"
"Seven Wonders", Fleetwood Mac

Day 14: Namche Bazaar to Lukla

Will's feeling much better today and spends breakfast moaning about the food. He's beginning to sound like a broken record, and I'm looking forward to a break from him soon. Tomorrow he's flying directly back to Kathmandu to volunteer in one of the local hospitals and gain some valuable work experience, while Joe, Lilly, Tim and I will be continuing down the mountain to Bupsa, where we'll be staying for the next two weeks.

Today we've got to trek back to Lukla. First, though, we have to navigate a path out of town, which is more challenging than expected due to the weekly Saturday market. Pemba tells me that porters carry their loads from villages located six to ten days' walk away just to sell their wares at this market, so it's understandably busy. There's also an array of produce for sale not ordinarily grown in this Khumbu region and this brings with it an excited energy.

The market zigzags its way up the side of the steep terrain of Namche, the goods displayed on material laid out on the ground on both sides of the small path. It's a rather lively affair, as much a sociable event as a market, as it brings together Sherpas from surrounding villages to buy and sell their goods and chatter with one another and share news.

It's a real treat for the eyes, as we carve a path through the many people, trying to have a peek at all the stuff for sale. There are all sorts of goods on offer here: upturned baskets containing live chickens, baskets of eggs, huge bags of white rice, all sorts of herbs, spices and grains that I don't recognise to name, a selection of fresh vegetables including cauliflowers, carrots, potatoes and green beans, bars of chocolate and an assortment of sugary biscuits.

There are piles of clothing including jackets, jeans, all sorts of trainers, warm socks and flip-flops, and piles and piles of thick blankets for sale too. You can buy material for making clothes, and shampoos and hair gel, washing liquid and cleaning products, and even kitchen equipment. There's also other household stuff like bright plastic cups, jugs, bowls, plates and flasks.

I grimace as I notice, across the path, huge slabs of meat hung on enormous silver hooks. It turns my stomach and I look the other way, where I see line upon line of cardboard boxes filled with packets of dried noodles, and tin cans of oil instead – much less distressing for the vegetarian! There are cartons of juice and bags of salt and toilet roll and everything else it seems that you could possibly need or want!

When we finally manage to navigate a path past all the people haggling with one another, we're able to increase our pace. I'm so happy to descend the hill that threatened to destroy me as we ascended it two weeks ago now. It's quieter on the trail today than it was back then and we're easily able to stop at the Mount Everest viewing point without having to hustle for space.

We're also able to take refuge from the bright sunshine as we trek under the shade of the pine trees, their needles making it slippery underfoot, so we have to concentrate on the path, using our walking poles to support us. At times, it feels as though we're skiing down the steep hill, side to side, holding on to tree trunks for support. I'm brought well and truly into the present moment, mindful of my every step.

Knowing that we're nearly at the end of the trek is exciting, but it has sent me into a bit of a spin today because it's a milestone reached. I've done a huge amount of thinking and processing while on this trip, and Lilly and I have chatted at length. I have had a growing sense that I really want to write about my experiences of life in Nepal and especially on this trek, so that I can share this with family, friends and students.

It is one thing to write for family and friends, however, and quite another to write for people who don't know you, because you open yourself up to a wider audience of judgment! So there is a vulnerability and a fear that accompanies this. But the trek has given me some strength, and I've really missed writing. It's something that I do regularly when I'm travelling, but I haven't been able to bring my laptop with me on this trek (funnily enough!) and I'm now keen to get back to it as soon as I return to Kathmandu.

I also have a sense that I will join the others in India after our stint in Kathmandu. But I still don't know what to do about B. Just before my brother and I sold our house and I decided that I needed to leave B to go travelling to Australia and focus on my yoga practice, B and I had paid the deposit for a no-expenses-spared, organised, two-week trip to Nepal and India. I think how different my life is now and how different my experience of Nepal and the Himalayas would have been on a two-week holiday, where my experience of the Himalayas and Mount Everest would have been limited to a private flight.

I would have had none of this experience. I wouldn't have known about the reality of life lived in the mountains, or the effect of altitude. I wouldn't have had any awareness of the challenges of trekking in this mountain range, nor would I have been touched by a sense of something greater than myself and yet a part of myself too. I wouldn't have learned the lessons that I am continuing to learn, about surrender and gratitude and faith in a positive outcome – and love and compassion.

I wouldn't have had an embodied experience. That's the biggest difference. There is no doubt that the energy of Tibetan Buddhism has worked its magic in my life, healing and opening my heart, and helping me to see things differently.

But there is still some resistance, some need to cling on to the familiar. B is a huge part of this. There is something that prevents me from making a clean break, and it is constantly playing on my mind. So the terrain, the manner in which it demands present-moment awareness provides a joyful break from my over-thinking mind!

Soon, we reach the seemingly endless steps leading to the river valley below. These are a real challenge on the knees and slow us down. I realise now that it's no surprise I was at my wits' end coming up here on our ascent. They're steep, unforgiving and relentless! My knees are soon hot and aching and I'm grateful to have both walking poles as they provide further support (unlike Joe who still only has the one!).

I chuckle to Lilly, "The altitude threatened to get us on the way up and now it's these steep steps on our knees on the way down."

"I know," she laughs back at me, all of us in good humour today. "They're hard work, but at least we're descending!"

"Hoorah for the descent!" I agree. "Oh look," I add, pointing down to the valley below, "there's the suspension bridge, which means we're almost at the bottom! Double hoorah!"

"Not long to go," Lilly adds joyfully.

And before we know it, we're all the way back down to the fast-flowing Dudh Kosi River at the bottom of the valley. Here we are greeted by the lengthy suspension bridge, covered in prayer flags, that challenged us on our ascent. Now these bridges don't faze us and, if anything, I feel a little melancholy that this may be our last one. It highlights again how the things that challenge us can lose their grip on us once we have stepped beyond the initial fear.

I question whether it's fear that is preventing me from making a clean break with B, or whether I'm doubtful and indecisive because I'm fearful to truly love. But I believe that we should be guided by whatever is in our heart. If I'm honest, I don't know if it is in my heart to spend my life with B. I may be better living a life on my own, than a life that is not properly aligned in true love. Deep down I know the answer, but matters of the heart are always tricky, and the situation needs to unravel in its own time – often to the frustration of family and friends.

Fortunately, I am not nourished by romantic love alone. I have a deep sense of purpose to help others through yoga, Reiki and the written word, and while I have no idea how this may unfold, I know without doubt that I must continue to follow my heart. This is not always easy, because it always feels a little uneasy when you're not quite sure which direction life will take you (after India, what next?).

But I know I'm lucky. I am very aware that living a life of purpose is what gives life meaning, despite the challenges it may bring. As I walk along the path on my own, I wonder how many people live with a sense of emptiness in their life, not because they don't have enough to fill their lives, but because they lack a sense of purpose in their lives.

I've heard many times of the loss that people feel when they experience a change. When their children grow up and leave home or they retire or even are made redundant. They lose their purpose and meaning in life and become disenchanted and sick. Ending a relationship is a big change.

All too often, or so it seems to me, people are limited by their beliefs in their own inadequacy, and confined by their lack of faith in themselves or in the support of the Universe. Repeatedly, they may deny their soul expression and therefore experience the emptiness, loneliness and pain that can accompany this. (I talk from experience here, I've felt that emptiness, loneliness and pain!)

Many give up on their dreams during childhood and many have no idea what it means to follow their hearts (and perhaps for some they feel that they do not have this choice because life circumstances prevent this luxury). Furthermore, society being as it is, with its emphasis on material gain and the notion of this as success (and being famous!), does not help. It's no wonder then that many find themselves adrift without any sense of anchoring, without any awareness of what it might mean to be truly alive and live with faith.

This is one of the greatest gifts that yoga has given to me – faith. While I may not be clear yet of my direction, I have a deep sense of faith that I will be guided to where I need to be and at just the right time.

This is what motivates me out of bed in the morning. This is what causes me to keep going when the darkness descends. This is the reason that I step onto my mat daily, practising yoga, praying and chanting mantra. This is what finds me standing in the light of a full moon giving thanks to the Goddess of the Moon. This is the reason I love to hold crystals and bring them into my life. This is the reason I seek silence so that I can hear more clearly what my heart is trying to say, and this is the reason that I nourish my soul with nature and the elements where I can.

We walk along the bank of the Dudh Kosi River, down the valley, walking across the pebbles, passing more and more porters carrying their ridiculous loads. "Namaste, Namaste, Namaste", heart-open, compassion, love to you all, we say. We're surrounded by the sights and sounds of nature, the water glistening in the morning sun, the bright green leaves on the trees, the roar of the river calming and reassuring, and the fresh air filling our lungs and invigorating us.

I've been touched by this beautiful land of Solukhumbu, as I've also been touched by the hearts of the many Sherpas and porters with whom I've had contact. The simple exchange of "Namaste" with those I don't know in person on a daily basis has been enriching, as if this act alone has awakened something deep within me, healing my heart.

Our heart can hold so much pain. My own heart has been holding on to so much from my past, which is shaping my current reality. There is fear of becoming too attached, of loving too much, and what that might mean if it all falls apart. And despite the faith, there are still moments of fear – when the darkness descends – of not living life to the full, of somehow missing out on something that I'm meant to be doing because I haven't listened to my heart's guidance, and ending up doing what I feel is expected of me by others instead.

However, despite all this, I've also become increasingly aware that life has a habit of providing us with a series of difficulties and challenges, or what the Buddha described as 'inevitable sufferings of existence' to help us live a life of purpose. We cannot escape these. However, if we are able to view these challenges from a more elevated and spiritual perspective, then we may recognise that these events provide the opportunity for our ongoing awakening and for us to become more aligned to our authentic self.

We continue along the path, climbing the steep bank all the way up to the entrance (and exit) to the Sagarmatha National Park. On the way we pass more prayer wheels and delight in spinning these, sending more good luck out into the Universe. "We're alive and all is well," I want to sing with the joy of the moment. Pemba checks us out of the National Park while we sit waiting for him, basking in the morning sun, not a care in the world.

I love these lower climes, where it's rich and abundant, invigorating us with its spacious, new and vibrant energy, where potential abounds. We pass hamlets where we see children playing happily with one another, lost in their imaginary world, dancing around the goats. Other times they stop to wave to us. "Namaste, Namaste, Namaste," we call to them, and they shyly respond. Occasionally, one will be bold and ask us where we're from. "England," we respond, "a long way from here."

Pemba chooses a lodge for us to stop for lunch and disappears into the kitchen while we sit together in the light-filled dining room and wait. We wait some more. And then we wait even more! We're wondering what on earth he's doing when the lunch finally arrives - rice and vegetable curry, of which I doubt I'll ever tire.

Pemba's still hidden away in the kitchen and we giggle as we spot the Sherpini collect two bottles of rum from the dining room, before disappearing back into the kitchen. "What is Pemba playing at today?" we ask each other and then laugh, as it seems he's getting drunk with the local ladies.

He keeps us waiting for some time.

"What's he doing in there now?" we each question. "He can't still be drinking rum."

"Pemba and the Sherpinis," Joe exclaims with a smile on his face, as he gyrates his hips.

"Oh don't," Lilly and I sigh together before bursting into a fit of giggles.

Finally, Pemba appears with a big grin on his face.

"What have you been doing?" we demand.

"I've been eating," he responds, acting all innocent before a bigger smile erupts on his face.

"Yeah, right!" we all exclaim.

"I've been catching up with my friends," he continues, and we laugh, because we get a whiff of his alcohol breath.

"Drinking rum more likely," Lilly and I joke. He laughs and gestures his hand as if to say, "No, no, no, don't be silly."

"The ladies!" Joe says, as he starts kissing the air as if he's Pemba kissing the Sherpinis.

Pemba laughs coyly before beckoning us on our way. "Come, come," he smiles.

We're a merry bunch of trekkers as we follow the path to Lukla. We lose Pemba along the way. It's one of those days! He stops at the lodge where we stayed on our way up the mountain in Phakding to have a drink with the owner and tells us to carry on without him. After a while, we make the decision to stop for tea, the first time we've done this on our own without Pemba, and choose a place that's near to where we stopped for our first lunch, by a large prayer wheel. We enjoy the novelty of ordering for ourselves and sit outside, keeping an eye out for Pemba.

Sure enough, there he comes, virtually falling at our feet as he stumbles over a stone. To say it's funny is an understatement. We're crying with laughter, holding our tummies to stop the pain of uncontrollably laughing, rolling around in our chairs, "Ha, ha, ha!" He couldn't have done that better if he'd tried. We joke to Pemba about his drunken condition and all the while there he is grinning at us and trying to make out he's not drunk.

The last few hours of trekking up to Lukla are hard work. Tim and Will disappear off into the distance while Joe and I continue to walk together just a little bit ahead of Lilly who is walking with jolly Pemba. We're tired and we start moaning again and demanding, "How much further Pemba?"

"Another hour," he keeps telling us, smiling.

Joe soon becomes angry and complains to Pemba that Nepal needs to get some roads.

"But we are a poor country," Pemba tries to explain to him, almost laughing at the thought of roads in the mountains. "We cannot afford to build roads."

"And anyway, why would you want to build roads up here Joe?" I ask. "This is perhaps one of the few places in the world where the physical terrain prevents the building of roads, and I think it's brilliant."

"Well, it's ridiculous," Joe continues. "I'll give Nepal some money. It needs to install some elevators or something."

Pemba chuckles. I think he'll be pleased to see the back of us soon.

Finally, after what feels like hours, (it's been an awfully long day), we walk around the ridge and can scarcely believe that we've made it, as we see ahead of us the stone entrance to the town of Lukla.

We did it!

Lilly and I hug and kiss one another. "We've made it, we've made it!" we sing to each other, with huge grins on our faces. Trekking up to Base Camp of Mount Everest is not something I ever thought I wanted to do, but now I've made an attempt at it, I'm delighted I've done it. I feel blessed and silently thank my angels for looking after us so well.

We virtually dance our way through the cobbled streets of Lukla to our hotel, smiling at everyone we pass. It feels so strange to be back here after all we've been through this last two weeks. There are people everywhere, trekkers and Sherpas alike, and we find it disorienting with children also running around, dogs barking and the general noise and activity of a hill town (and yet this place seemed so quiet in comparison to Kathmandu two weeks earlier!).

Tim and Will are already at the hotel when we arrive and we greet them with big smiles on our faces.

"We've made it, we've made it," we continue singing to one other as we collapse, shattered, onto the soft benches and chairs in the hotel's main dining room. I don't know whether to keep laughing or to cry with relief of making it here.

Before I get too settled, I rush off to an Internet café and try to telephone my parents, but again there's no answer and I feel a little deflated. I would have loved to hear their voices and tell them firsthand that we made it, but an email has to suffice instead.

It doesn't cross my mind to telephone B. There's been a shift. I'm aware of it now that we're back in 'civilization'. I feel different, stronger and happier within myself. I'm not yet sure what this means or how the on-off relationship will unravel, but I know that things have to change; life has to move on now (whatever that means).

Back at the hotel, we shower in our en-suite bathrooms, before meeting back in the dining room for celebrations. The boys are drinking beer and we share popcorn while chatting and laughing together.

Will is due to leave us first thing the next morning and Pemba tells us we will be setting out early in the morning too for Bupsa, further down the valley. Lilly and I sigh. We are tired and would welcome a rest day before we start all over again, but Pemba will not entertain such a thought. Joe is adamant that we won't trek, but Pemba is insistent. We're trekking and that's that.

Joe goes to bed in a sulk, while Will and Tim continue drinking beer. I sit with them drinking fresh mint tea, but there's a tipping point where drunk people become boring rather than entertaining. Sitting at the table, I'm very aware that my hands are sore with blisters from my walking poles. I have a cold sore developing on my lip and my throat is scratchy with exhaustion. It's time for another early night. I say goodbye to Will, as we won't see him in the morning, and head off to bed, still jubilant. *We made it!*

Lying in bed, I consider how much the trek has provided me with the opportunity to live yoga. I have come to recognise that transformation – physical, mental, emotional and, particularly, spiritual – is not simply limited to the guidance of others in yoga studios, on retreats or in yoga books, but can happen in any moment of life if we challenge our limitations, listen to our inner guide and embrace every heart-felt opportunity for doing something different (beyond the fear and doubt).

To me, yoga goes beyond definition and limitation. It is simply to be lived as a direct experience of the vast interrelatedness of all life and all things. And here in Nepal, in the Himalayas, where the environment is permeated with the energy of Tibetan Buddhism, well, it has given me an amazing opportunity to learn more about this and I've been truly touched by my experience.

I shall always be grateful to the powers that be for conspiring to bring me here and to my heart for knowing this and taking the first step.

Little did I know then how this trip to Nepal and the trekking in Solukhumbu would play such a pivotal role in directing my life over the next few years and beyond, or how Nepal would seep under my skin and into my heart and become like a second home. Nepal will always represent 'Never-Ending Love And Peace' to me. There is no doubt that this beautiful country has given me more love and peace and a greater sense of compassion for all beings.

Namaste!

Afterword

We continued trekking down towards Bupsa the following day as planned and spent two weeks living with a lovely Nepali family in their guesthouse. Lilly and I shared a room with views over the green terraced hills in the distance and a large expanse of green grass below us. Our hearts were warmed by the continuous presence of nature – green is the colour of the heart! We felt fortunate to have access to a clean, indoor squat toilet and a warm shower outside on the patio.

We spent our time volunteering in the local primary school, which was a short walk away, down a steep hill from the lodge where we were staying. I'd like to say that this was a life-changing time for me and perhaps it was in many respects, but I never felt that I was making a real difference.

The school was run by a drunken head teacher who had lost all passion for educating the children. We never did find out what had happened to him, but were led to believe that the Maoists had made life very difficult for teachers in the region. Looking back with the knowledge I have now, I suspect he was trying to do his best, but the village – like so many villages in Nepal – was so far removed from Kathmandu that there would have been very little support, if any.

While there were two stone-built classrooms (and another being built and funded by the charity), they were not being used and the children sat under a tree on a grass bank outside to learn instead. They were taught together, all 30 children or so of all different ages, although when we arrived they were split into two groups to make it more manageable for us. We split ourselves into two groups too and attempted to teach the children something, anything, but I found it frustrating and demoralising.

I couldn't speak Nepali and the children couldn't speak very much English (if any) and they were extremely shy, as is common in this region. The idea was that we would teach them English, but none of us had any training to help us achieve this. We tried our best, but often the classes were painfully challenging as we attempted to find a way to communicate with the children so that they would understand and respond to us, but it was tricky and we would frequently end the session wondering how we could make it more effective the next time.

A couple of the boys in our group (I forget who now) had been led to believe that they were in Bupsa to help build a new classroom. They made a fuss to our host and one day we were led to the new classroom to help with its construction. This meant that we each had to carry a couple of wooden poles from the nearby 'jungle' to the construction site where they would be used in the building. Lilly and I then got to sit down and watch as the boys removed their shirts and attempted to help move bricks and lay them in place. It was embarrassing!

The boys got the photographs they wanted to put on Facebook and show to their friends back at home: "Here, look at me on my gap year, building a school in a rural village in Nepal." The truth is, we were a pain in the arse to the local builders, who knew what they were doing, who have the skills to build a stone-building, and didn't need us getting in their way and indirectly making more work for them (clearing up the boys' mess). So that was that, we were off the job by lunchtime and the end of the school day!

So, we decided the best thing for us to do was to tidy the two classrooms which weren't being used so that the teacher could start teaching in them again. It took two days to do this as they were a shambles – desks stacked higgledy-piggledy in the corners, one resting on another, and books were strewn all over the place, with a thick layer of dust coating everything, so we were constantly sneezing and feeling dirty.

They looked better when we finished with them, but then we realised that the one head teacher wouldn't be able to teach all the children in just one room. We also quickly realised that being in the classrooms, sitting behind desks, made the children hyperactive and the din of them all chattering and us trying to control them was laughable at times. The environment was far too noisy for anyone to learn anything and we were soon happy to retreat to the grass bank or play volleyball instead.

Another time, we took a break from teaching and ventured an hour down the terraced land to the village below. Here, I saw a small screaming boy being whipped with a belt by his mother. The image still haunts me to this day and as a mother now myself, I appreciate more than I did then that children can be exhausting and drive you to your edge (let alone when you're extremely poor, that I can only imagine), but, nonetheless, my approach is gentle and I abhor violence of any kind towards children.

This incident woke me up to the suffering of poverty and the manner in which child abuse can be construed as 'normal' in different cultures and communities in this world. On another trip to this same village, we stopped for tea at a lodge and I found myself sitting beside a man from New Zealand who has spent a number of years visiting Nepal and has helped financially to support that particular village school.

He set up an inter-village football competition, which was well received by the local boys, especially as he brought with him new footballs and football kit, essentially giving them each new clothes in the process. (Clothes, new ones especially, are often in short supply in these villages.) At that time, he was also paying for the education of one of the village boys (essentially sponsoring him). He was also paying for the boy's remedial treatment in Kathmandu for a cleft lip, which alone would make a huge difference to the boy's life.

This was an impressionable meeting for me, as I was able to speak to him about our recent experience at the village school. He helped me to realise that it is possible to make a difference, even if you do not speak the same language, but ultimately, it's the money these places need, not us trying to build a school or even trying to teach them. They need stability and continuation, not gap-year students flitting in and out two weeks at a time. It's like promising the earth and then disappearing.

Which is actually what happened. Not that we promised the earth, but here we were, meant to be helping, but then we tired of it and Lilly, Tim and I left a few days earlier than planned to return to Kathmandu, as we were all missing civilisation. It's difficult now to believe that I made that decision, but back then I was bored of hanging around with very little to do and longed to start yoga classes back in Kathmandu and to have freedom again, after living with others in their home.

I resolved that I would return to Bupsa one day, although I felt strongly that I needed to learn how to teach English to foreign students first. I thought perhaps my parents would be best placed to do this, as both of them are ex-teachers and are always trying to make a difference in this world. I wondered if I could entice them to Nepal.

During my time in the village I taught yoga to Lilly, Tim and Joe, outside, with views of the terraced hills and the mountains in the distance. I got to practise in this environment on my own too, as I'd always hoped I would do, and often up by the small village gompa, which has been restored by the charity. This meant that monks were once again educated there; often that is the chosen path for a boy from each of the local families, as it provides a better life than toiling in the fields.

Back in Kathmandu, I relished the freedom to come and go as I pleased and started attending yoga classes with a male Nepali yoga teacher in Thamel, the main tourist area of the city.

We also volunteered in a school in the city, although this also didn't go as planned. It was a boarding school supported by the charity, and primarily schooling Sherpa children from Solukhumbu. Pemba's children had all boarded there, and so too had the children of our host in Bupsa. It was a proper school with a good number of teachers. We were given the delightful task of teaching the children 'health' as there wasn't a dedicated health teacher at the time. However, the dedicated health textbook needed some updating!

The children were often out of control in our presence, which we found both challenging and entertaining. Here they were being paid to go to school and yet they had no interest in learning. This was in stark contrast to the beautiful, shy children in Bupsa who desperately wanted to learn, but had very little opportunity to do so. Isn't this always the way?

We found the whole experience exhausting and were delighted in many respects when the teachers throughout the country went on strike, which meant no school for us. For the students, it wasn't ideal and I soon learned that at that time, certainly, the teachers often went on strike and schools would then close, so that the children were no longer being taught. This made me question how Nepal would ever change, because the politics and the poverty seemed so hopeless at times. None of this of course can ever be helped if the people are not given consistent access to quality education.

At the beginning of the strike, Lilly, Joe, Tim and I flew to Pokhara, Nepal's second largest city, for the weekend. Pokhara is everything that Kathmandu is not. (This is not to say that I don't enjoy Kathmandu, as I do, I love the craziness of it, but only for a short time.) Pokhara is laid-back and peaceful, set beside Lake Phewa with fabulous views of Machapuchare (known locally as Fishtail Mountain) in the distance. The air is clean and the pace of life slower. Furthermore, there are yoga classes – and it was these that I sought.

I'd seen The Nepali Yoga Centre mentioned in the Lonely Planet guide and I found it easily up a side road and in a small stone house, not far from the lodge where we were staying. It was set within a very tidy property with a vegetable garden that was well-tended. There was something about its energy that attracted me and I was surprised to find a female Nepali yoga teacher, D, taking the class. Nepal, certainly at that time, was a very male-oriented society, not at all like the West. The women's empowerment movement was only just beginning and it was extremely unusual to find a woman running her own business, let alone one teaching yoga.

I didn't exchange too many words with D beyond sharing our names, but she led the class in fluent English in a beautifully soft and gentle voice. D taught traditional Hatha yoga and in a way that was different to how I'd practised previously – there was very little flow. D was very keen on the energetics of the practice, and moving slowly. She was also keen for students to truly notice how the postures made them feel energetically and how this approach would help them to heal. The teaching certainly resonated with me and I began to feel my body and the energy within it in a subtler and liberating way – there was a coming home to myself all over again.

I had already been working and practising energetically – I'm a Reiki Master after all and Reiki is all about energy, and healing, and in my yoga practice I was also aware of energy – but this was different. I felt more stretched than I would do ordinarily, both in body and mind, and I liked the way that D wove into the practice breathing techniques, mudras and relaxation. It was a different dance, more graceful and lighter than the dance of my Western-influenced, vinyasa-inspired home practice. I was encouraged to slow down and go even deeper within.

The yoga classes and Pokhara made quite an impression on me. We took the bus back to Kathmandu – (five hours on a bouncing bus, versus the 30 minutes it took us to fly there in the first place!) – to find that the schools were still on strike throughout the country. With that, Joe, Tim and Lilly made the decision to visit a water park somewhere near the border with India, while I booked myself on a plane to fly back to Pokhara on my own, instead.

I felt terribly brave and proud of myself for venturing out alone in Nepal, and I loved every minute of the experience. I had already befriended a young friendly guy called Bijay who worked in one of the local restaurants we visited on our initial trip. Our friendship was cemented on this solo trip and he showed me around the town on the back of a motorbike that he had borrowed from a friend. We even went to meet his family in one of the local villages. I ate in the restaurant where he worked on my own every night and made friends with the other staff members. I felt safe. They seemed to genuinely care about me, and I certainly never felt it was just about the money, or about anything other than friendship.

As for the yoga, well, rather typically (although meant to be), D had left town while I'd been in Kathmandu, to head to India, where we were headed next too. Her friend, S, a male Nepali yoga teacher, was teaching the Hatha yoga classes instead, in a similar style to D. I attended these classes twice a day and was often the only student in the class, which felt a bit strange, but I enjoyed the opportunity to be led.

S was keen to chat and when he heard I was also going to India he insisted that I email D and see if we might meet up. Now, India is a huge country, but when I made contact with D it turned out that we were both going to be in Dharamsala (known as Mini Tibet) in northern India, at exactly the same time; it was a strange coincidence (not that there is such a thing as a coincidence!).

Lilly, Joe, Tim and I left Nepal for India a week earlier than originally planned as the strike was continuing indefinitely and we were merely kicking our heels by then. So, we bade Nepal a farewell, (I knew with certainty I'd be soon returning), and walked over the border into India together and caught a train to Varanasi, our first stop. There, the ashes from the burning ghats hung in the air and I felt uncomfortable breathing in the dead.

There was a heatwave too and I struggled with the lack of air conditioning and cold water – the water in the showers went hot with the rising temperatures so there was no way of cooling off – and the concern of getting sick from the food. I also wasn't prepared for the dirt, and I'll never forget seeing a frail elderly lady squatting in the street ahead of me defecating in the midday sun. It was eye-opening and made me question lots of things about life and our own morality, let alone mortality.

From Varanasi, Lilly, Joe and I headed up to Rishikesh, the supposed yoga capital of India. Here I happened upon a marvellous male Indian teacher who taught in the hotel where we were staying. Lilly and I attended his classes together – it was fun for me to have Lilly's company. By then Lilly was really getting into her yoga and I was very proud of her for making such steady progress and showing such commitment. However, it was so hot in Rishikesh that we spent much of the day sitting inside our room in the comfort of the air conditioning, nipping out to smoke roll-ups and order banana lassis. It was a relief when dusk arrived and we could enjoy life outside without the relentless sun beating down on us.

From Rishikesh we headed to Agra together to see the Taj Mahal. There is no doubt that this is a stunning building, a true testament to love, which made me long for greater love in my own life too. We left Tim in Agra feeling ill, and carried on, Lilly, Joe and I, to Amritsar to see the Golden Temple. This is another stunning building, but it was just so hot that we couldn't do it justice. We took a trip out to the border with Pakistan for the daily evening ceremony, not something I'd be rushing to repeat again.

From Amritsar, Lilly and I took a taxi on our own all the way up to Dharamsala, home to the Dalai Lama and the Tibetan community in exile. Within hours of our arrival, we bumped into D, quite literally, in the street. It was the strangest thing, as if we were brought together by the powers that be. D was as delighted to see me as I was to see her, which was strange, really, given that we'd barely said more than our names to one another in Pokhara.

Still, D came to teach Lilly and me yoga together at our hotel each morning and then she'd join us for breakfast. One morning, over our Tibetan bread with jam and masala tea, we talked about our hopes and dreams. I'd had some clarity by then and had this feeling that I needed to return to Nepal and do something to help empower women. D sat in front of me and told me that this was also her dream, that she too wanted to empower women in Nepal. We couldn't believe it! Clearly we'd been brought together for a reason!

We talked about how we might achieve our mutual dream and within the space of an hour we'd agreed that we would like to empower women through a combination of yoga, massage and Reiki. We were also both keen that they be given the skills to make a difference in their own lives – we wanted to teach them how to fish, rather than catching the fish for them, and to do this using holistic means.

I was inspired and desperate to make our dream a reality. D was also eager to move it forward and one morning when we were talking about how we might raise some money to get it going, I had the idea to sponsor her to come to Guernsey and teach yoga and use this as an opportunity to fundraise. It was exciting and we parted determined to make it a reality.

I'm not sure whether D ever believed I'd follow through on our plans, but I'm true to my word and as soon as I returned to Guernsey, I set about completing the mass of paperwork that would enable D to apply for a visa to visit the United Kingdom. It was serious stuff. I had to provide photos of the room in which she would be staying, for example, and copies of my bank statements proving I had sufficient funds to sponsor her, let alone references etc.

It took time to collate all the documents, but soon I was able to send these to her and just crossed my fingers that they'd make it through the postal system and safely into her hands. They did, and we took this as a positive sign. Still, it was a huge risk for D. She needed to attend the British Embassy in Kathmandu for an interview. If our application was denied, then she ran the risk of having a black mark put against her name, which would undoubtedly adversely influence any future applications.

It was a risk D was prepared to take and I'll never forget when she telephoned me from Kathmandu, full of joy, to tell me that her visa application had been approved. She was coming to Guernsey! This was exciting too, because it meant that the project was about to become a reality.

And a reality it became. The Nepali Yoga Women's Project was born and with that we fundraised in Guernsey and in London where a friend of a friend helped D to meet with some wealthy women who were keen to support a project like ours. My family, friends and students were generous and I shall always be thankful to them for believing in us.

The workshop in Guernsey was a success and I enjoyed bringing D out to the West. In Guernsey she also shared her Nepali cooking skills, while we tried to give her an experience of our lives on the island. From Guernsey, she travelled on to the UK to stay with her dear friend C, 'Mother England', in Worcester where they undertook more fundraising, before she returned safely to Nepal and set up the project in earnest.

There continued my love affair with Nepal, as I spent the next few years travelling backwards and forwards twice a year, and even attempted to learn Nepali on one of my flittings. Pokhara became like a second home to me. I stayed at the same hotel each trip, run by a lovely man called Narayan, who has always looked out for me, and I mainly ate at Bijay's restaurant where I never got sick. I made friends with a Dutch lady living locally, and I became a familiar face wandering around the town, to the yoga studio and to the pool at an expensive hotel.

I wasn't as hands-on at the project as I probably should have been, choosing instead to see my role as one of raising funds and awareness in the West. It was easy compared to D's role and I never truly grasped the extent of her responsibility, or the manner in which she gave so much of herself to it. She was the one who taught the women yoga and massage and set them up to make Nepali handicrafts. The latter tend to go hand in hand with women's empowerment projects in Nepal, and Pokhara and Kathmandu are full of little shops selling crafts handmade by women.

While we had never intended to venture down the handicraft route, it soon became clear that this would be the easiest way to help the women make money. It would also give them something to do that could be worked around their children – the children often joined them at the centre. However, we wanted to differentiate ourselves from the rest and while the women made the classic woolly Tibetan socks (sold throughout town), they also made beautiful cotton yoga-mat bags, yoga pants and yoga shawls, the latter based on a pattern from my mum.

D would send huge cardboard boxes containing all these handmade Nepali products to me to sell to students in Guernsey. We were lucky in that everyone was very supportive and keen to buy when they could. Inevitably it was trial and error initially, sizing being different between East and West and also the pattern and colours which may appeal. But we kept working on this, as the women became more skilful in their efforts and more aware of Western taste.

Backtrack to India, and after much heart-searching and yoga, I had a clear sense that I needed to return to Guernsey with Lilly after our month of Indian travelling. I was tired and in need of some stability and grounding. I was also beginning to feel a little purposeless and was keen to start teaching yoga again, and writing.

I had decided that I wanted to write a book about my two months in Nepal and this is what I returned home to do. I had warned my parents, so that there was no expectation of me returning to a finance job, at least for the short-term. I was keen to use what savings I had to support myself while I gave the dream of writing a book a chance.

So this is what I did. I sat on my bed each day and wrote. I also started teaching yoga again as I was keen to share all I had learned with my students, and this brought with it a wave of new students as my teaching style had subtly changed. This has happened many times since – a shift within me and my energy will present a shift in the people who are attracted to my classes, albeit there is a core of dedicated students who continue attending classes with me regardless.

While I might have started teaching again, developing 'Beinspired', my yoga community, was not the top of my priority list at this time, as I was keen to devote my energy to my writing instead. However, a month into the writing and an opportunity presented itself, (again, like Nepal, with no effort on my part), to help my dad set up a wealth-management company on behalf of one of his friends, and this I could do from the comfort of my bed.

For whatever reason, it seemed that I was always drawn back into the world of finance and to my professional skills as a company secretary. There is a part of me that likes this work and the manner in which it uses my brain, and it helps to ground me, especially when I'm doing lots of energy work.

I continued with the writing regardless and I finally finished the first draft of the manuscript while I was on retreat in Goa, seven months after returning from my trip to Nepal and India with Lilly. It was a relief to finish, as writing a manuscript is all-consuming and I spent most of my spare time on my laptop. It was here in Goa that I met a trainee editor who agreed to look at my work.

Her feedback did have some positives, but it was the negatives I focused upon. I was new to this whole writing malarkey back then and still had a lot to learn. It was one thing writing a first draft manuscript and quite another going through the editing process to get it to a publishable stage. I didn't realise this at the time. Instead, I thought that if the first draft didn't hit the mark then the book would never be published.

So I set it aside and got caught up in the company secretarial job, which quickly became time-consuming, albeit that I managed to retain flexibility and the opportunity to come and go from the office – (by then we had secured premises and I was no longer working from my bed!) – as I pleased, depending on my workload. In many respects, it was the ideal job because of this flexibility and the manner in which it could fit around my yoga teaching and Reiki commitments.

The Goa retreat was intensive, led by Emil Wendel and his friend Sue Pendlebury, and took place at Satsanga Retreat Centre, where we practiced yoga twice daily in the Shiva shala in front of a huge statue of Shiva. It is perhaps hardly surprising then that change followed this retreat – you cannot immerse yourself in the energy of Shiva and not expect some shift! Of course, the practice itself encouraged transformation as we practised a combination of asana, pranayama, mudra, meditation and chanting, and spent some of the retreat in silence too.

Back home in Guernsey, and six weeks or so after the retreat, I met E. It coincided with me finally accepting the fact that B and I were co-dependent, depending on one another for friendship and company alone, and that we were preventing each other from moving on. We both knew at heart that our relationship was not for the long-term, as we both wanted different things from life. The trouble was that neither of us was truly strong enough to make the break.

It was E's arrival in my life at a yoga class I was teaching, and later at a bar – (quite by chance as at that time I rarely drank alcohol and barely went to bars, but that night I was at the end of my tether and needed a blow-out) – that gave me the necessary impetus to move on from the relationship. Coincidentally, B met someone at the same time who he is still with to this day, so while we undoubtedly grieved for one another, this was eased by the new potential relationships in our lives.

It was painful because we had become such good friends, but it was also a huge relief. I had given so much energy to questioning whether our relationship was right that I felt lighter with the decision having now been made. It felt like I was now able to enter a new chapter of my life, and this is certainly what happened.

A week or so after I met E, I was booked to take my parents to Nepal with me so they could see the country themselves. We trekked in the Annapurna Range and they understood a little more of my love for this compassionate and peaceful country. They saw the women's project in action too and my mum gave them some ideas for the knitting, while others by then were learning massage with D. Often Western yoga students visiting the yoga centre on their travels would help by volunteering, perhaps some English lessons, or other times teaching in the studio and donating the takings to the project.

My parents ended up sponsoring the children of the two porters who accompanied us on the Annapurna trek. This meant that they committed to paying for their education, ensuring a good education and the provision of books etc. This cemented their relationship with Nepal too and has given them a reason to maintain contact and to return again one day to see how the children have grown.

As our relationship developed, I was desperate for E to come and visit Nepal and see for himself the country that had etched a path in my heart. The problem was, E and I are both free spirits and, at that time, we were both used to being non-committal. He saw a trip to Nepal with me as a form of commitment that might entrap him and he was not ready for that. It would take us some time to anchor down together; both of us were kites instead, flying!

Frustrated by his inability to commit, and desperate to continue to follow my heart and live my dreams, I decided to use an inheritance I'd recently received from my gran's passing to go travelling around the world over the course of five months, the first three of these to be spent in Nepal trying to live there for a full season. I resigned from my flexible company secretarial job and sent my students off to other teachers.

I loved my time spent in Nepal. I taught yoga at D's centre to visiting trekkers, and I enjoyed the diversity of nationalities and the stories that each brought with them. I relished the transient nature of the town. I never knew who might turn up at class from one day to the next, which was such a contrast to classes back home where you build a relationship with regular students over time and they come to class knowing you – this means that it took me out of my comfort zone because maybe students wouldn't like my style of teaching!

I enjoyed the simplicity of life too, drinking lots of Nepali tea while writing on my laptop, and then later in the day swimming in the pool at a hotel. I had friends, people who were keen to say hi and make me feel at home. Not long after I arrived, E booked a ticket, on a whim, to visit me for two weeks, the first time he had needed a passport for ten years. I saw this as a favourable sign.

We went trekking in the Annapurna Range and spent time in Pokhara, where he got to see the project taking shape, or perhaps it wasn't taking shape as such, just doing what it was doing – providing an opportunity for maybe eight women at that time to learn a new skill. It wasn't without its challenges. Often the ladies lacked the confidence to progress their learning of massage for example, and struggled with the yoga; it wasn't always for them.

Then there were those younger ones whom D tried to help who had a history that made life difficult for them. For example, in Nepal, if a woman is divorced even if through no fault of her own, then she is tarnished and the locals will turn their back on her. Often women in this situation will 'disappear' and try to make a new life for themselves elsewhere in the country.

It's tough to do this though, because there is no government support, financial or otherwise, so you are literally on your own. If you have children in tow then this makes it extremely difficult, as you have to provide for them too, and many end up giving their children away to children's homes in the hope that they can be fed and educated there instead. Sadly, there is the whole human-trafficking risk that accompanies this, but that's too depressing to even touch upon here – suffice it to say that those of us who live in the West have no concept of the poverty experienced by so many in Nepal.

Sometimes D would try to help a younger woman with a tarnished background, but this would create an issue for the other ladies because tarnishing runs deep in this society. The culture, with its caste system, is complex, and despite living in the country for many years, I would frequently speak to Westerners who would admit to me that they still didn't understand it. This alone makes it tricky to change perceptions, even among women.

By this same token, at other times, it became apparent that the project was failing. It was supporting women, but not empowering them to make a difference in their own lives as we had intended. They needed D to make it work. They didn't have the confidence, or perhaps the support from their families, or from the community, to take their skills out into the world.

It was easy for me to forget the extent of my own empowerment and of D's empowerment too. She was extremely unusual in Nepal. A woman owning her own business and travelling abroad is not commonplace. Even the fact that she wore jeans was unusual back then, when women, certainly those on the project, wore more traditional dress.

I was blinded to some of the issues that the project was experiencing. I was happy to write the website, to raise awareness, to produce newsletters and share these with students back home. I was also keen to sell the products and to teach the yoga, but it wasn't in my heart to do the on-the-ground work.

Perhaps that's how it should've been. After all, I didn't speak Nepali (despite attempting to learn it) and I didn't understand the culture and the way things were done. D absolutely needed to be at the helm as she understood all this and was embodying empowerment. She was the perfect leader.

My heart loved Nepal though, and I played around with the idea of carving out a life in this country of 'Never-Ending Peace and Love'. The trouble was visas. Yoga is not recognised as a business in Nepal, so getting a business visa to work in the country was not feasible. Perhaps I could fall back on my other skills either as a Reiki Master, or a company secretary? And yet the likelihood of the Reiki was slim and of course I knew virtually nothing about company law in Nepal.

Then of course I quickly came to realise that even if I was able to get a business visa to teach yoga, I was not going to make very much money from doing so. We charged about £2 per class, much less than at home, and it's seasonal work, October to December and then March to May. It would be impossible to earn enough to live off, let alone ever have any money to return home. My idea of spending the 'seasons' in Nepal was looking more like a pipe dream and I left Nepal after those three months unsure when I would return.

It was eighteen months later when I did return, for my fifth trip, and with E, his second trip, as he'd liked it enough to visit again. Between his trips we had split up and I had taken refuge in a static home on my cousin's smallholding in North Devon where I deepened my connection with nature and the land, and rewilded myself in the process. After this experience, and perhaps because of this experience (it grounded me and brought me back to earth), we got back together again, but still in a non-committal way.

Soon after, E had been gifted redundancy from the finance industry and decided to use his redundancy money to travel around the world, only he didn't want me joining him, as he wanted to do it with friends initially, and then on his own. We'd been together on and off for three years by then and I had moved into his cottage, so I found this a little difficult to accept. At that time, my life had been one of travelling and here he was choosing to go without me. It took a while, but eventually I came to realise that it was a blessing.

We started his trip together in Nepal, and here we explored a little bit more of the country, as well as spending time in Pokhara visiting D and the project and the other friends I had made. Sadly, by then one of the porters from the trek I had enjoyed with my parents (and then separately with E), had died. His name was Dill and he was one of the gentlest men I have ever met. He was hit by a bus on the walk home with his son from school. His son is one of the children that my parents sponsor, and we were all very shocked and saddened by his passing, and took comfort that my parents were helping Dill's widow and family.

It made me acutely aware that there is a timing to everything and that perhaps some greater force is really taking care of things. When our time's up, our time's up; best to get on with living. Not that this realisation made it any easier when E left me in Kathmandu to return home to join my parents on my own for Christmas, while he continued his travels to meet friends. It was not a joyful time, and I was incredibly angry about being abandoned.

Still, I survived, and the following February I spent five weeks in Canada, visiting a friend on Vancouver Island, before undertaking a yoga-therapy course in Vancouver, and spending time in this marvellous city on my own (in silence mainly) for a few weeks, practising yoga and coming to terms with my abandonment.

Needless to say, it was exactly what I needed, and gave me the clarity to recognise that if I truly wanted a future with E, with children too, then it was time to switch from being a kite, flitting around the world, and make a decision, take action then, to anchor down instead. I felt perhaps if I made that decision, it would make it easier for E to anchor down with me. So it was back to Guernsey for me and amazingly my flexible company secretarial job presented itself again, helping with the grounding and anchoring. I also stopped smoking, finally. Yoga Nidra, especially, helped with this.

Fortunately, E returned from his trip ready to commit too. Not that it was plain sailing, but slowly I started to settle myself more fully in the cottage. (My clothes had lain in piles on the bed in the spare room before our travels, but now space was made in the drawers in what is now our bedroom.) We women are good at weaving our way into a man's world, and that is what I did, and we soon became settled into our more settled way of being!

After a time, the question of children hung in the air. This had always been the dream and now I was keen to realise it. However, we met a stumbling block. Could E commit to this enormous undertaking at this stage in life: he forty-six years old and I thirty-six? Could he step beyond the fear and just see what might happen? Or was I going to have to call an end to this relationship that my heart told me was the one for me? I couldn't take the risk of not having children. This too was eating away at me (my ovaries were screaming that the time was nigh). I don't envy any woman who has to make such a decision.

As for E, well, eventually, yes, the decision was made: we would try for a baby. There was anxiety, but I took it upon myself to make it our priority; my biological clock was ticking. Only it didn't happen immediately as I had hoped.

So, our lives became consumed with trying to get pregnant, the natural approach initially and then through IVF, which I've documented separately in my book *Dancing with the Moon* and which was a spiritual journey all of its own. And all the while D was going through her own settling. She too had found love and the time had come for her and her American beau to commit and make a life together. It was also time to let go of the project, now that we had our own personal projects in which to channel our energy. So, the project ceased and any hopes I may have had for visiting Nepal were put on hold for the time being.

One of my long-held dreams is for my children to grow up with an awareness of life in Nepal, to trek in the Himalayas and embody this life lived so differently, to learn about the world from direct experience and to be touched by the compassion and love of the Nepali people.

We're almost there, perhaps another few years until our two boys are strong enough to tackle the mountain terrain without needing to be carried – well at least not carried *all* the time.

I'm delighted that the lives touched, mine, E's, D's, the children sponsored, the women on the project, my Nepali friends, and my family and friends who have visited Nepal on my recommendation, has happened all because my heart led me to sign up to trek to Mount Everest Base Camp and undertake some volunteer work – I've the Universe to thank for that!

This book is a result of the manuscript I wrote all those years ago now. It went untouched for a good seven years until I was pregnant with my younger son and I felt a calling to dust it off and begin the long editing process. It has taken a couple of years since and the version that you've read is only a small part of what was initially written, but it was the trek, really, that I was keen to share, and the editing process has been a journey in itself – Emil was right, you don't need to physically climb a mountain to climb a mountain!

They say we should follow our heart to live a life full of meaning. This allows our soul expression and provides us with an opportunity to share our gifts with the world and to be in service to something greater than ourselves, and yet a part of ourselves too. It's never an easy path, that much I have learned, but it is one of depth and love and light and purpose. This is what drives us on. I wonder now how the path will continue to unfold, for Nepal is never far from my heart.

I hope you enjoyed this book.
I would be delighted if you could
leave a review on Amazon.
Many thanks,
Emma Després

Thank you and with gratitude

There are lots of people without whom this book would not have come to fruition, so with enormous love, gratitude and thank you to my parents, Ron and Jill Després, my brother, Ross Després, Jo de Diepold Braham, Michelle Johansen, Hannah Larkin, Hayley Bougourd, Vanessa Lasenby, Dr Alyssa Burns-Hill, Dr Deepika, Dr Wathsala and the wonderful ladies at The Ayurvedic Clinic, all the amazing Nepali porters and Sherpas who helped us on the trek, Narayan Adhikari, Bijay Thapa, Devika Gurung, all those amazingly open-hearted Nepali people who made me feel so welcome in Nepal, all of the many yoga teachers and healers who have inspired me, all the Guernsey yoga students who supported the Nepali Yoga Women's Project and who continue to support me to this day, Leila Green and the team at 'I Am Self-Publishing', Steph Bisson, Charlotte Hill and the many other Earth angels who have helped along the way.

Special thanks and much love to my amazing Mum for reading and editing various versions of this manuscript and for encouraging me to keep going when I almost gave up, and to Jo Chapman for her friendship and laughter and for never giving up.

And finally a huge thank you to Ewan and our boys, Elijah and Eben, for putting up with my seemingly endless early morning and late night tapping, and for teaching me what it means to truly love.

Never Ending Peace And Love x

32125198R00171

Printed in Poland
by Amazon Fulfillment
Poland Sp. z o.o., Wrocław